Journeys

Journeys

An Anthology of Adult Student Writing

2021

Literacy Minnesota

First Edition
Printed in the United States of America

ISBN 978-1-7337440-2-7

Cover Design: Kasey Payette

Table of Contents

Foreword by Kao Kalia Yang   7

For My Loved Ones, Near or Far   9

Arrivals and Departures: Journeys to the U.S.   29

Pieces of the Past   41

We Persevere: Overcoming Challenges   61

Social and Racial Justice   81

Teaching and Learning in the Pandemic   85

Sketches and Snapshots   99

Exploring Culture and History   107

Fiction and Folktales   121

Wishes and Wonderings   125

Letters about Literature   137

Index   145

Curriculum Unit   150

Journeys Editorial Team   172

Acknowledgements   175

Foreword

In the pandemic, my Hmong-American family, like countless others across the world, lost loved ones.

A dear uncle contracted the coronavirus. He went to the hospital when his oxygen levels fell. In the hospital, he was placed on a ventilator. The days passed and his body deteriorated. We watched, family from across the nation, as the air left our uncle's body and his chest sank. We watched as the color dissipated from his skin and he became a statue of himself.

Before his illness Uncle had been a blur of movement. A lifelong early riser, even in America, Uncle got up before the dawn to the quiet crow of a morning rooster tucked somewhere within the body of his memories. With his death, Uncle took with him much of an undocumented history of what it'd been like to grow up as a boy in the tall mountains of Laos, as a young man called to respond to the destructive forces of war, and as a father and husband who had to flee the land of his buried father for the possibility that his children might live. With his passing, not only do we mourn the loss of a life that had been tied to so many's survival, we grieve the stories that he used to share and the ones we were waiting to share with him. Now, he is no longer here with us, a figment from a time we used to know, an invisible thread to those who lived and died before him, whose lives make ours possible.

I imagine that my uncle is now with my grandparents, a grandfather I never met and a grandmother I loved, and whose words I continue to carry and call on. I imagine that Uncle is young again, once more healthy and well, moving with flushed cheeks, among the trails of his childhood, in a country free from war, beneath a brilliant sky uncluttered by the debris of a hard life.

I remember the words of my grandmother, "Our only offering to the world when we die is the strength and the power of our stories."

Since my uncle's death, I've not only looked to what I know of Uncle's stories but that of others around me to be reminded of the incredible strength of the human being, the source of our power. It is in our stories of resilience, the gifts of our treasured memories, and our individual human experiences that I find pieces of the life my uncle had lived, the one I shared, the one we share together.

It is my fondest hope that this anthology offers you not only a glimpse of lives faraway, but a look into the heart of your own life and loves.

Kao Kalia Yang
March 14, 2021

For My Loved Ones, Near or Far

Featured Author

Veronica De Alva

SHAFER, MN

Veronica De Alva was born and raised in Mexico City. She is the oldest of four siblings. She has one brother, Edgar, who is thirty-four years old, and two half-brothers, Eduardo and Andrea. Her dad, Salvador, was born in a small town of Guadalajara, and he moved to Mexico City looking for a better life and a good eye doctor. He was diagnosed with glaucoma when he was eight years old. Veronica's mom is from Mexico City, and she immigrated to the USA trying to find a better life for her family.

Veronica was a smart girl but mischievous; she was always in trouble at school. She went to a strict Catholic school, but she is grateful for the discipline and values she learned from the mothers and teachers from that institution. Veronica's favorite time of the year was the summer when she used to go on vacation to her Grandpa's town, Jantetelco Morelos. She loved to play with her cousins, swim in the river, and explore.

In 1999, Veronica was accepted to one of the best high schools in Mexico, the National University of Mexico (UNAM), and her life changed for the better. She is a graduate of the UNAM School of Dentistry, specializing in Endodontics. Veronica immigrated to the United States with her family in 2018. She lives in rural Minnesota with her husband, two teenage sons, and two chihuahuas. She plans to earn her U.S. dental license and return to her passion of practicing dentistry.

My Hero

When we are little, we have the concept that a hero wears a cape and has superpowers. As we are growing up and we learn the values of life, that concept changes. Our superheroes become people of flesh and blood, who do extraordinary things, and always seek to transmit an example of life and essential values to live in peace and help our fellow men.

My superhero is my dad. He was born and raised in Jalisco, Mexico. At the age of six years old, he was diagnosed with glaucoma and since he lived in a situation of extreme poverty, he did not have the resources to receive medical attention. When he was eighteen years old, he moved to Mexico City. He started to work, but it was too late to get a treatment. He lost his sight when he was thirty years old. He joined a school for the blind. He learned braille, orientation, and mobility skills that helped him face his new reality.

He applied for a Guide Dog Program in Leader Dogs for the Blind in Rochester, Michigan. He got accepted, and he completed the training with Sparkly, a beautiful black lab. For the final test, they boarded a bus, and the bus dropped him off in a park, and he had to find the way back to school with the help of his guide dog.

He and Sparkly were the first ones to arrive at the school. Their coach was happy. Sparkly and my dad went back to Mexico, and since then, they are inseparable, and my dad's life has been easier and more productive.

Sparkly became the most important thing in my dad's life. She is my dad's eyes, friend, and protection. She is always ready when my dad is ready to go to work. It's impressive to see how they work together and how Sparkly has been adjusting to Mexico because down there we don't have an inclusive culture, and they have been facing a lot of inconveniences.

It has been a challenge for Sparkly and my dad, but they solve everything together. My dad always says the disability is only a state of mind. We are capable of accomplishing whatever we want, and the only limit is heaven. They love and take care of each other.

Veronica De Alva is 39 and originally from Mexico.

Puppies

DEVENORIS MCCRANEY, DULUTH, MN

So cute and cuddly

Slow but suddenly

Furry pups

that keep you emotionally

Pit bulls and terriers

that strive for the best of us

warm and gentle

Don't forget to pet them though

Young and gay

Happy and stray

Big tall fuzzy

Always licking on the face

Devenoris McCraney is 42 and originally from Minnesota.

Thank You Mom

MICHAEL WARREN, DETROIT LAKES, MN

Things   you do
for me that no   one else could
do. When I was growing up you always
made me go to school. As a baby you always
bathed me and made sure clothes were on my back.
And as I grew older and got myself into some trouble
you never stopped loving me. You always come to
my court for me. And when it is your time to go,
Mom I think I will be very lost. You are my
best friend, Mom. I tell you everything.
And when it is your time to go, Mom
rest in peace. Don't worry about
me Mom. I promise when
you are looking down
on me I will make
you happy.
Love you
Mom
!

Michael Warren is 24 and originally from White Earth, MN.

Leaving My Family in Somalia

HAYAAT MOHAMED SHEIK ALI, ST. PAUL, MN

I lived with my family until I finished high school. Then, I married a man from the United States of America. After one year of my marriage, I had my first baby boy. We lived a happy, sweet life. After four and a half years, we moved to the United States. It was so hard to leave my family and go where I did not have family. After a long time of living with my family, I decided I preferred to have my son see his dad and make them both happy. The night I was leaving, my family all came to see me to say their final goodbye. It was a very emotional night with sobbing and kissing. My family asked when I would come back to them. I was shaking and crying a lot because leaving my family was not easy, but living with my son and husband was very important to me. My son could not wait to see his father.

At last we got to Washington, DC. It looked like another world with a lot of snow. It was a shining, beautiful place. I was so happy when we landed in the Minneapolis, Minnesota airport. I did not know where I could get my bags and where I was supposed to go. I needed help, and I didn't know how to ask for help. Finally, I was with my husband who was waiting in the lower part of the airport. It was such a happy moment.

Hayaat Mohamed Sheik Ali is 33 and originally from Somalia.

Myself

THA BLAY EH, WORTHINGTON, MN

My name is Tha Blay Eh. I'm from Thailand's Karen refugee camp. I have three brothers and two sisters. I arrived in the U.S. in 2017. In the USA, everything is difficult for me. In the USA, many people come from different countries. Different languages. It's too hard for me, but I never give up.

Tha Blay Eh is 35 and originally from Thailand.

Fall in Minnesota

SANDRA ESTRADA, COLUMBIA HEIGHTS, MN

The fall in Minnesota is beautiful; I enjoy the clear sky, the sun, and the awesome foliage of fall. Walking through the parks of Minneapolis or St. Paul, the cool breeze relaxes me as I see the red-orange leaves falling from the trees. If you live here in Minnesota, I invite you to explore these places; it is a really beautiful experience. I love the fall season! In my country, Guatemala, I remember the fall was completely different. The trees would dry, and the leaves would fan. The fall in Minnesota is more colorful.

Sandra Estrada is 38 and originally from Guatemala.

Family

TANYA TROMBLEY, MAPLEWOOD, MN

I love both sides of my family. On Thanksgiving my dad, my mom, my little brother, Tom, and I would split the day into two parts. First, we would go to my Grandma O'Connor's house. She had seven grown adult children in a small house. Along with their own children and husbands and wives, it was very crowded. My Grandmother O'Connor could not cook if her life depended on it. She attempted to make dishes of wild rice casserole and mashed potatoes. Other dishes included yams, cranberries, and biscuits.

The other part of the day, we would go to my other Grandpa and Grandma's house on my dad's side. They had a much better variety of food because they were not as poor. They had only three boys and grew up in a better setting. My mom was one of two sisters and four brothers. Her food was much better. Grandma Trombley would make real apple cider and crackers with different types of cheeses.

I love food and could tell which dishes were good and could not wait for more, and I knew which dishes to put a nice face on while eating them. Happy Thanksgiving.

Tanya Trombley is 38 and originally from Maplewood, MN.

My Family

MU AYE, WORTHINGTON, MN

My family is from Thailand's Karen refugee camp. We are a family of five. We left the refugee camp on April 25, and we arrived in the U.S. in Indianapolis, Indiana on April 26, 2017.

We have two bedrooms and two bathrooms in our apartment. One bathroom is upstairs and downstairs is the living room, kitchen, dining room, and one other bathroom. We all like it because it is clean and quiet.

Mu Aye is 36 and originally from Thailand.

A Good Mother

SAI DUONG, ST. PAUL, MN

I live in an extended family with a lot of people. My mother has had a big responsibility to take care of us. She is fifty-five years old, has medium height, short black hair, and is a little bit chubby.

My father is too busy with his work, so my mother has to spend a lot of effort to make sure everything in the house is fine. Every morning, she wakes up early to prepare breakfast for the rest of us. When I was young, my mother prepared meals and drinks for me to bring to school, and when I went to college, she continued to do that for me.

I have many siblings. We all went to school, except my older sister who stayed home to help my mother. During the upland season, my mom had to work until night before coming home, but she still smiled at us. When I asked, "Mom, are you tired?" She said, "No, I'm not. I'm very healthy and strong, so don't worry about me, daughter." Even though I knew my mom was very tired, she just didn't want us to worry.

I remember when I was in primary school, my mother was very sick, and we thought she could pass. I cried and feared losing her forever. When she was cured, I was very happy. I hope my mother is always healthy and always smiles at us forever.

Now, we are grown, but my mother has to take care of my grandparents. They are old and need her help. I know my mother will do a great job when she takes care of them. I went far away from her. Every time I see her on the phone screen, she cries because she misses me.

My mother is the one who I love the most in my life. I really appreciate my mother's effort, patience, and her hard work to conserve the family's happiness. I want to be a woman like her.

Sai Duong is 26 and originally from Vietnam.

Someone I Admire

SAMAR MOHAMED, ST. PAUL, MN

I admire my teacher. She is very kind, generous, and very smart. She knows how to build confidence in her students by giving them compliments. I am really grateful to have a teacher like her. She is very patient and knows when to be strict in a kind way.

She has many excellent qualities that are worth learning. Therefore, Brenda at South St. Paul Adult Education is a person I admire.

Samar Mohamed is 51 and originally from Sudan.

The Woman I Love

ANGELICA PINTO, ST. PAUL, MN

I was born and raised by the best woman ever. Who is she? She is my wonderful mom, Elina Maria Garcia de Pinto, a strong woman, my Wonder Woman. She was born and grew up in a small town in Venezuela called Guiria.

She had a very difficult childhood, because she lost her mom when she was six years old. She lived with her brothers, sisters, and dad. She got married when she was twenty years old, and she had three sons and two daughters. I'm the youngest daughter, my mom's baby girl. She always showed me how to be strong, and the most important thing she said was, "People need to work hard to get whatever they want, but always think about God."

When I was a child and I cried, she wiped my tears, hugged me, kissed me, and told me everything would be okay. Now, she continues to wipe my tears. She loves me more than life itself.

She is an independent and super strong woman. She showed me how to make my own wings to fly.

Today, she's not with me because she's in Venezuela, but I want to say thank you God for giving me my mom. She encourages my dreams, understands me, forgives my mistakes, and has always been so proud of me. She's my Supermom, and I'm so proud of her, too. I love her so much!

Angelica Pinto is 40 and originally from Venezuela.

The Worst Day of My Life

MESERET FANA, ST. PAUL, MN

A few months ago, my phone kept ringing in the middle of the night. I couldn't ignore it. I picked up. It was one of my cousins on the phone. He told me my dad had passed away. I immediately felt shocked, nervous, and I couldn't control myself. I fell on the floor. You can imagine how difficult it is to hear this sad news from back home. Also, it was so hard to travel due to COVID-19. My daughter was six months old, so it wasn't easy to take her with me. Since that day, I am always thinking about my dad. It remains, the worst day of my life.

Meseret Fana is 44 and originally from Oromia.

My Family

TIGIST GEBREMARIAM, BROOKLYN PARK, MN

I am from Ethiopia. I have a big family. My family is made up of my mother, my father, three brothers, and four sisters. I am the oldest of my siblings. It is sometimes hard to be the oldest in my country because there are many responsibilities like cleaning, cooking, and taking care of my younger siblings.

My family still lives in Ethiopia. My mother is a very hard worker, and she has a business of selling cow's milk. My father is a merchant and runs his own store. As children, my siblings and I had a lot of memories and a lot of fun together. I especially liked to play outside with my youngest brother and sister. We enjoyed playing games together, like football and hide-and-go-seek. I was closer with one of my brothers because he understood what I was thinking, and he listened to my ideas.

I met my husband in 2009. He too is from Ethiopia but was living in the United States. We were able to communicate with phone and email. After two years, he returned to Ethiopia, and we were married.

In 2013, I came to the United States. I love and miss my family very much. Because I am now in the United States, we sometimes talk on a video call. Mostly, it is only my brothers and sisters. With my parents, we talk on the phone.

Now, I have plans to bring my family to the United States. My parents would like to visit the United States. I have applied for a tourist visa, but because of the coronavirus, we must wait.

A friend of mine from Ethiopia now lives in St. Paul, Minnesota. She also has two children, like me, so sometimes we spend time together. We meet every week together at church. Together with my family and other friends, we like to have a coffee ceremony in the park, when we eat and drink. The children like to play together. We all love each other very much.

Tigist Gebremariam is 38 and originally from Ethiopia.

Loving TV Shows So Much

ANONYMOUS, ST. PAUL, MN

One night there was going to be a wedding. My sister's friend was going to get married. It was my sister's friend's wedding in the town where I was born and grew up. We celebrate the weddings a week before the actual day of the wedding, and mostly we do the dances at night.

One night, my sister went to the party. I decided to watch a TV show by myself. However, I was not allowed to watch because it was at night, and my mom did not let me. If my sister was there, I would watch with her, and my mom wouldn't say no.

So, I decided to sleep early. I went to my bed and pretended like I was sleeping. I wanted my mom to sleep early before the show started. She

thought I slept, and she went for her bed too. My mom and I used to sleep in the same room.

After my sister left, my mom slept. I got up and turned on the lights in the house, so she wouldn't notice the TV was on. Unfortunately, she woke up to use the bathroom. She turned the bedroom's light on. She didn't see me on my bed. She was scared to the death. She looked for me in the house. She couldn't find me because I hid myself under the table. Then she realized my sister was not home too, and thought I was gone with her. My mom tried to call my sister. She couldn't reach her on the phone.

I was scared my mom would show up. I let her do whatever she was doing. She was panicking when she called her best friend. Her best friend's house is next to our house. They both went to get me at the wedding place. When they got there, I was not there. I was home watching the show. They did not find me there, so they came back with my sister and two of her friends. When I heard them coming, their footsteps and their conversations, I turned off the TV and pretended like I was sleeping again. I could hear my mom and sister arguing. My sister was like, "She is at home," and my mom was like "No, she is not."

When they get home, I was on my bed. My mom was like, "Wait, what?" I knew what was happening, but I acted like I didn't know anything. I was like "What's going on?" My sister told me, "Mom says you were not home!" I said, "I was sleeping."

Families and Friends

BIANCA YOUNG, MINNEAPOLIS, MN

Now more than ever, it is very important to have someone in your corner through hardships. Friends and family can be a huge piece of your success. Whether it's starting your own business or thriving in your education, having a support group is needed. I moved to Minnesota eleven years ago. I remember my junior year in high school. I did not know a single person there. I felt lonely and missed my friends and family from Chicago and needed that drive of support. Minnesota seemed like such a small town compared to Chicago, but my mom convinced me to join the dance team.

Joining the dance team brought me lots of friends and popularity. Even to this day, my friends have become like family and have been a major piece in my life and goals that I want to achieve. I don't have much family here now, but my circle of friends has grown over the years. Life is so precious and short that I try to make time for all the important people in my life and let them know that they are appreciated and loved. I recently helped fund my sister's hair care business because she has always been a huge support to me.

Bianca Young is 28 and originally from Chicago, IL.

My Daughter's Graduation

FOSIYA SHIREH, BROOKLYN PARK, MN

Two years ago, my daughter graduated from eighth grade on May 30. We had a fun time; the whole family went for her. She was so happy, and I was happy too. We went to dinner, but we went to different places. Me and my mom and mother-in-law went to a buffet, and my husband and my kids went to the Cheesecake Factory. We gave her a new phone as a gift to her. She was so happy, and it was the best day.

Fosiya Shireh is 39 and originally from Somalia.

Looking for Bamboo Shoot in the Forest with Sister

PLAE MEH, ST. PAUL, MN

When I lived in a Thailand refugee camp, I was young. I was fifteen years old, and my sister was eleven years old. We had a playground next to the house. Every afternoon after school, we just played volleyball or soccer at the playground. After we were done playing, we went to the river. We used to swim together at Mae Surin river. We went back to our home to cook dinner together. We lived like that every day in the Thailand refugee camp.

One day, me and my sister made a plan. We told each other that we were going to find bamboo shoots in the forest on Saturday. We will go to the forest that is near to our house. We will start at nine in the morning. The next day at 8 a.m., I woke up and prepared some food for breakfast. After, I took all the stuff that I had to bring with me. Then I started to go to the forest. When we got in the forest, I started to find bamboo shoots. We saw many bamboo shoots. We used the knife to dig bamboo shoots and put them into our bag. We used the knife because it is too bristly.

We got too many bamboo shoots now. And we took a time for eating. I took out my rice and chili paste, and we ate together. After we were done eating, we were ready to go back to our home. At 6 p.m., we left. On the way home, we happily sang a song together. We were tired, but we were happy. We spent the whole day in the forest. We also had so many bamboo shoots.

Plae Meh is 23 and originally from Thailand.

My Friend Abel

GIZE LEKULU, NEW HOPE, MN

My friend Abel was raised by a woman who was not his biological parent. His biological mother left him in the church at the age of two. He was then adopted by a single mother with two daughters. His adoptive parent took him in, cared for, educated, and raised him with her other kids. When he was fourteen, sadly, his adoptive mother passed away.

After she passed away, there was a disagreement between his stepsisters and him, and they told him to leave the house. He was shocked, very sad, cried a lot, and felt lonely. Then he started asking himself, "Where do I come from? Who is my family? Where is my family? Why haven't they contacted me?" and he didn't know where to go. Because he was a student and didn't have any money, his life became complicated. He left the house and started living his own life as a homeless person for a while. After looking for a while, he found a job. He was feeling better and had hope and was eventually able to rent a house with another person.

Abel worked during the day time and went to school in the evening until he graduated from high school. Because he got very good grades, he was able to attend the university for free for four years. He graduated from the university with high honors, and the university hired him as an assistant lecturer. His life changed, and he became successful.

But, he still didn't have any answers about his family. Today, at twenty-eight years old, he is still looking for his family on social media and in the news. He is asking his mom to come and see him as a grown man and to have that special love between a mother and a son.

Gize Lekulu is 36 and originally from Ethiopia.

My Best Friend

FARHIYO SHIRELLE, MINNEAPOLIS, MN

My best friend, Faiza, moved back to Kenya two years ago, but we still talk with each other every week on WhatsApp. Even though she is the same age, I will never forget her because she is like a mother to me.

Faiza helped me prepare for my wedding because my mom wasn't here. In my culture, it's very important for a mom to be with her daughter to prepare for the wedding. She went with me to find everything I needed for my new home and wedding clothes. I was very young when I married, but she was already married, so she helped me learn everything I needed to know about marriage and child care.

When my babies were born, my best friend and her husband, who is my cousin, came to visit and brought many gifts. She also brought a special food, which in my culture, is given by the woman's family when they visit her home for a special occasion. This special food is made from beef or camel meat and called *oodkac*.

We were neighbors when we were very young, but when the Somali Civil War came, our families fled different ways. We lost contact with each other for ten years, but later, we found each other and became close neighbors again in Nairobi for five years. Later, she married my cousin, who had been living in the USA, and moved back to the USA with him. Soon after I came to the USA, we were reunited again.

Faiza is a good person, friendly, helpful, smart, and very active. She is the same age, height, and size as me. Faiza is my best friend.

Farhiyo Shirelle is 36 and originally from Somalia.

Life of My Grandma

SHA RUAN, LAUDERDALE, MN

My grandma is over eighty-five years old, and her life was full of suffering. She was born in 1934 in a small village in the Hunan province, in southeast China. At that time, China was fighting a war with Japan, and people's lives were very poor.

When she was six years old, her father was forced into the army. There was no harvest that year because of a heavy drought. In order to not starve to death, her mother and siblings begged along the road and finally settled in a village more than eighty miles away. Her mother was unable to raise five children on her own, so she had to send my grandma to a landowner's family as a maid. In 1942, her father escaped from the army and found them, but he only collected his wife and three sons, leaving his two daughters behind.

The Chinese Civil War broke out in 1945, and in 1949, the People's Republic of China was established. My grandma was liberated and was no longer the maid of the landlord's family.

In 1951, my grandma married a carpenter. In the beginning, their relationship was not bad, but her mother-in-law didn't like her. She looked down on her because her family was poor. At the request of his mother, my grandma's husband divorced her in 1953. My grandma walked for two days and returned to her parents' house more than eighty miles away, but her father refused to let her stay, saying he wouldn't accept a daughter who was divorced.

In 1955, someone introduced my grandma to my grandpa, and they soon got married. Unfortunately, my grandpa was addicted to gambling and didn't take responsibility for his family. My grandma had to work very hard to earn money to raise their children, and she needed to hide the money carefully so my grandpa wouldn't steal it.

Sometimes, when my grandpa was angry, he beat and abused my grandma. One time, my grandma couldn't bear it and jumped into the river to commit suicide but was rescued by a nearby fisherman.

In 1981, when all four of her older children (including my mom) were independent, my grandma found a better job and left my grandpa. She raised the two younger children, who were still in middle school, on her own. They lived apart until my grandpa died in 1996.

Fortunately, my grandma has been living happily in her old age. She now lives with my parents and is well taken care of.

Sha Ruan is 34 and originally from China.

My Country Life
MEKDES TRITE, WORTHINGTON, MN

Hi, nice to meet you. I would like to tell you a story about myself. First of all, I was born in Ethiopia. My family was born in Ethiopia. I have a big family. Every Saturday and Sunday, I go to church with my family. I love all my family. School life is very good. Every morning, I go to school with my best friend. My favorite school subject is biology and IT. In my free time after school, I like to watch movies. It's very good.

Mekdes Trite is 27 and originally from Ethiopia.

My Brother
PAXOUA YANG, ST. PAUL, MN

There are many people in my family. I have two brothers, three sisters, and me. I was close with my big brother. His name is Khu. He is two years older than me. When we were young, I liked to play with him everywhere. He always asked me to go with him.

One morning, my mom told me to take care of my younger sister. After eating breakfast, I heard my brother say he is going fishing. I really want to go, but I have to take care my younger sister. I ask him if I can go with him, but he says, "NO." It made me sad.

After I saw my brother was gone, I told my sister to watch the baby because she was sleeping. After that, I followed my brother and went to find him at the lake. When he saw me, he was angry and asked me to go home but I did not. When we got home, my mom was very angry to me. She said, "Why don't you listen?" She didn't let me go with my brother anymore. I would stay home and help my mom take care of the baby and help my mom sew Hmong cloth called the *paj ntaub*. I felt sad. I was just a little tiny bit mad.

Now, I have lived in the U.S. for almost three years. When I miss them, I would video chat with them on Facebook. I plan to get my U.S. citizenship and go back to visit my family again.

Paxoua Yang is 23 and originally from Laos.

The Difference between Family and Friends
TRESOR KEMPOUK HERMEN, OAKDALE, MN

My name is Tresor Kempouk Hermen. I am thirty-five years old, and was born on February 28, 1985, in the city of Kumba, in Cameroon. I was a businessman and was involved in politics.

I am a father of three children: two girls, ages eight and one, and one boy, age five. I am not married, but I have a fiance named Flavie. We met in 2008 and started living together in 2012. Flavie is from the French-speaking part of Cameroon, but I grew up in the English-speaking part of the country. Flavie and our children are still in Cameroon, but in the future, I hope to bring them here to the United States with me.

I came from a small Christian family known as the Nulla family, which was my father's family name. My father was a truck driver, and later he became a farmer. My mother was also a farmer, and later she started her own business. My father died in 2011.

I have five siblings: two brothers and three sisters, one of whom has died. We were all born of the same parents. Currently, three of my siblings, my mother, and I are living in the United States. I live together with my two older brothers.

I had many friends, but never had someone serious, someone I can call my real friend, someone who can fight for me.

I was thinking that they were my friends, but instead, I was making a fool of myself. I realised that they were not my friends, because they were always expecting things from me. When I told them, "I don't have something," they would not believe me, because they wanted to take advantage of me and my business.

Tresor Kempouk Hermen is 35 and originally from Cameroon.

Lydia's Lost Battle
LAURENT GUEHI, ST. PAUL, MN

Cancer is a serious deadly disease that does not sort out its victims. Children, old people, men, and women can be affected. Breast cancer took my dear oldest daughter from this life. I was so looking forward to walking her down the aisle at her wedding.

I am in immense sorrow. I asked God, "Why are you letting me suffer this loss?" I made a decision to be an activist for a cancer foundation, or create my own foundation in the memory of my dear daughter, Lydia.

Lydia Guehi, we will never stop loving you. You will always live on in our hearts.

Laurent Guehi is 57 and originally from Côte d'Ivoire.

My Personal Narrative
HALIMO ABDALLE, FRIDLEY, MN

I came to America from Somalia in the year 1996. I was very close with my mother. She wanted me to leave with my older brother for America, which she viewed as a land of opportunities. I thought I would see her again soon, but it would be almost twenty years before the next time I saw her. I missed her dearly all those years. Life continued here, and I got married and had six children, and I finally decided to go to Somalia. It was a long and hard trip, but when I saw her again, it was like I had never left. I was very sorry that I had to come back, and I had hoped to visit her again soon.

The year 2020 was supposed to be a good and joyous year. That was the plan until coronavirus happened. A lot of people I knew became sick here in Minnesota and some passed away, and I was sad by their loss, but I never thought I would lose someone too. My husband's father was a great man who was always kind to me and treated me like his own daughter. He became sick around August, and my husband went to Egypt and took care of him. However, the week after my husband came back, we got the news that my father-in-law had passed away. The news was too emotional for me as I had hoped he would recover.

Around the same time, my beloved mother also became sick and experienced a stroke that left her bedridden. She was taken to a bigger city, and they tried to treat her, but she went into a coma and became unable to talk that well. Three of my siblings who lived abroad went to help out. I too decided to leave but sadly, it was too late. We received the call from my younger brother who told us she passed away. I was in a state of shock for a long time, and I couldn't even talk. I had wanted to just see her one more time, and I never got the opportunity.

The deaths of my mother and father-in-law had a big effect on me. I loved them both very much and they treated me with lot of kindness and care. It took me a while to recover from their deaths, and I am still sad when I think about them. However, I know that they are now in a better place, and I hope to see them again someday.

Halimo Abdalle is 36 and originally from Somalia.

My Grandmother "My Moon"
SARAH A, FRIDLEY, MN

I still remember grandmother. She was a strong woman, beautiful, and had a big heart. My mother told me when I was born, she was very happy. In 2001, suddenly she didn't remember who she was. She asked my grandfather, "Who are you?" She asked many questions. My mother did not know what was happening. In the past, we did not know what "Alzheimer's" is.

I was afraid if she forgot me. Every morning before I went to school I asked her, "What is my name? Who am I?" Every time she remembered who I am. She never forgot me.

The year 2009 was very hard because my grandma was sick, and in the last days of her life, she stopped talking. I don't know why, but one day before I went to my school, she told me, "I pray for you to pass your test." I was surprised and so happy because she did not forget me, and she still prayed for me after that. In the afternoon, when I went back to my home, my mother told me, "My mom is very sick. I will take her to hospital." I didn't know, but I was sure this would be the last day I could see her and touch her.

At 11 p.m., I got a big feeling she was dead. After midnight, my mother told me to be strong and pray to her. I'm in every prayer I pray for her. I did not forget her, and I will not forget her.

I can say she was beautiful all the time. I love you, MY MOON!

Sarah A is 25 and originally from Somalia.

Story about Baby Teething

YASMIN ALI, MINNEAPOLIS, MN

My son Mahad is fourteen months old. Mahad was nine months old when he got his first tooth. Mahad had two white dots in his mouth and was drooling a lot. Sometimes he was fussy and cried a lot. He liked to chew on a plastic toy. He needed extra love. Sometimes I gave him some Tylenol. The pain killer medication made him feel better. I sang a Somali and English lullaby that made him comfortable. I remember the teething time was not funny.

Somali Lullaby

Hobeeya hobeey hobeeheyaa

Hooyo markaad dhalatood dhawaaqday

Hooyo dhulkaa iikala iftiimay

Hooyo korkayga dhadaa ka duushay

Dhalaalaayow ha dhaylmin.

Dhul iyo dhagax haw dhaxaynin.

Dharaar habartaa ma ooydo.

Dhallaamada kaama waydo.

English Lullaby

You are my sunshine.

My only sunshine.

You make me happy

When skies are grey.

You never know dear

How much I love you.

Yasmin Ali is 27 and originally from Minneapolis, MN.

Busy Mom

TOMASA ROMERO, FRIDLEY, MN

On the weekend, I'm very busy because my sons play soccer and my younger son plays in a soccer club. His soccer practices start on Friday from 6:30 to 8:30 p.m. in Brooklyn Park, and then he also plays on Saturday with his soccer team in a place called Soccer Blast that's in Burnsville. He usually plays around 3 p.m. When he finishes, after his game is done, he comes out very tired. Sometimes, when we get home, we watch movies or tv shows but also go to sleep early, because he also plays in the morning. At 8 a.m. he plays in the YMCA in Minneapolis, and then after that he plays in another place in Minneapolis. He plays U12 and then after that, my oldest son plays in the same place but a different field. He plays U16. He sometimes plays goalie or defender. That is what I usually do on the weekend.

Tomasa Romero is 33 and originally from Mexico.

My Best Friend in America

EDGAR DE ALBA, LINDSTROM, MN

I never thought that my best friend would be an American. Let me describe him to you and see what are your thoughts. His name is Connor. He became my roommate on Thanksgiving Day, 2018. The first day that I met Connor, we had to ride together, and he wasn't quiet all the way home. He had a lot to say. He's tall, strong, young, blonde, has brown eyes, and long hair. Connor has blond eyelashes, and he's very fast.

Connor was rude to everyone that came to visit the house. Over time, he learned to be kind and polite. Connor went to school in 2019 to learn to be kind and patient. Now he smiles.

Even though he is an adult, Connor still likes to play with toys and balls. He is really good at hunting mice. He likes to be up very early every morning before the coffee starts. He likes to take hikes and to go for a swim in the summertime in the afternoon. Connor used to sleep under the bed, but now he sleeps in the bed. Now Connor knows when to speak and when to be quiet. He learned to share his space with others.

Connor didn't like to shower, but now he's learning to accept that it has to be done if he wants to live in the same house with me—especially after rolling in stinky stuff. If you give him a couple of treats, he will sit, lay down, roll, speak, or shake. His best friend is a Chihuahua. He learned not to bite people. Actually, he has a certificate for a S.T.A.R. Puppy from the American Kennel Club.

My best friend is a four-year-old German Shepherd, Chow Chow, and Golden Retriever mix. He came from the Humane Society. If you ever consider finding a good American friend, the Humane Society is a good place to look. If you consider having a pet, maybe consider rescuing one.

Edgar De Alba is 34 and originally from Mexico.

My Neighborhood "Luluvizinhas"

CRISTIANE REIS, PLYMOUTH, MN

Anytime when I must decide to move, this is a very emotional situation. My family moved from Brazil three times. All of these were very difficult for family, friends, and of course, for us.

The last move out of Brazil was memorable. We lived in an incredible neighborhood called Luluvizinhas. The neighbors were very special, and we did many things together. The children were friends and always played together. We always had parties,

commemorations, and most important, the families helped and supported each other when necessary. We had different opinions, cultures, religions, beliefs, thoughts, attitudes, and customs, but the feelings of friendship, compassion, and support were very intense.

In situations of joy or sadness, health or illness, birth or death, or simply because we thought that person needed attention, we were there as neighbors. All these situations had an attitude of love and friendship. A flower left in front of your door or a surprise birthday party, anything was a reason for us to be together. One family helping another with a single feeling: friendship. In a selfish world, it is very difficult to find people with good attitudes, and we were blessed.

One month before we came to the U.S., the neighbors had a big and emotional party for me, and at the end, I went home, put on my pajamas, and went to sleep. The bell rang, and I thought, "Who will it be at this hour?" It was unbelievable to see almost all my neighbors in front of my house with their cell phone flashlights on, simulating a candle, and singing a beautiful song. All were crying, and I almost had an emotional heart attack. This surprise made me believe that my neighbors are important for me and my family. The song was "Friends for Life."

I wrote this story using verbs in the past tense, but my neighbors still have the same attitudes in Brazil. We always communicate, and I miss them. They can count on me, and I can count on them ALWAYS. After all, the distance doesn't separate true friendships.

Cristiane Reis is 47 and originally from Brazil.

Ten Years

MIRIAM AGUSTIN, WORTHINGTON, MN

Ten years ago, I left my country, Mexico, my home, and my family. I left my two children, a ten-year-old girl and an eight-year-old boy, with great sadness but with the hope of giving them the best. I got to Minnesota first. I have worked a lot during these years. Although I have missed them and I had to be without them, I know it has been worth the sacrifice. Now they are studying at the university. They are excellent children and very good students. In about three years, they will graduate. I am happy and very proud of them. I have my husband and my nine-year-old son here with me. My husband is my support. My son is my everyday company. He is also a very good son and student. After these ten years, I have the hope that, very soon, we will all be together.

Miriam Agustin is 39 and originally from Mexico.

My Older Brother

ALI TUSSA, ST. PAUL, MN

First, me and my older brother are really close, more than the other brothers. I have three brothers from same mom and same dad, and then I have three brothers and three sisters from different mom. I could say we have a big family. All my brothers are close to each other, but me and my older brother from my mom, we are super close than the other brothers.

We went to the same religious school. We always walked together to go to school. We had to walk at least fifteen to twenty minutes to get there. When we went to school, we had to cross one river. That river was so clean and not deep. We liked swimming so much, sometimes we would leave early from home because we wanted to have enough time to swim. Before we swam, we throw a coin to the water. Then, we ask each other, who can get the coin first? Then, we jumped from the bridge at the same time. Then, we started swimming.

After we were done swimming, we went to school. When I was in fifth grade, my brother was seventh grade. We went to different classes but we saw each other on break time. Then, we played soccer games with our friends after we finished class. We did not walk. We ran for a competition. Most of the time, he got home before me, and I was mad but, rarely I got home first, but he was not mad.

In Oromia, we had two shifts for school. It switches every month. One month is morning shift and another month, afternoon shift. During, I learn morning shift and after class, I help my family then I study little bit, and play marbles with my friends and brothers. I am always mad and cry when I lose.

Finally, I miss that time, and all my friends and my brothers. I did not see them for four years. Especially my older brother. I miss him so much. I hope I see him one day.

Ali Tussa is 26 and originally from Ethiopia.

My World

BRANDON KERTSCHER, DETROIT LAKES, MN

Kacen. My Son. My World.
He brings joy to my life. We
bonded from the start. Even
though he was a little fart. I got
to bond with this son more because
I was sober. Not like for my others. He talks like me, and he acts like me. He even has to be naked to go poop. Just like me. I know it's weird, but it makes me laugh. Kacen is a hard worker. He even helps me cut my grass. It's awkward 4x4 but fun. Even though I have to step wide. He bent in front hand on the first bar helping me push. He got my looks, but he gots her eyes. But he gots my hair so you know he's my heir. He likes his dog and cat. Mom and I separated when he was two. He is the protector like me. He won't lie. He would hint around. Mom was in a rough relationship. We play cars a lot. He got a remote control 4x4 and walks it like a dog. I watched it on a video. Just know Kacen. Daddy loves you. Daddy misses you. Daddy will always be here or there for you.

Brandon Kertscher is 30 and originally from Detroit Lakes, MN.

Family and Friends

SAFIA AHMED, ROSEVILLE, MN

I have a big family: my mom and my dad, four brothers, three sisters, and five cousins. We live in Minnesota. I live with my parents and my sisters. My cousins also live in Minneapolis. My brothers live in other cities like St. Cloud. I love my family a lot. We have a lot of fun cooking together, watching TV, going outside to the park, and going shopping at the mall. We always make some rice and chicken and sometimes spaghetti. I watch TV with my sisters. Sometimes we watch shows. We watch Netflix in English. Last time I watched "Witches," and we liked it.

I'm new here. I don't have a lot of friends yet. I just have one friend here from Cairo; I met her in Cairo, but she is Somali like me. Now she lives in St. Cloud. I like people who are funny. My best friend is very funny. I like shopping a lot, and I like to go shopping with friends. I like clothes and makeup. It is hard to make new friends now because of COVID. When the coronavirus is finished, I will get a lot of new friends.

Safia Ahmed is 22 and originally from Somalia.

The Best Time of My Life

MARYAM JAMAC, MINNEAPOLIS, MN

The best time of my life was when our first child was born. We were happy when our son was born. I am excited when my son grows, because I see him when he helps me. We are happy with our son every time. Also, my husband feels happy when his son grows. Now he is twelve years old. My son does everything. He uses his bathroom and prepares his food and cleans dishes and even washes clothes. He takes out the trash. We are happy with our son.

Maryam Jamac is 47 and originally from Somalia.

My Favorite Place Is Mexico City

MIRIAM SAUZ, WORTHINGTON, MN

My favorite place is Mexico City because my father and brothers are there. Mexico is very beautiful for the people, for the traditions. My family lives in Culancengo. I like to eat tacos. Tacos are my family's favorite food.

Miriam Sauz is 28 and originally from Mexico.

My Cute Niece

ANONYMOUS, MINNEAPOLIS, MN

Yesterday was the birthday of my little niece, and I was really happy because she has just one year. She doesn't know what is a celebration but was happy because all my family took a lot of silly pictures with her. There was a lot of desserts and food.

A Peanut Memory

CRISTINA MOROZUMI, ST. PAUL, MN

I would like to share how baby Peanut came into my life. My oldest daughter adopted our first dog named AJ. She drove from Minnesota to Chicago to adopt AJ. She wanted to give the dog to her brother as a gift, but my husband didn't agree. So, my daughter gave AJ up for adoption.

One month later, my youngest daughter was crying and crying for one week because she missed AJ. They used to play together after school. So, my husband decided to approve bringing another puppy home. After Peanut came to my house, everything was happy around Peanut.

Peanut did stuff that was not very common. For example, she stayed with the kids and protected them when they slept. Automatically, she learned to listen and obey. She even respects our food and knows not to touch it. And that is why we enjoy her.

Cristina Morozumi is 46 and originally from Mexico.

My Last Pregnancy

LUDMILA LERICHE LEONNE, ROGERS, MN

I didn't know that I was pregnant. I went to the hospital because I felt tired for a couple days. At the hospital, the doctor took my urine sample and did the test. After that he said, "You are pregnant." My husband and I were so happy.

The first two trimesters were very good because I didn't feel bad. I was strong, I worked a lot, I didn't have nausea, and I didn't sleep a lot. All of these things were really different compared to my first pregnancy. For this reason some of my friends said maybe it would be a boy because I felt so different than my first pregnancy.

But the last trimester, especially the last two months, was so hard. I felt like my baby wanted to come early, but it was a false labor. I had cramps in the night, but in the morning they disappeared. A couple weeks later, I had contractions, and I went to the hospital. They said, "The baby is not ready, so you need to go back home." Three times, I had contractions during the night, but in the morning they disappeared. I felt so bad and very tired, and I didn't know what I could do.

One day, I started to pray to God, the Creator of the Universe. I called the name of "Jesus." I gave my life and my soul, and I prayed more than before. I prayed every day, every morning, and every night. I called the name of my baby, and I said, "It's your time to come because I know you are ready. I know you want me to take you in my arms because it's your time." I waited four more days, and my baby came in the morning after my morning prayer. She came this day very quickly, and I was surprised. One thing was very interesting. She came two days before my due date. I was happy to see finally my baby girl, Leona.

Ludmila Leriche Leonne is 30 and originally from Gabon.

Four Little Girls

ANONYMOUS, TWIN CITIES, MN

Emoni never cared from the start

La'Shay on her face will always be a frown

You broke Praiza's heart

You let Olaina down

Oh you mad, you filled with anger

To these four little girls you are not and

Will always be a stranger

You feeling hurt, now you want to cry, you a dead beat

Daddy.

Rehabilitate yourself don't even try

Oh you get to keep in touch, you get fifteen min
    phone calls

You pathetic, a disgrace to the family and by you I am

Appalled. You want a standing ovation, you deserve an

Applause. Quit, you was headed to the touchdown and

You fumbled the ball. Justice was absent, you wish the

Jury would die, the verdict wasn't fair

You lied to four little girls, looked them in the eyes and

Said, "I'll always be there." What's gonna happen if
    a man

Disrespects them? Shut up sir, you in prison you can't

Even protect them. Oh you gotta plan to make up

Lost time and things right… please dude, they'll be
    grown next time you see the light.

You said, "See you later" you might as well said,
    "See you goodbye"

Another man gonna step up to the plate and teach
    your daughter how to drive, get them off to
    college, and show them a better life.

What's wrong… you feel neglected? Forget yo feelings, imagine how these four little girls will be affected. Their little precious hearts more hurt than chemo.

They will spend a lifetime searching for you but you won't be found like finding Nemo. You went from a king to a zero. Life put you at the line and you air-balled a free throw. How does that make you feel Richard? Just another dead-beat father who left the picture, and to think you was your families' hero. I'm done with this conversation, where the heck is Rico?

My Successful Uncle

JIALING LIN, MAPLE GROVE, MN

My uncle, Bruce, is the most successful person I know, even though he has had many obstacles on his road to success. First of all, my grandparents are very poor. They are farmers, and they have five children. They are not able to keep my uncle going to school; therefore, my uncle quit school. But my uncle is very smart. He helped my grandparents do farm work and taught himself. Later, my grandmother sent him to the United States. He worked very hard to make money, hoping to help his family live a good life. Then, he met my aunt, and they fell in love. A few years later, they opened the first restaurant. However, my grandpa passed away. My uncle was very busy in the restaurant, so he could not see my grandpa for the last time. This is his biggest regret. Now, my uncle already has several restaurants of his own. He has a son and a daughter. My uncle also helped his brothers and sisters a lot to make them live a better life. He is our hero.

Jialing Lin is 24 and originally from China.

A Little Help Can Go Far

COLETTE TINKPON, EAGAN, MN

The person who impacted me the most in my life besides my parents was Madame Attolou, one of the best people in the world. She was my neighbor who lived beside my parents' house in Africa. She lived with her husband and two boys.

I met Madame Attolou for the first time when I was in third grade when they moved to the house near mine. She always wanted to be a friend of mine, and she was very friendly towards me. Often times she would invite me to her house, and a lot of times I would help her clean. At the end of the day, she would give me some money so I could get lunch for the day. I loved going to her house, and I loved helping her. She didn't have any daughters, and she wished she had one. I think she thought of me as a daughter to her.

The following year, I moved on to fourth grade, and once I got done with that, I moved on to fifth grade. After two months, I was sent home to get the tuition for the school, which was thirty dollars. My parents didn't have the money, so I dropped out of school and started helping my mother with her daily activities. At first, my mom didn't want me to leave the house during the school time because she felt uncomfortable, but eventually I was doing most of the work with her. Then, one day, Madame Attolou saw me outside running errands for my mom, and she asked, "Why aren't you going to school anymore? Did they let you out today?" I told her no

and that I wasn't going to school because my family couldn't afford the tuition. She nodded and went home, and I continued helping my mom out for the rest of the day.

The next day I woke up, ready to start helping my mom again, but someone came to our door. It was Madame Attolou. When I opened the door, she greeted me and asked for my mom. When my mom came to the door, she handed her some money. When my mom asked her what it was for, Madame Attolou told her that I could go back to school. I thanked Madame Attolou and my mom, and I got dressed to go to the school. We went to the school and paid the tuition, and I was allowed back into class.

That day changed my life, and I was able to receive an education because of her kind actions. From that day, I learned that no matter who you are or where you're from, there will be someone willing to help you out.

Colette Tinkpon is 42 and originally from Benin.

My Story

KA LER, FULDA, MN

My family and I like the United States. I like Fulda. Thailand was a little bit good, but America is better. I stay in Fulda, and I meet my teacher. My teacher is good, and I like my teacher. I will go to church with my teacher when COVID is gone. I like my friends Mike and Sharon, and I love my family. I like the beautiful town of Fulda and the good people. I came to America on August 8, 2012, and I became a citizen on December 17, 2020. Life is good in America!!!!

Ka Ler is 50 and originally from Thailand.

Halloween during Covid

AMY TONG-YANG LEE, OAKDALE, MN

In the past years, I took my children trick-or-treating around our neighborhood. Children were dressed like ghosts and were scared to walk towards people's houses. Some of the houses made noises and frightening sounds. Sometimes, we ran away without taking the candy. We would be scared to walk to the next house. I would call my children to come home. I was happy to be home with my children this year because of Covid-19.

Amy Tong-Yang Lee is 31 and originally from Laos.

How I Met My Husband
YADIRA SALVADOR, BROOKLYN PARK, MN

My husband's name is Rubén. We met when I was thirteen years old, and Rubén was fifteen years old. We were in high school and were introduced by a mutual friend. Rubén was very popular in school and caught my attention, but he took the first step for us to get to know each other. One day, Rubén asked me if he could walk me home, and I said yes. Four days passed, and Rubén asked me to be his girlfriend. I said yes, and we were together for three months when I saw him with someone else. At that time, I told him that is was all over between us. After that, we would see each other as friends and Rubén still wanted to be with me, but I didn't want a relationship with him anymore.

For six months, I didn't see my ex-boyfriend Rubén. One day, Rubén went to my secondary school and surprised me with roses, but I had a new boyfriend called Ramiro. At that moment, Ramiro came by, and I introduced him to Rubén. Ramiro knew that Rubén had been my boyfriend and got angry and asked me if I wanted to leave him. I said no and explained that he was just my friend. I told Rubén, "I'm sorry but my boyfriend is angry, and I have to go with him."

Eighteen months passed before I saw Rubén again. He had suffered an accident and had had an operation on his stomach. He offered to take me to school, but he was always with a friend. I asked him, "Why don't you leave your bodyguard behind?" He said no because he still was not well. It was about a month before Rubén asked me to be his girlfriend. I asked him if he had changed or was still the same as before. He laughed nervously, and I told him not to worry because I had learned my lesson, and if he hadn't, it would be the last chance for us.

I stayed with him, and after fourteen months, we decided to get married. I was turning seventeen and he was nineteen years old.

We have been married for almost twenty-three years now. We have two daughters: one is twenty-two, and the other is thirteen.

Yadira Salvador is 39 and originally from Mexico.

Hamdi's Graduation
HODAN FARAH, BROOKLYN PARK, MN

My second oldest daughter, Hamdi, graduated on December 14, 2019. I was happy that day, as much as my daughter. Our whole family went out to eat and have fun all day. It was one of the happiest moments in my life.

Hodan Farah is 47 and originally from Somalia.

My Younger Brother
H. PIERRETTE SANTANNA, CRYSTAL, MN

My younger brother's name was Isaac. At the age of seven, he hated school. He didn't like to obey the rules of the school. He didn't like to hear talk about school. My father decided to send him to a boarding school, but my mother refused. One day, we looked at a movie on TV which talked about school's advantages. After the movie, he decided to study hard at school and become the first in his class. He began to study hard. At the end of primary school, he was the first person in his class. It was the same at the end of middle school.

He became our father's favorite. Our father bought him good things like shoes and clothes. He accompanied our father everywhere. He became a friend of everybody. I wanted to be like him. He gave me a good example. He was successful at school. He graduated from high school. After high school, he enrolled in the medical analysis program. He studied hard.

At the third year of his study, he suddenly got sick. The doctor told us he had renal failure. Despite his illness, he continued to work hard. On February 2015, I was at work when my younger sister called me to tell me that our brother had died. I was very sad when I heard the news. I didn't eat for two days. Every member of the family felt very sad because first, he was the only boy of the family, second, he worked hard, and third, he was at the end of his study, and he wanted to begin some work and continue to study.

After his death, I got married on September 3, 2015. I gave birth, and the baby was a boy. He looked like my brother, his face, his head. It was wonderful. Everybody was happy. They said our Isaac had returned.

H. Pierrette Santanna is 31 and originally from Togo.

My Wonderful Mom

EVAN MAHMOUD, FRIDLEY, MN

My mom was my hero. I lived with my mom for twenty-six years. I never left her for any reason, but she left me last year on June 26 because she passed away. The first night she was not at home was the blackest night in my whole life. It was the saddest day in my life. It's a day I'll never forget. I never ever thought that day would come. It's not easy to understand it. I'm the second child in my family. I always see her in my dreams. She was my best friend and my mom at the same time. She is always with me to reach my goals and to be a strong woman in the future. I had many great times and memories with my mom. I learned many good things as experiences for life. I learned how to be a strong woman like my mom. She never gave up. My life was happy when we were all together. I have a very big space in my life now. My mom will live in my heart forever.

I remember how much we were happy when we first came to the USA. My mom was the most important person in my life. I know she knows that and also she knows how much I LOVE HER. She was the one who took care of me and all my family. God blessed her because she was a wise woman. This month will be seven months, and I still miss her so much in my heart. It feels like years passed. I will never forget all the sweet things that she did for me, because she will still live in my heart. My mom is an amazing person if you ever met her. I am so thankful for my mom because she was the person that gave me birth. She was the person that took care of me before I came, for nine months. That was not easy for all women. I'm very proud of my mother. I'm always thankful to GOD for my mom because she was a wonderful mother. They say, "Anybody without a mother is nothing." I am so glad I had my wonderful mom, even for a short time. I would not be the same without her. I will be a good role model like my mom, for my children.

Evan Mahmoud is 26 and originally from Iraq.

My Brother and Me

FILSAN ISMAIL, ST. PAUL, MN

My brother and I are close friends. His name is Kunil. He is a dancer and also a soccer player.

Kunil is a very quiet man who does not interfere with people. He is not a bad person, but it is his nature to be silent, but he talks to me every time.

He wanted to buy a PlayStation 5, but every GameStop has only two PlayStations, so the opening time of the store was 7 a.m. on Black Friday. We went to the front of the GameStop on Wednesday night. There we sat for two nights and one day.

It was too cold. What we were doing, as it was very cold, was I turned on the car, then my brother and I changed places. Each of us sat in the car for a while. Then, on Thursday night, my older brother, Adnan, who is older than both of us, came. He told me I had to go home. I went home, and at 8:30, they came home, and he bought what he wanted.

Filsan Ismail is 22 and originally from Ethiopia.

My Mother

GABRIELA LARA TELLO, ST. PAUL, MN

The person I admire most is my mother. She is my hero in so many ways. She is a great person who likes to help other people. She is always kind and caring. Another reason I admire her is because she is hard working. She has worked hard to make her dreams come true. She immigrated to the United

States twenty years ago for a better life and future for us. She went to a new country to work. She had to learn a new language. She worked two jobs to earn money to bring us here from Mexico.

After four years of living in the United States alone, she brought us here. Coming to the United States was a dream come true for us. After many years apart, we were united again.

My sisters and I will always be thankful for the wonderful mother we have. We thank God for her. She will always be our hero and inspiration. Mother, we will always love you and thank you for everything you have done for us.

Gabriela Lara Tello is 32 and originally from Mexico.

My Busy Life
SHADA ADAM, ST. PAUL, MN

My life is very busy. I am the mother of eight children: five boys and three girls. It is not easy caring for eight children and my husband. I have to wake up early in the morning, make breakfast, and make sure everyone brushes their teeth. While they are attending online classes, I check on them often. My oldest son helps me take care of them.

We do many things together. The whole family plays games and reads books together. We love homemade food. After lunch, we all take a nap. I am proud to say, I have good kids. They help me to become a better mother each day.

Shada Adam is 45 and originally from Oromia.

Marigold
ANONYMOUS, ST. PAUL, MN

Her thick hair seems like a ruffled marigold, gleaming with golden luster. What it frames inwardly is her watery oval eyes, supple lips, soft round cheeks. Her smile reveals concealed dimples, the shallow imperfection making her countenance more perfect. Yet it is her faint blush that captivates even the most nonchalant heart: a tinge of scarlet flushes through the silky face, all the way down to the neck. It fades to a creamy yellow and mingles in the snow-colored skin, smoothly shifting from one shade to another, without any trace of transgression.

Such a familiar and glamorous smile! It seems a savory smile when the family tastes a crude salad platter spiced with marigold petals, a mixed flavor of sweetness, pungency, and subtle sourness. A smile of satisfaction of delicious and chilling food on a scorching summer night; it seems an exuberant and exhilarant wedding smile when a couple scurries through marigold-ornate arch, across the tang of fragrance toward the altar. A blissful smile of ready to bind the lifelong vow with the other part of soulmate; it is also a peaceful smile of the deceased when he or she motionlessly lies on the marigold-overlayered bed and is embedded in the dazzling floral radiance. An etched stagnant smile after fulfilling the life purpose and embarking on the pure journey to heaven.

Her smile, like marigold, condensed all the pleasurable senses into one single lustrous flower.

Arrivals and Departures: Journeys to the U.S.

Featured Author

Ayub Mohamed

COLUMBUS, OH

My name is Ayub Mohamed. I was born in Somalia, a small country in Africa. I grew up in a family of eight, and despite the poverty-ridden environment and slums, my memories of childhood are happy, content, and adventurous.

My family and I moved to America with the same dream most immigrants possessed. We settled in Columbus, Ohio. I was acquainted with snow and became ecstatic beyond measure; not even the subzero temperature could pierce my excitement. I was enrolled in school but didn't speak English, which was the prerequisite for all curriculums. Therefore, I had to adapt and integrate forthwith. Because of the constant moves, new challenges presented themselves, and preadolescence was a battle of its own. My personality throughout school was taciturn. I became disinterested in school and started flocking with individuals vilified by most. I was unaware of their motive because their approach was very subtle. For the first time in life, I had to thread the needle and exercise my mental faculties in order to produce solutions to my tribulations.

I eventually received my GED, and a world of possibilities seems endless. I've received my dreams of the past that were suppressed long ago. My journey has just begun, and I have no regrets. In succession, my life was a hurricane of problems, but I also enjoyed the better part of life. Today, I'm blessed with a support system that always loves and cares for me, and at times I wonder if I deserve them.

Trials

In the midst of my adolescence and early twenties, I was unaware of the company I kept. Unbeknownst to the severity of my choices, a prison sentence became a reality. Early on, the signs were visible, and the numerous times spent in jail became a constant headache for my family because they always bailed me out. Somehow, this cycle didn't seem to bother me until the doors of the penitentiary became visible.

Upon entry as I was going through the gates and bars of prison, I felt abandoned. I felt alone. That first night, I silently cried. Wishing for a second chance, while hoping for this part of my life to subdue and not become repetitive, but hope can at times be a blind leader. As I witness the world and my peers excel before my eyes with ease, a sense of defeat prevails. Oblivious and uniformed of the consequences ahead, I wandered aimlessly through most of my life. Therefore, sleep became sporadic, and I resented my life of the past. It's unfathomable, like the depths of the ocean. Layers of darkness and confusion provide no solutions, yet I'm still smiling. Once again, I remain hopeful, however futile.

A glimpse of the seeds I sowed puts an emphasis on my hopes and dreams left behind in a dust of hopelessness. Dreams of making my poor immigrant parents proud, so your efforts and sacrifices were not in vain. So, come join me in this journey of patience, alleviate my burdens and don't you cry no more. A cold night departs, and the morning falsely deludes. It speaks volumes of things I took for granted, hopes of chasing my dreams and living a life of tranquility, of exploring the horizon and beyond, of pursuing my academics and becoming a somebody. But a reminder of life in prison ensues. Throughout my days, I contemplate about the futility of hope and wonder, why am I consumed in regret? Associating with pernicious individuals, most were eager to see my downfall and demise. Such nefarious individuals will never concede their dark motive, for misery likes company. In the future, I hope to differentiate between friend and deception.

I'm glad I went down this road. So much can be learned from failure, as this became my unforgiving teacher. Through darkness and ignorance, I've become cognizant and vigilant. In bondage, I've awakened a beast inside of me and for that, I feel liberated; no longer incapacitated. One shouldn't be too concerned with what was, and what will be because yesterday is history, tomorrow is a mystery, and today is a gift.

Ayub Mohamed is 27 and originally from Somalia.

My New Journey in Minneapolis

LEMMA TUFA, MINNEAPOLIS, MN

I was born in a small village called Siltana, Oromia. It is located in Ethiopia. My parents never attended school because they are farmers, and they devoted their time to a plantation.

I am the last person born in a family of eight. I am the first person in my family to earn a high school diploma and a Bachelor of Arts degree in accounting. That was a big achievement for our family.

I came to Minneapolis at the beginning of 2020 when COVID-19's transmission was becoming extreme. I survived interviewing fifteen times and finally got a job. I thought my English was good, but while interviewing so many times, I realized that it is not as good as I thought. I want to see another version of me. I'm starting my life over from scratch in this country. That is what I'm fighting for.

I understand that there will be more obstacles and barriers in the future, but I believe that pain is a thing to be prized. Someone who does not know the pain would not appreciate joy, nor would he obtain the strength to make the journey worthwhile. I'm thirty years old. I know I can do more than I expect. Wish me well as God blesses my new journey.

Lemma Tufa is 30 and originally from Oromia.

Coming to America

SARA JAMA, MINNEAPOLIS, MN

When I went to Ethiopia from Somalia in 2011, my husband was living in America. I moved to Ethiopia to interview for a visa to go to the United States. I didn't speak the language. I didn't speak Oromo, so I didn't understand what people were saying. I could have hired someone to translate for me, but it costs a lot of money. I lived in a hotel for four days. Then my husband's cousin who lived in Ethiopia helped us find a house. After six months, my daughter, Barwato, who was six years old, was able to speak Oromo. She was then able to help me when I went to the grocery store or the clinic or took the bus.

I lived in Ethiopia for two and a half years, and then I came to the United States. We landed in Fort Worth, Texas. Texas was a good place—not that cold. But it was difficult to find a job because I didn't speak English. I lived for four years in Texas, where I had two kids. Then I came to Minneapolis in 2015 so that I could get a better job and get an education. They didn't have classes for adults in Texas. I attended Open Door to learn English. Now I understand English pretty well. In 2019, I applied at the Amazon warehouse. Now I can understand everything about my job. Things are going very well.

The future is good. If my English gets better, I hope to attend college someday. I would like to be a teacher. I would like to teach kindergarten.

Minneapolis is a good place. Right now I am able to help others who don't speak English. Last week, I was at work, and a woman I work with needed help speaking to the manager. He said, "What do you want? I can't understand you." I said, "I can help translate." I helped her get everything that she was asking for. She said, "Thank you, thank you! I didn't know what he was saying to me!" That made me feel good.

Sara Jama is 41 and originally from Somalia.

Snow! For the First Time

ABENA POMAAH, CRYSTAL, MN

My name is Abena Pomaah, and I came from Ghana, West Africa. When I came to the United States, I saw different people. The U.S. is full of rules and regulations, and everything is in order. When I came to the U.S., I saw snow for the first time, and I loved it! When I came here, the first week in 2013, it was wintertime, which is January. I have serious asthma, and they rushed me to the hospital. I was there for two days. When I came here for the first time, it was difficult for me to eat American food because our food is so different from American food.

Abena Pomaah is 69 and originally from Ghana.

My Name Is Almamy Sillah

ALMAMY SILLAH, MAPLEWOOD, MN

My name is Almamy Sillah, and I'm from the West African country of Gambia. I was born in a small town called Bnaiko. I came to America in the year 2000. It was March and springtime. I stayed with my sister for a while in New York for about forty-five days and then moved here to Minnesota and have lived here ever since.

When I came here to Minnesota, I lived with my brothers and friends. They have all since moved away. Some are staying in New York, and some are living in Canada, while some are living in Spain!

However, I'm still here. They ask me why I'm still living in Minnesota. "Minnesota is very cold, how do you handle it?" I tell them, "I like Minnesota healthwise, and it has the best quality air that I know of in the United States."

I started working at different temp agencies. One day, my friend told me about being a personal care assistant and asked me if I knew about it. I said, "No, I couldn't do that job," but he told me, "Yes you can, they will train you." I said, "I will try," and then went in to be trained for a week.

Almamy Sillah is 47 and originally from the Gambia.

My Memory

ZAYNAB AL WAHAH, FRIDLEY, MN

I remember my first travel when I came to America, and that was in November 2007. All my family was very sad, especially my mother. Her sisters came to support her to be strong and to say goodbye to me. When I rode in the car to the airport, my mom ran behind the car, and she was screaming, "Zaynab my dear, don't leave! I cannot live without seeing you!" That was a scene I will never forget in all my life. I am sorry Mom, that I put you in this situation and make you feel sad. I hope one day you can visit us and see this beautiful country. All my children love you and hope to see you again.

Zaynab Al Wahah is 44 and originally from Iraq.

My Journey to the United States

DIEP HA, COON RAPIDS, MN

My name is Diep Ha, and I am thirty-seven years old. I am from Camau, Vietnam.

I came to the United States on April 12, 2017. I remember the first day I came here. I felt very worried about everything! Because I didn't know how to speak English, everything here was difficult for me.

After two weeks my husband took me to school, and I learned English. I met many people in school! First, I met Ilse Hogan Griffin. She was so beautiful and very friendly! Then I felt better because I know all the teachers here are very nice and friendly! But when I learn English, I feel English is difficult.

After three months, I can hear some words of English. I also became friends with Ilse and Lisa. I felt excited about that!

After six more months, I can write, read, and remember some words of English. I felt so lucky and happy, too!

And everything here is better than in my country! The buses are very good to use. The school is so beautiful and very secure.

In the spring, many flowers grow up, and they look so beautiful! In the summer, the air is very fresh, and the sun is so beautiful! I can walk and grow vegetables. In the autumn it starts to get cold. The leaves turn beautiful and start to fall. In the winter, snow starts to fall. The first snow season is so beautiful! But after that it gets too cold, that makes me scared every time I go out.

Now I can speak a little English. But I need to speak English well. Then people can understand easier when I speak. And I can look for a job easier, too!

First, I want to say thank you to my parents for giving birth to me and teaching me how to be a good person. Second, I want to say thank you to God for keeping us safe and healthy! Third, I want to say thank you to my teachers for teaching English to me! Fourth, I want to say thank you to my husband because he took me to school four days a week. Fifth, I hope COVID-19 will soon end to return peace to all people around the world! Then, I can visit my family in Vietnam!

The last thing I pray for is my family and everyone to be healthy, peaceful, and have a good life! I love my family, and I love you all. May God protect and bless everyone!

Diep Ha is 37 and originally from Vietnam.

Coming to America
HALI ABDI, WAITE PARK, MN

I was born in Somalia. My family and I fled to Ethiopia. After staying in Ethiopia, we moved again to Seattle, Washington around 2011. The first time I got on a plane was the trip from Addis Ababa, Ethiopia to Seattle, Washington. When I was on the plane, it was fun. The plane ride was about twenty hours. The UN took us to the United States of America. My kids and family lived in Seattle, Washington safely for about three years until we moved to Minnesota.

Hali Abdi is 45 and originally from Somalia.

My Life in America
VICENTE VITAL CORTEZ, ST. PAUL, MN

When I arrived in the United States in 1995, I was having many feelings in my heart and in my dreams. For example, I felt these good feelings. I was free, happy, and excited. I also had bad feelings, as I was worried and sad over leaving my country. So much so that I cried for many days.

The most difficult thing was the language, but I'm learning little by little a bit every day. After one year in America, I had my first daughter. I felt happy and at peace because I had the best opportunities. One thing that was hard was my job at the restaurant, Superhut. The pay was low. I missed the love and warmth of my family, as well as the Mexican food, which is the best.

I love many things in the United States now. For example, the hospitals and healthcare is better than in my country of Mexico. Also, I love the laws in the U.S., for they are fair in all ways, especially in the care of women and children. When women and

children suffer abuse in my country, there are no existing laws to protect them. The laws in Mexico make women feel ashamed, and women don't feel safe. Never have I felt unsafe here, and I am glad that I can spend my whole life in the United States. I have three adult children and two grandchildren, all who were born here. I feel proud because they will have a different life than me. I will never forget my country. It is my second family, but I have decided to stay here because I love the USA for these awesome reasons.

Vicente Vital Cortez is 47 and originally from Mexico.

Journey to the U.S.
ANONYMOUS, MINNEAPOLIS, MN

My journey to the U.S. was by plane. I flew for eighteen hours, and it was a big challenge for me. I had never been on a flight for such long hours. I was so scared, tired, and worried. I kept praying a lot to land safely.

I felt like I would not go back to earth. I imagined how astronauts go to space and stay there for six months or more to calm my self down. Finally, after such a long flight, I landed at New York.

Coming to America
MICHELLE GEORGETTE ZABALOU, MAPLEWOOD, MN

My name is Michelle Zabalou, and I'm from the Ivory Coast (a West African country). Coming to America for me meant leaving my beautiful country and all of people that I love. But I had to come to America for a better future. I left behind my mother, father, my many siblings (ten brothers and four sisters), and my lovely grandmother, "Ekoun Kouass," that I lost later on. That loss was very painful for me and affected my life in America. The idea that the last day that I saw my grandmother was the day I came to America made me not able to focus on my new life.

I came in March 2003 to the state of Pennsylvania, precisely Philadelphia, where I spent seventeen years of my life before deciding to come to Minnesota, where my son is. The weather was the first thing that amazed me in America because in my country, it is always summer (one season). In America, I discovered four seasons, and this was strange to me. Out of the four seasons, I prefer the winters and springs. Winter because of the snow falls and spring because of the flowers. I had heard that the winters in Minnesota are hard, that they can have sometimes over twelve inches of snow. I'm waiting to see that!

I have also discovered that we have some differences in holidays. In America, they celebrate Halloween and Thanksgiving, and we don't in my country. I can say that I'm learning a lot about American culture.

Michelle Georgette Zabalou is 51 and originally from Côte d'Ivoire.

When I Moved to America

JOHANNA CHAVEZ MENDOZA, MATOMEDI, MN

I moved to the United States on March 5, 2020. I was very excited because I wanted to know all of the different places in Minnesota. However, I would not be able to do this because one week later everything was closed because of the Covid-19 virus. I felt happy when I was about to start English classes online. I got a job, and I had many activities at home because I didn't have many more options.

Some days were good, but others days I was bored. It is not comfortable wearing a mask all of the time. I have tried to make the best of it in the United States during these difficult moments. Every day I was curious for more information about the pandemic because I was worried for my family in Columbia.

I think when the pandemic is finished, I'll have more activities to enjoy, because for now, I need to take care of myself. I think that this year is very difficult for everyone, especially because of the big changes all around the world due to the coronavirus.

Johanna Chavez Mendoza is 43 and originally from Colombia.

My Family around the World

ELSA OLIVERA, ST. MICHAEL, MN

I was born in Venezuela. I have one sister who lives in Greece. Her name is Carolina. My other sister's name is Judith. She lives in Scotland. My mother lives with Judith in Scotland. My son, Carlos, is in Venezuela. I have two daughters. One is thirty-three and one thirty-six. I came to the United States two years ago. I live in St. Michael with my daughter, Carla, and my granddaughters, Amelie, eight, and Camilie, five. I went to school in Venezuela. I went to high school. I went to a course for pharmacy assistant for two years. I liked working as a pharmacy assistant. I worked as an assistant in a pharmacy for sixteen years. When I have learned English, I will get a job.

Elsa Olivera is 58 and originally from Venezuela.

My New Relatives

ZHANNA KIM, PRIOR LAKE, MN

My husband and I wanted to move to the United States because this country has many opportunities for everyone, a good economy, and equality. My husband applied for a green card. It was the first time for me and the third time for him. Six months later, a friend called me and said that she hadn't won the green card, and she wondered about us. I had completely forgotten about it and asked my husband to check. We were so surprised and happy because I had won. I played once and won! How could this be? I have no idea! The next day, we began to worry about our new life in America. We had relatives in Minnesota, but we had never met each other. We found them on the internet and sent them an email asking if we could live at their house after we arrived. They agreed.

When we arrived in the USA, they met us at the airport. Alina is the sister-in-law of my husband's mother. She is married and has three children. Her oldest son gave us his room. The end of our first day in America was a surprise to us. Our new relatives threw a big "welcome party." Their friends, probably fifteen people, brought traditional

Russian food and many gifts, supplies, and toys for my little daughter. The living room had been decorated, and there was a delicious three-tiered cake on the counter in the kitchen. Then they helped my husband find a car and a job. Soon, we became dearer to each other.

We have been living in America for five years now. Alina is one of my best friends. Once I asked her why she and her family helped us so much. She answered that when they arrived in the United States, many American families helped them. She smiled and said, "We are just returning what we owe them, by helping your family."

Zhanna Kim is 37 and originally from Kazakhstan.

I Love St. Cloud
AMINA MUSE, ST. CLOUD, MN

I like living here in St. Cloud because it is a nice and beautiful place. It's not too big or too scary. It is safe. Immigrants don't have problems with the police, like in Minneapolis. There are a lot of jobs. A lot of my relatives live here. It has great schools. Students get help with homework. The community is supportive and friendly.

Amina Muse is 48 and originally from Somalia.

My Favorite Athlete
HAE THOO, ST. PAUL, MN

My favorite sport is soccer. My favorite soccer player is Sergio Ramos. He is a good defender. This is my favorite defender. Sergio Ramos lives in Spain. The professional soccer player plays for Real Madrid and the Spanish national team. Ramos is one of the best defenders of all time. He was born on March 30, 1986. His height is six feet. Right now, he is thirty-four years old. Defender Sergio Ramos will leave Real Madrid on June 30. He needed more contract, but the president did not give him more. I am feeling so bad for him. I think so many people don't want him to leave Madrid.

Hae Thoo is 23 and originally from St. Paul, MN.

My Happy and Scary Experience
ARACELI MORALES, BROOKLYN CENTER, MN

In November of 1995, I had a scary but happy experience.

When I was eighteen years old, I came to Phoenix, Arizona to take care of my nephew. I drove from Mexico in a car with my brother. It was scary because I didn't speak or understand English. It was happy because later, I met my first husband and had two daughters and one son in the U.S. I still did not know the alphabet. When people spoke to me, I said, "No English!" In 2011, I went to school at Winnetka to learn English. I wanted to help my children with their homework. Now, I can understand more English, and it's not scary.

Araceli Morales is 43 and originally from Mexico.

When I Came to the United States
FAHIMA YASIN, MINNEAPOLIS, MN

I came to the United States on May 15, 2009. I arrived at the Washington, DC airport. My husband was waiting for me and my daughter, who was two and a half years at the time.

The weather was beautiful, and the ground was green. Everything was gorgeous. I was very happy. But we had to leave Washington, DC and go to Minnesota. Some of my family lived in Virginia. I stayed with them for three days. Then I flew to Minnesota.

When I landed in Minnesota, it was nighttime and not very pretty. I was worried. My daughter and I didn't like Minnesota, but we couldn't change anything. The food, weather, and language were hard. When I got here, I wanted to learn English right away because it was hard to talk with people. I am a shy person. It was embarrassing.

One year later I had a son. Everything was hard for me. I have to overcome many challenges. When I got to Minneapolis, I had two young children. I took care of them all by myself. I learned about transportation and how to ride the light rail and bus. I studied for my driver's test and I passed. Also, I studied for my citizenship test. And I passed that too.

I have always wanted to keep learning. I take care of my children and try to go to school and work. Now I am back in school, and I want to improve my skills. I want to get my GED, and maybe in the future, I can go to college.

Fahima Yasin is 42 and originally from Somalia.

New Beginning
CARALYS SANTIAGO, MAPLE GROVE, MN

Puerto Rico is small in size but around every corner, you'll find a celebration, food for the soul, and very friendly people. In 2015, I began to work in the Head Start program. I was teaching parents how to follow the special diets for their kids. I loved my job because I was traveling around the island to different sites, and my work was a new adventure every single day. I met my boyfriend at a reggae concert on the island in 2016. Two years later, my boyfriend got a new job in Minnesota. He proposed we move together to Minnesota. It was a shock for me because I never imagined living outside Puerto Rico. I didn't speak English, and it was very difficult for me because on the island I had everything: my job, family, and beautiful beaches. It took me about a year to make the decision, but then I decided to venture to a new beginning, new country, language, weather, people, and much more.

During the first month, it was very difficult for me because people spoke to me, and I didn't understand them. The wife of my boyfriend's co-worker recommended English classes from the Crystal Learning Center to me, and little by little, I learned more English. In these classes, I met people from around the world. When I got to Minnesota, I was a little sad because I missed my family and my lifestyle. I arrived in Minnesota at the beginning of the fall season. My boyfriend took me to see the North Shore, and then we visited Lutsen Mountains. I felt that I was in a calendar picture. I was impressed with the colors of the trees. I never saw anything like this. In my country, Puerto Rico, it's always summer, and the trees always are green.

During these months that I have spent in Min-nesota I have been impressed by the cultural variety and the friendly people. When I talk to people, they try to understand me. Now, I'm learning about the winter. I will never forget my first snow here in Minnesota. I went to the balcony of my apartment to feel the snow in my face. It was amazing. I would love to bring my whole family to visit so they can see how beautiful Minnesota is. I hope it's the beginning of new adventures.

Caralys Santiago is 31 and originally from Puerto Rico.

My Dream in a New Country
KARLA LUNA, MONTICELLO, MN

My story begins in Mexico. I finished my studies and made a career as a dental technician, of which I am very proud. Thinking about coming to the United States was very difficult since I would get away from all my family. Arriving in this country was not easy. I had good days and bad days, but even so until today, I have known how to face things by myself. I took time to learn English. I never thought English was so essential until you really have to live in another country. I am proud of my family and myself since, even if they are not present with me, I always have their support in a message or a call. I would like to study again in this country to find a job that I can really enjoy doing. For now, I will continue working in the company where I am. I work making egg products, breakfasts for schools, gas stations, and McDonald's. I hope very soon to tell a different story about a new job or studying at a college.

Karla Luna is 24 and originally from Mexico.

My Trip to Minnesota
ANONYMOUS, MINNEAPOLIS, MN

I'm originally from Djibouti, and my first language is Somali. I came to America in 2016, and I lived in Kentucky for four years. Every state in America has their own history or their own traditions. Kentucky is known for horses, the Derby, and bluegrass. It is not as cold as Minnesota.

Six months ago, I moved to Minnesota, and this is my first winter here. Minnesota seems like the coldest place in the U.S. I've ever experienced or seen. But one thing I like about Minnesota is there are a lot of resources like ESL and schooling. Now, I feel like Minnesota is my second home, because here there are a lot of Somali people or immigrants. Where I lived in Kentucky, there were no Somali or immigrants like Minnesota has. One thing I like about Minnesota is everywhere I go, there are lots Somali and Ethiopian restaurants. And people are nice and kind. I'm very grateful to be in Minnesota.

Coming to the United States

FATUMA ADAN, ST. MICHAEL, MN

I was born in 1974 in Mogadishu, Somalia. When fighting began in Somalia, it was dangerous. In 1991 my mother, father, two brothers, and my uncle were killed.

In 1992, my husband and I went to Mombasa. In 1995, we moved to Nairobi. My husband drove a taxi there. My children and I went to Kakuma camp.

The money my husband earned bought us food when we were in the camp. My son lived at my brother's house in Nairobi. He went to high school for four years. My other children went to elementary school. We had to pay fees for their schools. My husband got sick in 2005 and could not work anymore. I started working in a store to pay for school. On September 28, 2015 we came to the United States.

We went to Connecticut first. A Catholic church helped us. They found us an apartment. They gave us food, clothes, blankets, and shoes. Winter was coming! We needed warm clothes. The children went to school. On June 9, 2016 we moved to St. Michael, Minnesota. We did not know anyone. My cousin got us an apartment. My older son worked at Walmart in Connecticut, and he could get a job at Walmart in Minnesota. My older son went to Anoka College. He graduated. In January 2021, he started the University of Minnesota. One daughter is in college to become a nurse. My other daughter is in twelfth grade. My younger son is in ninth grade.

Now, my husband is very sick. He is on dialysis treatments three times a week. A treatment takes four to five hours each time. He also has high blood pressure and diabetes. Medication costs a lot of money. He can't work. I worked at Albertville Outlet Mall for four years. I did housekeeping in many stores. I worked four days a week. I liked my job. I only made a little money. The job became too hard because they don't have enough people to do the work. I will need to get a new job. I am happy to live in the United States because my husband can get good medical care. It is still not good in my country. St. Michael is safe for my family.

Fatuma Adan is 46 and originally from Somalia.

One Big Success

IKRAM YUSUF, EDINA, MN

I came from Oromia, Ethiopia in 2010. When I came to the United States, I didn't speak English, and I didn't drive a car. My husband took me wherever I wanted to go because it is very hard to drive when I don't speak English. I came to the U.S. with my daughter. She was six months old. After a few months, I started high school. My sister took care of my baby. After a few months, I was pregnant with my second child. I stopped high school. After I had my second child, I started Adult Academic Program. I learned a lot of things from Adult Academic Program. Now I read, write and speak English. I even studied for my citizenship there.

Ikram Yusuf is 31 and originally from Ethiopia.

My Journey to Come to America

GANO HUSSEIN, ST. PAUL, MN

First, when I give DNA, I wait for two years. After my DNA comes back, I'm so excited and nervous too. I'm nervous for interview because I'm thinking they will ask me so many questions. But they just ask me two questions. They ask me my dad's age and my DNA paper. After I finish my interview, I will get my visa in two weeks. When my visa comes, I'm so excited to come to the USA, and I'm excited to see my dad.

I'm excited to see how America looks like. So many things are different, and so many things are hard. For example, after I came to the USA so many things were hard to me. Speaking English, finding a job, and getting new friends. It was hard the first time I came here, especially in the winter time. I came to America in winter time. It was hard for me to go outside because I never saw snow before in my country. It was hard for me to start work and start school. My dad was old, and he did not drive a car. My brother and sisters live in another state, so I don't have anyone to give me ride. I stay home more than two months.

When I stay home, I feel lonely. I remember my mom and all of my friends. Sometimes, when I call my friends, they ask me how was America? When I'm in Ethiopia, we been talking about America with some of my friends. We think everything was easy. I told them America was not how we thought when we were talking before. I told them everything was hard, especially when you are not speaking English.

Gano Hussein is 27 and originally from Ethiopia

How I Met My Husband
SONITA SOY DJOA, ST. PAUL, MN

In late September of 2006, my aunt who was living in America called me to say she had a friend who was curious about a picture he had seen of me. He wanted to talk to me and get to know me. Back then, my English was not very good. I could write in English, but I couldn't speak it. So, we wrote letters to each other every day. Two months later, he asked me to be his girlfriend. I told him that in my country we could not be boyfriend and girlfriend. "If you love me, you have to marry me." He said, "Okay," and he came to Cambodia in December of 2006. We were married on December 30–31. In my country, our tradition is to have one and one-half day weddings.

Two days later, my husband and I visited a couple of different places for our honeymoon. On the first day we traveled to Kampong Sum beach.

It is a beautiful white sand beach. Then, we went to Angkor Wat and saw the old temple. There is a small park in front of Angkor Wat that is filled with lily pads. In the evening when the sun sets, it sets right over the top of the temple, and the shadow falls across the park, and it is so amazing.

My husband had to return to America. It took eleven months to do all of my paperwork. I finally got an interview with the United States Embassy in the middle of December. I passed on the first try! I arrived in Minnesota on December 24. It was the most beautiful place I had ever seen. The next day was Christmas Day, and there was snow on the roads, and the trees were white.

I am so happy to have a new life in Minnesota. This country has given me the freedom to speak that I didn't have in Cambodia. Before the pandemic, I had a good job and hopefully, I will be able to return to it and still go to school to continue learning English at no cost. Now, I have a nine-year-old son, and he goes everywhere we go. I have been able to travel to many countries such as Canada, Mexico, Central America, Belize, and the Caribbean. After the pandemic is over, my family and I will continue to travel to more countries. Someday, I will reach my dream to visit more places around the world.

Sonita Soy Djoa is 39 and originally from Cambodia.

My Story
HAE MOO, FULDA, MN

My name is Hae Nay Moo, and I came to the United States in 2009. Thailand was not good for me.

I have five children—three daughters and two sons. One daughter and one son live in Fulda, two daughters live in Texas, and one son lives in Utah. Three of my children are citizens, and I will become a citizen on December 17!

I like the United States, and Fulda is good! I like my ESL class, and I am happy!

Hae Moo is 50 and originally from Burma and Thailand.

What Surprised Me about the USA

THANY KUONG, ST. PAUL, MN

When my husband and I came to the USA, we met our family. We met my son-in-law, my daughter, and my grandchildren. My husband and I were so very surprised because they thought that living in the USA was safe and not dangerous. They thought that all grandchildren will have a good future. I was very surprised because in my country, it is not good; it looks like it is good, but it is not good.

Thany Kuong is 57 and originally from Cambodia.

My Life in the USA

BER DI, ST. PAUL, MN

My name is Ber Di. I live with my mom and dad in the USA. I have two younger brothers and four sisters. One sister is older, and three are younger than me. I am a student. My school name is GAP School. I take construction class, and then I learn about tool names. I learn how to take measurements, how to use sawzall, circular saw, hammer, chalk line, drill, drill bits, and more.

Every weekend, I go to buy the food. I cook chicken curry and *ma-ma* (noodles), soup, rice, and fish paste. Sometimes, we eat together, but sometimes not. I have one car. My car is a red Ford. Sometimes, I have a party and sometimes hang out with my friend and my cousin. Usually, I wake up at 6:30 a.m. I see the snow every year. Snow is beautiful. I take pictures with my brother after snow is falling. Sometimes I go to the park, and I ride the bike around the park.

Ber Di is 23 and originally from Burma.

My Refugee Story

SAHRA WALI, MINNEAPOLIS, MN

I was born in Somalia and had two brothers and five sisters. My country was in a civil war, so my family decided to go to Kenya. My parents passed away in Somalia. My auntie took us to the Utange refugee camp in Kenya. I liked it okay, as it was safe and good. We did not have any opportunity to go school. Lutheran Social Services sponsored my family to go to New York and then Sioux Falls, South Dakota on September 12, 1997. It was very cold and snowy and difficult to go outside. I didn't know how to live in the winter. We were in Sioux Falls for three months in the winter. I went by myself to Wilmar, Minnesota to my mom's family. I went to school in Wilmar for one year and improved my English. I then came to Minneapolis to go to work at the airport and worked for a rental car agency. I worked about ten years. I got married and had two boys. I now work another job, and I am happy. America is the best country and best people. I always see nice people. I am very excited to be in the United States.

Sahra Wali is 48 and originally from Somalia.

Immigration

MOZHGAN PAZOAKI, ST. PAUL, MN

I immigrated from Iran to Minnesota, where my daughter and husband live, when I was fifty years old. Immigration at this age is extremely difficult. Suddenly, everything in my life changed: country, culture, and especially a new language. I left my hometown and moved to this much larger city.

In this huge country, I had to start all over. Upon arrival in Minnesota, I enrolled in classes at the Hubbs Center to improve my English skills. My instructor, dear Stacy, helped me a lot. She helped me obtain a SafeServ certificate from the state of Minnesota, which led to a job a few months later.

My only hope for the future is to have my older daughter and her family join us here. Her absence in my life leaves a big void in my heart and soul. I pray to have her with us soon.

Mozhgan Pazoaki is 57 and originally from Iran.

Pieces of the Past

Featured Author

Daisuke Ishizuka

MINNEAPOLIS, MN

I am Daisuke Ishizuka. I am from Japan. I grew up in Kushiro city, Hokkaido, Japan until I was eighteen years old. My hometown is a very peaceful place. It has a moor, mountains, farms, rivers, and the sea. Yes, they have hot springs too! My hometown has great fresh food, so I am still healthy and strong. The people are kind, friendly and love tourists. If you go to Kushiro city, you are going to be a hero because they have a wonderful customer service with empathy. Also, cranes arrive there from October to March. Cranes are a Japanese symbol which is very special to us because it means good fortune and long life. I love my hometown and I miss my family and hot springs! After high school, I worked as an airman in the Air Force at Misawa Air Base in Japan. I was working in fuels - I operated a special oil vehicle while I refueled oil for airplanes. After that, I went to English school in Minnesota for a short time as a student. Then, I became a kaiseki and sushi chef in Tokyo, Japan. Nowadays I am in Minnesota and I have a wonderful spouse, Kai. I am studying English at the International Institute. I enjoy kayaking, fishing, bouldering, and hiking in Minnesota.

Memory of Being Bullied

As a child, I had bad experiences with bullying in Japan, and I found it hard to trust people; I was afraid of what they might do to me. As I have gotten older, however, I have been able to overcome these bad experiences, and now I am not afraid of people anymore.

In junior high school, three months before I graduated, my friends ignored me. I asked one of my friends what's going on. He said, "I can't talk to you because Kimura told me not to." One day in gym class we were playing basketball. I did not like his style of play because he did not play as part of a team. Kimura heard I had been talking about him. That was why he was upset and hated me. Kimura was a bully in my class. Everyone was afraid of him.

I learned from my girlfriend in high school how relationships could be good and healthy. I then tried to overcome my anxiety about not being able to trust people because of the pain of bullying. But, I had always hidden my experience because I was ashamed to talk about it. At least twice a month, I would have nightmares about a friend and me being bullied in junior high school.

In 2018, I moved to America as a Japanese chef. If American people do not like things, they say "no." However, if Japanese people do not like things, they say "yes" patiently. Also, Japanese people have to be the same way. I do not like this because we have our own identity and personality. So to be honest, I really respect American culture. It helped a lot with my anxiety.

In 2020, I met a psychologist. I took therapy from her for four months. It helped me a lot. Not many people in Japan care about trauma and anxiety. They should care more about their mental health. I wish I would have known the therapy when I was a child. After therapy, I did not feel stressed if I thought about bullying and was able to talk about it with people.

In conclusion, I'm happy to be living in America because I could overcome my anxiety from bullying. In the past, my parents said, "Don't go to another country." I respect my parents, but I do not regret my decision to come to America. I met a wonderful spouse, overcame my trauma, and took valuable education from the International Institute. I believe I can do it even if it is hard. I can do it!

Daisuke Ishizuka is 31 and originally from Japan.

Memories of My Favorite Childhood Holiday

LIDIA LOPEZ, MINNEAPOLIS, MN

What do we imagine when we hear the word "holiday?" Do we imagine gifts, a lot of food, a journey away from home, or do we just remember how beautiful our memories are?

Let's look at a little piece of my favorite childhood holiday from many years ago.

I lived about four years with my sister-in-law in Cajola, Quetzaltenango, Guatemala. People there celebrate a variety of holidays, and I'm not completely sure why they celebrate all of them. The ways the holidays are celebrated have also changed over time, but I remember well how they celebrated one of them: Easter. Easter was celebrated by Catholics and non-Catholics, and it was celebrated with dried fish and less sweetened breads, which are my favorite foods.

A week before celebrating Easter, close neighbors, friends, and families started exchanging about five pieces of their bread for each household. We had a lot of the breads, and I ate them for breakfast. For me, it was not boring to eat the bread for about two weeks because it is my favorite junk food, and people also bought their breads in different towns, so it was fun to try different types of them. And that was not all that we did to celebrate.

Holy Thursday was my awaited moment at that time. That Thursday, the parties began at six in the morning and continued until sunset, and the closest neighbors and relatives were invited to each other's homes to finish the celebration of Easter. Each person was served with a big fish, five breads, soda, beer, and tortillas. It was amazing to me because sometimes we ate fish only once a year and sometimes none, and we rarely drank soda, and when we did, one bottle was split by two people. I put the fish on my tortilla, and I dipped it in the fish stew. It was so delicious! I think fish will always be one of my favorite foods.

The last thing that was my favorite about that holiday was that after the party, I had permission to do whatever I wanted. That meant freedom. I could do whatever I wanted, like go for a walk or play with my friends.

It doesn't matter how many holidays we've had, or which ones are our favorites, or even how we celebrate them. What matters is how we treat the people around us and how we feel when we celebrate them, because the beautiful memories are the ones that turn into our favorite memories.

Lidia Lopez is 32 and originally from Guatemala.

Surprise

IBTIHAJ ALZUBAIDI, COLUMBIA HEIGHTS, MN

In 1971, I was thirteen years old. It was the first evening of Eid (an Islamic feast). My father and my brothers went to visit some relatives to exchange congratulations. My mother and I stayed home. I went up to my room and started reading a book. Suddenly, I heard the sound of the main house door strongly opened. It was a strong sound because it was made out of metal. I looked out the window and I saw the open door. I said to myself that my family members may have returned, but why did they leave the door open? I decided to go and see for myself. My father's office was next to the stairs. I heard the murmuring of men coming from my father's office. I was curious and decided to open the door a few inches. I saw two men standing, looking at a third person. I did not see him because he was behind the door where my father's safe was. I could hear the sound of the keys trying to open the safe. The moment I opened the door, the two men turned and saw me. I trembled, and my nerves were cramped from the intensity of fear. "Thieves in my father's office!"

My mother was astonished and threw everything from her hands, and with all her courage, she ran and screamed towards the office while I was behind her. I was afraid and terrified of what the thieves could do to us. When my mother reached the office door, I rushed up the stairs. I did not go beyond five steps. My mother swung the doors open, shouting, "Thieves!" Suddenly there was a moment of silence when our eyes fell on the third person who was opening the safe. My mother took a step back and I fainted.

I opened my eyes, and everyone around me

said, "Are you okay?" A new visitor caught my attention, sitting on a table. This was my father's surprise for us on Eid. Yes, our new visitor was a television. My father bought the television from the electrical appliances store owned by my father's friend. The television was heavy, so two friends of my father came to help him carry the TV, and then he handed them the money. After that, all of my family gathered around the TV, and we spent that night chatting and watching TV.

Ibtihaj Alzubaidi is 60 and originally from Iraq.

A Legacy

TJ LARSON, MINNEAPOLIS, MN

Sometimes you just need one person to believe in you, say a kind word to you, stand beside you, or see the potential in you.

It's not easy growing up in the projects surrounded by poverty, gang fights, drugs, prostitutes, teenage mothers, and so many struggling to survive. When I was twelve, my father put a six-foot fence around our yard. I often wonder if that fence was to keep the gang fights out or to keep us kids safe inside.

My father once repaired a school bus for a parochial school in the suburbs, and he worked it out so that my siblings and I could attend this school. It was a huge change in my life. I went from a school with hundreds of kids in one grade to a classroom of seventeen. I am forever grateful.

Later on in school, I had an amazing teacher named Mrs. Dietsche. I sometimes needed extra help and would reach out to her. She was encouraging, supportive, and a positive influence on my life. She could see the potential in me that others overlooked. The most incredible thing happened when I graduated from high school. She gave me a book of quotations, with two quotes marked, and a handwritten note.

To TJ
From Mrs. Dietsche
This is my legacy I leave to you
Page 298.
"Anyone who stops learning is old, whether at

twenty or eighty. Anyone who keeps learning stays young. The greatest thing in life is to keep your mind young." – Henry Ford
"The brighter you are, the more you have to learn." – Don Herold

I've held onto that book all these years, reaching for it for quotations or witty humor when writing cards or hoping to inspire others. It sits on my shelf, reminding me that I am valued, worthy, and loved. And now that I find myself back in school again, recovering from a brain injury, this book calls out to me, reminding me of Mrs. Dietsche and her legacy. I don't know where she is, or what she is doing, or even if she is still on this earth. As I hold her book, I think of the student that I was back then and the student that I am now, relearning how to read and write. I think to the future, when I will be that teacher or volunteer who reaches out to others, to mentor, to assist, to bring out the potential we all have within us as we learn and relearn together.

Respectfully and forever grateful,
TJ

TJ Larson is 38 and originally from St. Paul, MN.

Trip with My Friend

GANA IBRIHIM, ST. PAUL, MN

I remember when I lived in Ethiopia, I was going to the park. It is a fun and interesting way to spend time and a fun day.

When I was going to the park, I was sixteen years old. The year was 2014. The first time I went to the park was during summer time. That time I think it was 3:00 in the afternoon in the city of Adama. I went to the park with my best friends, and it was a trip that I can never forget. I am happy and my friend is too. My best friend's name is Mubarek, and Seyfu was driving the car. We saw all kinds of animals, birds, wildlife mammals, turtles, giraffes, monkeys, and many other kinds of animals, and a swimming pool or splash pad at the park. I could hear and smell things like popcorn and yucky things like manure. Some animals made loud noises, like when I heard a bird singing and it surprised me.

After that, we went to the swimming pool. Then my friend says, "Let's go swimming," and then one of them says he's not going swimming. He is scared to go swimming. He likes to swim but doesn't know how to swim. I say, "Let's go," and change clothes and then swim with one friend. Then we finish swimming, change the clothes, and we go to eat. After we eat, we go to the hotel and then sleep. There were lots of people at the park. I am happy to go with my best friends. My feeling right now is missing my friends and my country, Ethiopia. I hope I can go again.

Gana Ibrihim is 23 and originally from Ethiopia.

What I Miss about My Country

ASHA MOHAMED YAHYA, MINNEAPOLIS, MN

I am from Somalia. What I miss the most about my country is my family and my friends. I also miss the animals, which are camels, goats, sheep, cows, elephants, and giraffes. All those animals. What I miss about my friends is going together to the river for swimming. We also went out of the house together at night, sitting outside the house, talking and playing with each other.

The person I love very much in my family is my grandma because I lived with her since I was three years old, until I came to America. When I came to America, I was nineteen years old. I remember all the time the way she was talking to me and loving me, and she's my friend too. And she still gives me a lot of advice today. She says, "Do this," and "Do this," and what is good and not good. She even tells me how to talk to my kids. She is my friend. I love her.

Asha Mohamed Yahya is 34 and originally from Somalia.

What Surprised Me about Minnesota

ALVES SESEBI-MUPEPE, ST. PAUL, MN

My name is Alves. I am from D.R. Congo. I was born in Generation Y (Millennial). I have lived in Minnesota one year, but there are many things that surprised me when I first came to Minnesota.

First of all, I have respect for the people of Minnesota for their reception of me because I don't have family in Minnesota. But, the people of Minnesota happily welcomed me with smiles.

Secondly, the trees don't have the same leaves as the trees in my country. I asked someone, "Why don't the trees have the leaves?" He said to me, "You came in the winter season, and each year you will see this phenomenon."

Third, Minnesota has many more places to spend time outdoors than my country, like playgrounds, parks, and many lakes. Next, it has 10,000 lakes, but my country doesn't have the lakes like Minnesota.

Finally, the biggest lake in the world is located in the U.S. In my opinion, Minnesota is the state that will never lack water.

Alves Sesebi-Mupepe is 37 and originally from the Democratic Republic of the Congo.

Immigrant Life

NASRO SHEIKH ABDULLAHI, ST. PAUL, MN

Moving to America was the biggest change in my life. I was born in Mogadishu, the capital of Somalia, in January of 1978. I went to Mogadishu Academy for primary school. I lived in Somalia until I was a teenager.

Everything was going good, until one day the Civil War happened. On an early January morning in 1991, my family and I were getting ready for school when we heard gunshots. We didn't know what was going on, nor why people outside were screaming. After a couple hours of chaos and fear, we got to know that our country was falling apart, and all of my friends and family members were moving to different places.

At last! After a couple weeks of fear, we finally left Somalia and got transported to Kenya. Kenya wasn't like Somalia. It was colder, the food was different, people were different, and the most difficult thing was the language, because all we knew was Somali. My family and I got put in a refugee camp, and life really got hard. My education stopped, and I didn't have many choices anymore.

We lived in the refugee camp for a long time, and we endured many struggles. Finally, I left the camp, got married to my American husband, and that's when life started to become easier for me. I gave birth to my beautiful daughter in my second year of marriage, my husband finally got a visa for me, and we came to America. America had so many choices for me and my family. I took every opportunity I had and made something out of it, like helping my family who are still in the camp. Life in America as an immigrant isn't so hard.

Nasro Sheikh Abdullahi is 43 and originally from Somalia.

My Story
ANONYMOUS, ST. ANTHONY, MN

I'm from Ethiopia. I was born in 1997. I went to high school in Addis Ababa, Ethiopia. I met my husband in 2017 when he came to Ethiopia from the USA. We got married in January 2018. He sent me my visa, and I came to Minnesota in May 2019. I was thirty-four weeks pregnant with my first baby girl, and she was born after one month and twenty days. After that, there are a lot of things that happened, and I got another baby in October 2020. Thanks, thanks to God! I have two kids now in November 2020. When I went to the Ethiopian Airport, all of my family was with me, and I was very sad to leave them and cried a lot even in the plane, but I was happy to meet my husband. He prepared a welcome party for me. He's such a lovely husband.

Kitchen Accident
NIKY NOENURAI, ST. CLOUD, MN

When I was a child, about three or four years old, I lived in Thailand. It was winter time, and in the morning, after I woke up, I went to the kitchen with my sister to get warm heat from the wood stove. I got up close to the stove and fire burned my skirt. The fire burned my thigh and my belly. I was shocked! My sister pulled me out and called my mom for help. My mom stopped the fire and took off my skirt. Then she gave me first aid. At that time, my father had gone to another county far away from home. On the weekend, my father came home. He checked up and took care of me. Since then I'm not dead, but still have a scar on my skin.

Niky Noenurai is 64 and originally from Thailand.

Meeting a Lion for the First Time
MOHAMED DUALE, ST. CLOUD, MN

When I was very young, around ten years old, I had one job and that was going with the sheep every day. Then one day, a lion attacked one of my sheep before I could do anything. At that time, I didn't know what a lion was. I yelled at the lion and threw a rock, and then it put down the sheep and ran. The people that were watching me said to me that the animal that attacked me was a lion. After that I was frightened of the fact that it was a lion, not a regular animal that had attacked. I was sad that one of the sheep died and when I came home, my father said, "Why would you let the lion kill one of the sheep?" At the time, I couldn't answer his question.

Mohamed Duale is 28 and originally from Kenya.

My Life
VIMLESH (VIMMI) SHARMA, ST. PAUL, MN

When I was a child, I lived in a village in the north part of India. I spent some of my childhood with my grandparents. I lived in a joint family with my uncles. My father had a job in Agra, the city famous for the World Heritage Site, the Taj Mahal. My grandma did not want to send me with my parents, because I was an only child. When my grandma got two grandsons from my parents, she kept one of my brothers and me with her in the village.

When I was five years old, my mom took me with her and enrolled me in school in Agra. However, my grandma was angry to see me going away from her. After moving to Agra, I always missed her. My uncle visited my parents and brought me back to the village. I was back and forth several times between village and city, where my parents lived. Finally, I got used to the city and started living with my parents in Agra.

I finished high school. After that, my uncles and grandparents were worried about my marriage. They started searching for a boy for me to marry. After marriage, I went to my in-laws' house. My father-in-law had a business, and my husband was doing his bachelor's degree.

After a few years, my husband completed his bachelor's degree and soon started a job in the capital city, New Delhi. By this time, I had two daughters, and I moved to New Delhi with them. A few years later, my husband was transferred to the United States by his employer. I have been here since June 2015. When I came here, I could not speak a single word of English. I was so scared and worried and wondered how I would spend my time here. Sometimes I cried. Then my daughter searched for adult education on the internet and found a few schools.

Finally, I started going to Sandburg Learning Center in Golden Valley. Initially I was scared, but I say thank you to every single teacher for helping me learn English. Now, if I have a question, I can ask someone, and I can do grocery shopping. I say thanks to my family who helped me by translating and helping me with English. I can speak, read, and write English. I cannot speak fluently, but I have hope. Thank you to the United States and my teachers. Because of them, I feel more confident than ever before.

Vimlesh (Vimmi) Sharma is 47 and originally from India.

When I First Came to Minnesota
DA RA PAW, ST. PAUL, MN

When I first came to Minnesota, I liked it because it has many places. When I first came, I saw many lakes and waterfalls. It also has the Mississippi River. I like Minnesota because it has beautiful cities. When I went to Como Zoo, I saw many animals for the first time, like the zebra. In Burma, we don't see zebras.

Sometimes, when I go to the parks in Minnesota, I see many flowers. I like that Minnesota has four seasons; the names are winter, spring, summer, and fall. All the seasons are beautiful. I like many people in Minnesota. Minnesota is beautiful.

Da Ra Paw is 23 and originally from Burma.

Memories of Burma
SAW BO, ST. PAUL, MN

When I was a child, I lived in a small village in a rural area. Sometimes, I played soccer with my friends. I walked to school with them. My school wasn't in my village, so we had to walk to another village. As we walked to school, we were scared of tigers, and when it rained, we were afraid of falling trees.

In the new year, my parents invited some people to my house. We thanked God for all of our blessings. We cooked pork and chicken to eat after we prayed.

Saw Bo is 44 and originally from Burma.

What Kind of Clothes Should I Wear?
LUCIANA CARDOSO, MINNETONKA, MN

My husband and I were invited by a Brazilian friend, who lives in Minnesota, to go to a Rod Stewart concert at a Casino with her and her husband. I thought that the location of the concert would not be a problem.

When the day came, I was excited about what I would wear to the concert, especially because I had brought several dresses from Brazil, and it was a good opportunity to use them. So, I chose very formal clothes for my husband to wear, and I chose a very beautiful dress for me, obviously with thin high-heeled sandals to complete my look, because it is normal to dress like that to go to a concert in my city.

However, it was a Rod Stewart concert in a casino, and I had never been to a casino.

When we arrived at the casino I was surprised! The concert was going to be outdoors on the lawn and we would sit in plastic chairs! How could I get to the chairs with those sandals without sinking my heels into the grass? By walking on the tops of my feet, which was very uncomfortable.

And, to my surprise, as if it was possible for me to be more surprised, everyone else there was dressed in jeans, t-shirts, and comfortable shoes. Obvious? Not for me.

Everyone was looking at us, amused because we were dressed in a different way.

At first, I was very embarrassed, but then I got used to the situation and enjoyed the moment, especially because I had never before received so many compliments on my dress!

Luciana Cardoso is 39 and originally from Brazil.

My Blessed Wedding

LINDA CHACON, MAPLE GROVE, MN

I left my family and my country to get married in the United States. This was a hard decision. I felt so devastated when I saw, through the window, the airport disappear between the clouds. I cried throughout the trip.

When I arrived in the United States for the first time in California at night, I saw through the window a big and illuminated city. I had mixed feelings. When I met my future husband in the airport, it was a happy moment.

We only had a few months for the wedding preparation. I was blessed because my mom got a visa before I decided to come to the United States, and my father and sister got visas to assist in my wedding. This was a gift from God. I was blessed to find a beautiful church for the ceremony and reception. I was blessed because the pastor of the church gave permission to my father, who is a pastor too, to officiate my ceremony. I thought this would be impossible, but God gave me the privileges that my father could officiate at my wedding.

Finally the long awaited day arrived. This day was my birthday, too. One cousin of my future husband decorated the church with beautiful bouquets of roses of white, peach, and pink colors. My boyfriend and father were the first to arrive at the church. All the friends and family anxiously awaited my arrival. Then my mom and I arrived at the church. My future husband was nervous and I was, too. My future husband was waiting in the front. Two little kids started to walk down the white carpet that led to the altar, tossing petals all the way to the altar. Then I entered with my beautiful parents.

The ceremony started. We sat at one side of the altar in front of the audience. We felt really happy to share this moment with family and friends on this unforgettable day. We received the blessing of God; this was a gift. After the ceremony, we had a reception on the second floor that was decorated and prepared so that the guests enjoyed delicious food. My husband and I left the church and visited a pretty park to take professional pictures.

After that, we came back to the reception and enjoyed the delicious food and greeted the guests. We had a toast to our life together. When we were going to cut the cake, my husband started to sing a birthday song for me. I have many memories of this amazing day.

Linda Chacon is 47 and originally from El Salvador.

Lovely Mom Jennie

PING MECHTER, BLAINE, MN

Jennie was my husband's mom. She was a beautiful woman. She is also my most unforgettable person. Although she has been away from us for three years, her voice often comes back to my ear. When she was alive, we visited her once a week and talked to her on the phone almost every night. She liked to talk on the phone with friends all day, so she seemed to know everything. She was a very kind woman and a great mother. She liked to play the piano. She was a faithful Christian. She had a beautiful voice, often singing in church. Her husband passed away early, so she raised four children by herself.

I first met Jennie on my first day in the USA. I remember that evening. When we arrived home from the airport, I saw all the families in the living room welcoming me. Jennie gave me a big hug and my fatigue of flying for several days disappeared instantly. She was already eighty-nine years old. First, I came to a new country, and I wasn't used to many things. Jennie often talked to me on the phone, although I didn't entirely understand what she said. But I understand she was concerned about me and made me feel very warm. Also, she would speak slowly so I could understand her more easily. When we visited her, she showed me how to play find the word games.

I remember one day, I was making curtains at home and the phone rang. I picked up the phone and it was Jennie's rapid voice. She told me to run to the basement immediately because a tornado was coming. Outside it was dark. I turned all the lights on, then ran to the basement to hide. I was afraid… Fortunately, the tornado turned the other way. But I still very much appreciated her call. We have lots of relatives in Minnesota and get together every year for a family picnic. Jennie always attended. She had a wonderful sense of humor. For example, when she was watching TV and someone blocked her view, she wouldn't tell you to walk away. She would just say, "You make a better door than window." So we realize and laugh. That's Jennie. She never complained that life was hard, always happy and kind her entire life. We really miss her…

Ping Mechter is 52 and originally from China.

Dream
ABHINI VENNIKKAL, PLYMOUTH, MN

I didn't see my grandfather in my life. I never saw a single photo of him. But I heard a lot of stories about his kindness and helping mentality. In my childhood days, one of my wishes was to see my grandfather. I knew it was impossible because he died when my dad was fourteen years old. My dad always told us about his love and affection.

When I was in sixth grade, I went to my grandfather's house for a sleep over. That night I saw a handsome man in my dream. His hand was full of chocolates. He played with me and paid a lot of attention to me.

When I woke up, I missed that man very much. I told my dad about my dream. My dad asked me

what he looked like. I told my dad his features and clothes. That time my dad was silent for some time. Then he told me, he was your grandfather.

It was a beautiful dream. Now I am forty years old, and I still remember that dream.

Abhini Vennikkal is 40 and originally from India.

Thanks Minnesota
BLANCA MAYORGA, ROBBINSDALE, MN

Minnesota is the place that I first arrived when I came from Mexico. I have been here for twenty-six years. In Minnesota I learned to drive, speak and understand English, use the GPS, and more experiences. I have met very nice people—Americans and people from other countries.

Minnesota, I will always remember you—your winter, your spring, your lakes, and many more things.

Thank you Teacher Barbara and the students and volunteers, too.

At the end of December, I will move to San Antonio, Texas. I will miss you, Minnesota. Maybe some day I will come back here to live or for just a visit, but I will come back!

Blanca Mayorga is 59 and originally from Mexico.

My Life in Guatemala
MARSI PIVARAL, ST. MICHAEL, MN

I was born in Guatemala in 1975. I have two sisters and two brothers. My two sisters and one brother live in Guatemala. My younger brother lives in Virginia. There are many teachers in my family. My father is a retired teacher. He taught elementary school. I studied at college in Guatemala in 1995. I was an elementary teacher in Guatemala for eight years. In my school I taught first, second, third, and fourth grade. I was very busy. It was difficult because there were no supplies. The economy was very bad. The students tried hard to be good students. It was the best time when there were more teachers. I rode a horse to get to school for three years because the streets were very bad. In the year

2000, the streets were fixed, so then I could ride in a car.

Now, I teach children at church. I met the man I would marry in Guatemala. He moved to St. Michael, Minnesota, in the United States in 1996. I came to the United States in 2006 to get married. I have been in St. Michael for fifteen years. We have two boys. They are twins. My boys were born in 2011. My wish is to finish learning English.

Marsi Pivaral is 45 and originally from Guatemala.

My Childhood
VERÓNICA CELLERI, ROCKFORD, MN

When I was a little girl, I was very happy, and I liked to play with a doll. I lived with my parents and siblings. When I went to school, I started to like numbers, and since then my favorite subject is mathematics. Now, I live in Minneapolis with my husband and my daughter. It was very difficult to get used to my new life away from my family with new people, different customs, and a different language. I don't like winter because of the snow. In my free time I like to watch TV. My favorite memory is my mother's smile in the morning when I would wake up.

Verónica Celleri is 30 and originally from Ecuador.

About My Life in the United States
EH RAY, ST. PAUL, MN

Every memory brings me memories. The most memorable thing that I want to share with you is the reason why my parents chose to be here in the United States. They chose to be here for better opportunities and better education. First, I always remember that the reason my parents came to the U.S. is for better opportunities in education and more freedom for my younger siblings and our family.

It became more challenging for us when we first moved to a new country, since everything was new for us, such as different cultures, new languages, and difficulty finding transportation. My parents work really hard, encouraging us to get a higher education to be able to help back in our community.

Second, I am glad that I have a chance to get my high school diploma at GAP School. When I first started to go to school, it was hard for me to communicate with other students because I didn't know how to speak English very well. Also, during class discussion time, I was afraid to speak up and share my ideas. As I slowly learned, I realized my speaking and listening in the English language had improved. I complete every assignment on my own and have time to help my younger siblings as well.

Overall, I learned to depend on myself, and now my parents mostly rely on me because I am the oldest child. I provide transportation for my family members, and whenever we receive mail, I have to read and translate it for my parents.

I am hoping that someday I can help my family more if I keep improving my English.

Eh Ray is 23 and originally from Burma.

To Fly
JOLENE (JIALING) LIU, BROOKLYN CENTER, MN

When I was a young kid, I liked looking at the sky and thinking about something interesting. Sometimes, when I saw a bird flying I thought, why can't a person fly, but a bird can? Wings got birds flying, in my opinion.

To fly paper planes or paper birds that I made was my way of keeping myself from boredom. I would fly them from a high place rather than on the ground so they could fly further, but actually, they were just gliding. Did wings allow birds to fly, I asked myself.

However, not every bird can fly, even though it has wings. Chickens can jump high and glide far by using their wings, but they can't fly. They should fly. A long time ago, the ancestors of chickens had powerful wings. They were good hunters in the air until they were tamed by humans. After that, they didn't want to flap their wings, they put on weight, and in the end, lost their flying ability. Did wings really allow birds to fly? Again, I asked myself.

Tom and Jerry, a cartoon which I like, showed

me how a bird learns to fly. One day, a woodpecker was hatched, but he got separated from his mother. Tom, a cat, saw the woodpecker and wanted to catch it for a meal. Jerry, a rat, knew that Tom had bad intentions for the woodpecker and tried his best to prevent the woodpecker from being eaten. At first, Jerry asked the woodpecker to try flying, but the woodpecker could only stay in the air for a few seconds. At last, the woodpecker was almost eaten by Tom, but finally, at the last minute, he ran as fast as he could, jumped, and used all of his power to flap his wings. Excitedly, he flew! At that moment, my opinion was changed. Did wings get birds flying? No, flapping gets birds flying!

To glide, eventually to land.

To fly—no limit!

Jolene (Jialing) Liu is 30 and originally from China.

My New Life in the U.S.

SNOW YANG, ST. PAUL, MN

Moving to a new country is not easy. When I arrived in Minnesota, it was summer. The weather was beautiful, like back home in Laos. A couple months later, the leaves started to change colors. They were red, yellow, and so many colors I had never seen before. It was very cold. I asked my husband, "Why is it so cold?" He said, "It is winter." In November, I saw snow for the first time. I stared out the window for a long time. That was in 2013.

Starting school was difficult for me. People were speaking English. I didn't know any English, so I could not talk with them. I felt so lonely. My husband always helped me with my homework. I had to stop attending school when I was seven months pregnant, because I went to school by bus. I felt it was too dangerous while I was pregnant. After giving birth, I still could not attend school because I didn't have a babysitter.

One thing that is very important in the U.S. is being able to drive, because you cannot wait for someone to take care of you all the time. It was difficult for me when I wanted to go to the store and had to depend on my husband. If he didn't have time to help me, I could not go to the store.

I enjoy my life here now because I have opportunities to do so many things in my new life in the U.S. The first step was to get my driver's license. The second was to get citizenship.

Right now, I have a job and go to work even when I am very tired. I also go to school after work four nights a week. Finally, my husband is very happy because I can do things for myself. He said, "You don't even need me anymore." I go to school online these days because I want to get a better job in the future. I know I can achieve my goals, if I never give up.

Snow Yang is 46 and originally from Laos.

My Beautiful Country

MIRIAM FLORES GONZALEZ, ST. PAUL, MN

Mexico is my beautiful country

Where I was born,

In a little ranch called Las Animas

Where I lived in my childhood

With my amazing family and my great friends.

Miriam Flores Gonzalez is 31 and originally from Mexico.

I Visited New York City

NGA TRAN, MINNEAPOLIS, MN

During the summer four years ago, my family visited New York City. I wanted to see the Statue of Liberty in New York Harbor. We flew to New York and stayed for one week. Before visiting New York, we arrived in Massachusetts with my cousin. We stayed in Massachusetts for many days.

While there, I visited the biggest dam. Second, I visited a company that made these candles. Third, we saw the temples of the Japanese and Cambodians on the hill. Fourth, I went to a rose park that was created for an American family. The plants were donated in their honor after they passed away. In the evening, I looked out at the front of the capital of Massachusetts. The top of the capital sparkles because they made it with twenty-four karat gold.

On the last two days of our trip, we visited New York City where the streets were noisy and crowded. Although I located streets smaller than in Minneapolis, there were so many things in the streets: cars, buses, taxi cabs. The mall in the center displayed everything, but it was very expensive, and looked like a fast Hollywood film.

Next, I saw two buildings they didn't finish. Now, I remember 2001, the September terrorist attacks... they made thousands of people and children die! I saw at the moment where they had written all of the names of the people and children who had died on tables in the water pool. I am a little sad and my eyes tear!

We ate food in Chinatown; it was good and cheap, but the streets were very small and dirty due to trash. It made me remember Chợ Lớn, where there are many Chinese people living in my country.

Finally, we took the subway to where we bought tickets to go to New York Harbor. We waited more than two hours to get the tickets, before going into a big ship with about 500–700 people. The ship arrived on the island after about thirty minutes. The first time it was surprising! The statue is huge! It has been there for more than a hundred years, made of iron and changed to the color green. It is very nice! In her right hand, she holds a torch and in her left hand, she holds a book. We did not go into the body of the statue. We only looked at it from the outside.

One week of travelling went quickly. The Statue of Liberty made me remember. With two hands humans can build huge wonders.

Nga Tran is 74 and originally from Vietnam.

My Memory of Mae La Oon Camp
KYAW WIN NAI, ST. PAUL, MN

In 2007, I was ten years old. I lived in Thailand's Mae La Oon camp. Sometimes, me and my friends would go play soccer together. Their names are Bon Wah, Pa Ko Lo, and Che Poe, who is really my best friend. After we play soccer, we go swimming in the river together. We have a lot of fun. But sometimes we have sad days too because we drink together, talk bad too much, and we fight. I remember my friends. Sometimes I miss them. I think one time I can go back and see they are aging.

Kyaw Win Nai is 22 and originally from Thailand.

Moments and Happiness
PAH DAY, ST. PAUL, MN

I was fifteen years old in 2016 in Thailand's Mae La Oon camp. This is the best memory, and I chose to write about it because it was the happiest time of my life. That time, I was playing outside of my school with many of my friends. We were playing soccer. We had so much fun because people were screaming and laughing. It was so much fun. We were happy. We had so much fun to the point where we didn't worry about anything else. It was all about that moment and happiness we had at that time. I really miss that time because I wish I could have that old day while I'm in America. I miss it because I don't really have fun like that day in a long time, and I wish I could have it again with my old friends.

Pah Day is 22 and originally from Thailand.

My Life in Minnesota
AKOSSIWAS AGOSSOU, ST. PAUL, MN

I immigrated from Togo to the U.S. in 2015. I first lived in Minneapolis. Moving to a whole new country with a totally different environment and language was hard. I adjusted with the help of family and friends.

I first started school on Nicollet Avenue in Minneapolis. Going to school opened a new door for me in this new world. I learned many things about American culture. It was not an easy process, if I am going to be honest, but I tried with all I had. In a year, I moved to Crystal and started a new school: the Adult Learning Center. This school helped me improve my communication and listening skills, which helped me speak and express myself better. With all the challenges and hard work

I put into learning English, I can look back and say I did it. I am ready for what comes next.

A friend referred me to the Hubbs Center. She told me how the Hubbs Center helped her to become a nurse. When she came here, she did not know any English, but with the help of the Hubbs Center, she got prepared for college. Going to school totally changed her family's financial situation and issues. My goal while at the Hubbs Center is to become a more fluent speaker of English, get my GED, and go to college to become a better person.

Akossiwas Agossou is 42 and originally from Togo.

2008 to the Present

NYSOMAKORN SOUTH, ST. PAUL, MN

I came to Minnesota from Cambodia on November 22, 2008. On that day, I saw snow falling for the first time in my life. It was so beautiful that it amazed me. On the way home, I saw people driving in an organized way. They respect each other by staying in their own lane, and if they want to change lanes, they signal. No one drives through red lights. This is very different from my country.

After living in Minnesota for three months, I had a baby. It was very painful. I didn't have any relatives around me. I did have my doctor and nurses in the room to help me. They took very good care of me and made my pain go away.

After having a baby, I went to school at the Hubbs Center. At that time, I didn't speak and understand English very well. I was afraid and nervous to talk and answer questions. I was shy to see everyone. All these feelings left on my first day at school. Everybody made me feel comfortable, especially teachers. They are very nice, very friendly, and they pay careful attention to students.

This past year, 2020, has been terrible. It has been the year of COVID-19. People have lost their jobs, schools are closed, and some people have lost family members. Even though we have had a very bad situation, the government is still strong and is helping people. They help those who have lost their jobs with unemployment and are trying to make

vaccinations available for everyone.

I love the United States! I plan to work and live here for the rest of my life.

Nysomakorn South is 39 and originally from Cambodia.

My New Bumbershoot

SHAGITU RAFERA, ST. PAUL, MN

I just bought a new purple bumbershoot this past summer from JCPenney, and I keep it in my car in case of rain. I use this bumbershoot when it it raining outside. However, most of the time I use it when it is hot outside to protect my skin from the bright sun.

Shagitu Rafera is 51 and originally from Ethiopia.

My Trip to Guinea

SANA BANGOURA, MINNEAPOLIS, MN

In 2018, I checked my passport and saw that it would expire in 2019, and I decided to go to Guinea and visit my family. We talked about the trip. After a few months, we checked a lot of different flights. I bought two different tickets because we decided that I would sleep in New York and leave the next day. My first flight was Delta Airlines from MSP airport to JFK on December 15, 2019, and my second flight was from New York to Guinea on December 16, 2019. When I came to Guinea, there were my two sisters, one brother, and my friend at the airport of Guinea. It was 11 p.m. when we went to the house, and I stayed there.

The next day, my sister and I went to the passport office. It was Wednesday. We paid the passport fees, we took a photo, and they said we would get the passport in forty-eight hours. We came back to the office on Friday. They hadn't finished my passport, and they said it would be ready on Monday.

After a few days, I moved to my sister's house because there was a lot of traffic and also a lot of construction. It took two weeks to finish my passport because they were too slow, and there were some difficulties at the office. I was frustrated and worried at that time. When I got my passport, I was very happy! I bought some drums and brought them to my sister's house.

Three days before leaving, I visited my uncles, cousins, and aunts. On January 3, 2020, we went to the airport before my departure, but the flight was delayed because they said there were protests in France, and they didn't have a flight. I asked some people at the airport, and they said it happens sometimes. Delta Airlines is connected with Air France. We stayed at the hotel for two days. Then we left around 11 p.m. on December 5. It was delayed for two days. I came back to the USA on January 8, 2020.

Sana Bangoura is 40 and originally from Guinea.

Lost in the Woods

TATIANA USHAKOVA, OAK GROVE, MN

Have you ever been lost in the woods? When I was a small child, I got lost in the woods. I loved the fall because on the weekends my parents and I used to go mushroom hunting. I always looked forward to going, but that weekend was special. I got a puppy for my eighth birthday. I called him Umka, the name of a little polar bear from the famous Russian cartoon. I was very excited to take my puppy along for the hunt. I woke up early that day.

"Come on, Umka! Get up! We have to get ready for our trip!" Umka looked at me, yawning, and wagged his fuzzy tail. I packed my stuff and Umka in the car, and we were patiently waiting in the back seat.

When we got to the forest, my parents told me not to go too far from our car. Then they went into the woods to gather mushrooms. "Let's go, puppy!" I commanded. I went uphill into the woods, keeping my eye on the car. Umka followed me, barking happily.

After searching, I saw a big mushroom area. I was jazzed, but the more mushrooms I found, the deeper into the woods I went. I filled the whole basket. When I stood up and looked around, I didn't remember which direction I came from. Nothing looked familiar because I was staring at the ground hunting mushrooms.

I went back downhill. Umka was beginning to pant. I stopped. I was certain I was going in circles. I heard my heart beating. I was out of breath. It was before cell phones, so I had no communication with my parents. I went uphill again. Panic began to set in. I was a little girl compelled to save my puppy. I got upset and began to cry.

I calmed down. I made a decision to turn to the right and go downhill, following my intuition. I almost started running. Umka couldn't keep up with me, so I took him into my arms and kept running. After running quite awhile, my prayers were answered, and I found the car.

"We are saved, Umka!" I shouted. Umka and I were exhausted and thirsty but happy and relieved. Then I heard the voices of my parents as they approached us. I noticed the smiles on their faces. They picked a lot of mushrooms. They saw my full basket of mushrooms and said, "Wow, good job, dear. Did you have fun?"

I just nodded. Umka kept my secret forever.

Tatiana Ushakova is 38 and originally from Russia.

My First Time Learning English

NTXHI VANG, ST. PAUL, MN

January 6, 2020 was the first day I went to school at Open Door Learning Center. I met teacher Patrick, and then he took me to teacher Barbara's class.

Teacher Barbara greeted me saying, "Hi, what's your name?" I answered, "Hi, my name is Ntxhi Vang." And then she said, " Ntxhi, welcome to my class." I said, " Thank you." I was very happy to see my teacher and my classmates. They were all very nice.

Our school had English classes Monday to Friday 9:30 a.m. – 1:30 p.m. Every Friday, Miss Barbara had to attend the meeting, and we had other teachers who were volunteers to teach us. I studied in my English class with Miss Barbara for two months and two weeks. Our school had to stop teaching because a virus called COVID-19 is happening in the world.

After that, our school opened to teach us on

an app called Zoom. Miss Barbara had to move me to another English class because I have improved on my English. When I moved to my other class, I went to Miss Mya's English class, and she was my new teacher. Miss Mya is a nice teacher, along with my new classmates! My class logs onto Zoom to study English Monday to Thursday 10 a.m. – 11:30 a.m. I like our English class very much.

Ntxhi Vang is 25 and originally from Laos.

How Shawn Became My Husband

KANNIKA NELSON, VADNAIS HEIGHTS, MN

On October 19, 2018, my boyfriend took me to a fishing spot at Lebanon Hills. Before he picked me up, I had been waiting for him almost one hour past the scheduled time with our photographer. Shawn and I had scheduled a time at 2 p.m. but he showed up at about 3 p.m. and that made me upset. I was quiet in the car and had a bit of an attitude, but after we met our photographer, I felt better because she understood. We were taking pictures together to keep as a memory of the day.

That day the weather was perfect. It was sixty-five degrees. He then started to read a letter to me that he had written. I was so flabbergasted when he knelt down and proposed to me. This was such a beautiful moment, and it was captured by our friend forever. After we finished with our pictures, we decided to go to Minnesota Landscape Arboretum to have a picnic. That concluded our special day, and it was an emotional rollercoaster.

After he proposed to me, we decided to get married on January 10. I remember the night before my marriage, I couldn't sleep because I was very excited for my big day. I tried to write my vows, hoping to make him cry, but it did not work. However, to my surprise, he cried while reading his vows to me, which then made me cry as well. Our wedding was more than we could have asked for, and we were so thankful for all the support from both sides of the family and friends. I'm so happy that I married the love of my life. After our winter wedding was done in Minnesota, Shawn and I decided to have a small wedding in Thailand for my Thai family on the beach.

In March, my husband and his family went to Thailand for our wedding celebration on the beach. The day after our wedding, we thought it would be cool to go to see the pink dolphins in the gulf of Thailand. We went on a traditional long tail boat and saw a few pink dolphins. We learned that this species of dolphins is born white or gray and turn pink when they mature. We also learned from the cetologist that they eat small fish and seaweed. The babies feed off of their mom's milk for two to three years. We thought these dolphins were so cool and want to go back to see them again.

Kannika Nelson is 20 and originally from Thailand.

My Life in Africa

ABDINASIR OSMAN, MINNEAPOLIS, MN

My name is Abdinasir Osman. Today, I want to talk about Bosaso. Some things I did there are: I went to school, played football, and shopped at the supermarket. Sometimes, I played games with my friends. In Bosaso, I loved to go swimming in the sea when it was hot. Also, I worked sometimes, I helped my parents, and I liked to drive a car.

The things that I miss about Bosaso are: my job, my friends, my school, the nice weather, and visiting other regions like Erigavo City, Hargaisa, and Mogadishu. I do not miss that there was no mall, no good education, no rules, and sometimes no peace. I don't miss home.

The foods I ate there were pasta, bread, juice drinks (strawberry and mango), and especially Somali foods like *anjero*, rice, beans, maize, and meat. Also, I like to travel by airplane.

I also spent time in Djibouti. In Djibouti, I went shopping, played games, made friends, saw people dressed in traditional clothing, went to the sea to cool down, went to famous places like the Presidential Palace, and visited other cities like Obock.

Abdinasir Osman is 20 and originally from Somalia.

A Good Value in My Heart

ESMERALDA GARCIA, LINO LAKES, MN

"A tree grows big and pretty because it is well rooted in the ground."

Like the tree, I feel that my parents planted good values in my heart. One of the most beautiful things that my parents taught me when I grew up was to be humble and help people when they most need it, according to my abilities and without expecting anything in return. They told me to do it from the heart, for example, to help others with love and compassion. My mother used to tell me to help people who were sick or who had nothing to eat and that it was the right time to help.

For this reason, I feel the desire to help people. I have had the opportunity to help people, and I feel the joy of seeing in their faces a little relief from their needs. Life is very short, and one day, we will leave this world with nothing but the good things we have done. I'm thankful for all the people who have allowed me to help them and be part of their lives. Thanks to my parents for putting in my heart the love and compassion to help others.

Esmeralda Garcia is 42 and originally from Mexico.

My New Life

ADA ZEPEDA, ST. PAUL, MN

I arrived in the United States from Honduras two years ago with my son, Joseph. Oh, how time has flown by! I have a new life now. Everything here is different and new for me, from food, to the weather, and everything in between. There have been many challenges moving to a new country, the biggest of which has been learning a new language, English, which I need to use for everything.

I have learned many things here, too. One thing I have learned is that people have respect for time and are expected to be punctual. In my country, people do not respect time, and things always start later than planned. I have also learned to recycle and compost, two things I never did in Honduras. I have learned about and experienced the deep love and care that people have for animals and pets. I have met many people here who have helped me without even knowing me.

I currently work in a senior living home where I practice my English with residents. I am also improving my English by taking Hubbs Center English classes online. It is a bit difficult for me to understand, but I try because I know that one day I will be able to understand this new language and might even be able to be a translator!

Ada Zepeda is 31 and originally from Honduras.

Lost in the Jungle

EH MOO WAH, ST. PAUL, MN

I was eleven years old in 2010 in Thailand's Mae La Oon camp. Me and my friends Saw Dah, Saw Eh, and Pu Lah got lost in the jungle. We went to the jungle in the morning. We lost our way when we went to the jungle to find food. We looked for rice and water. We couldn't find the road to go back. We were scared and thought we cannot make it back home. We found some people, old men, and they showed us the way. We were lost for six hours. We came back in the dark.

Eh Moo Wah is 20 and originally from Thailand.

Magic Ecuador

MARITHZA RIVERA, COLUMBIA HEIGHTS, MN

On a calm and sunny day where the monotony of the time invaded my family, we decided to take a trip visiting three of the four regions of Ecuador: Coast, Sierra, and Oriente.

On Monday, June 24 of the previous year, my family and I excitedly started the tour at 5 a.m. The salsa and the lambada were part of this great adventure.

As a first stop, we were in the coast region, Guayaquil, a beautiful port city of Ecuador. Malecon 2000 and the Santai islands were two tourist places that caught our attention.

The next day, we were in the Sierra region. We went to El Chimborazo, which is the highest volcano in Ecuador, then we went mountain climbing, and we learned about rites that the Incas practiced in this place as part of their traditions.

Finally, we visited the Ecuadorian Amazon Napo, a place surrounded by endemic (species native to a single place or region which does not exist anywhere else) fauna and flora unique in the world.

Marithza Rivera is 23 and originally from Ecuador.

When I Was Young

CADNA A., ST. PAUL, MN

My name is Cadna. I was born in Mogadishu, Somalia in 1982. When I was young, I used to go to school. I had two really close friends. We used to go to school together and come home together. We were also scared of lions, and I have never seen a lion in real life. I have only seen it on television, and at night, I used to be scared of cats. I also had (still have) a family that I loved, and they loved me, and also my country was beautiful and peaceful.

Then in 1991, a civil war happened. Then we emigrated from Somalia to Kenya in 1991. My family and I lived there for a long time. After that, I came to the United States. And I had no idea how America and the people of America were. Then I came to realize that people here were really kind and nice. So, I am very happy to live in America, especially Minnesota.

Cadna A. is 37 and originally from Somalia.

Picking Mushrooms: A Russian Tradition

EKATERINA PERSHINA, PLYMOUTH, MN

Every autumn, our family goes to the forest to pick mushrooms. We take baskets, wear gumboots and jackets, and walk in a forest looking for mushrooms. We brought this tradition to America from Russia. This tradition comes from our parents, then grandparents, then great grandparents.

One day, we met with our friends to pick mushrooms. We got up early in the morning. Mushrooms must be picked early in the morning. The early bird gets the worm. Our cat was very surprised by our early rising. She usually waits for us to wake up in the morning. On the way, we saw fog spread over the lake. This was an amazing spectacle. After driving for an hour and a half, we found ourselves in one of the most beautiful places. The sun was shining, the birds were singing, and it smelled of autumn freshness.

A mushroom hike is not only interesting, but you also relax your body and soul from the rush of the city. This is a way to forget pressing problems and to get the energy of nature. This is to improve untouched nature and realize its superiority over man. There are many varieties of mushrooms and, as they say, you need to know them by sight. Mushrooms are both edible and inedible. A beginner can easily confuse them. Collecting mushrooms is not an easy task. You need to look into different parts of the forest, look under the leaves and branches of trees, go into ravines, and walk on bumpy forest ground. Sometimes it hides under the grass and moss. The successful mushroom picker has a sharp eye. The observant picker will collect a lot, and the unobservant picker will stay empty-handed.

After arriving home, the mushrooms need to be washed and peeled. Then the cooking process begins. Mushrooms are boiled, fried, and salted. There are many recipes for every taste. If you collect a lot of mushrooms, then they can be prepared for the winter. When you open jars of mushrooms in winter, you smell the forest and remember the wonderful mood you were in when picking mushrooms.

Ekaterina Pershina is 43 and originally from Russia.

My Young Life in a Small Village

ZONG XIONG, ST. PAUL, MN

I was born and raised in a small village. My village was a nice place. Around the village, there were many mountains and caves. The weather was very good. It was not hot and not cold. Each family had three to four farms. Some planted rice, some planted corn. And we also planted banana and sugarcane, too.

Our village didn't have electricity to use. My

parents just used candles for light. Because we lived in a village far away from the city, we never saw cars. Sometimes we saw an airplane in the sky, and every child looked happy until the airplane was gone.

When we were still young, we had a lot of fun playing together. The kids played with small rocks, small sticks, and dolls. The rocks game had like five or ten small rocks, depending how you wanted to play. But we had to do rock, paper, and scissors first. We also played hide and seek in the evening time. When we played hide and seek, I hid in a dark place because I didn't want other kids to see me, but when I waited a long time, I felt scared. And I still remember some nights the moon was full, so we could see it while we played. If the sky was clear, we could see all the stars at night time, and the stars were so beautiful.

Zong Xiong is 39 and originally from Laos.

My Favorite Place

SEANGCHAN "SUNSHINE" GUDIM, MAPLEWOOD, MN

When I was young, my favorite place was the Wanon Niwat morning market where my mom sold food in Thailand. The market was similar to a farmer's market in St. Paul, Minnesota. It was in the middle of a busy Wanon Niwat District. Hundreds of people participated each morning. In the morning after we arrived at the market, I did small work like wiping the banana leaves for wrapping food and putting the food in paper bags for customers. I remember the fresh air in the morning and the eclectic smell of the market.

My mom used a lot of banana leaves each day to wrap her food in portions for one serving. She sold a variety of food and rotated different menus each day. Mom always had five to six menus each day. For example, she sold spring rolls, fried rice, fried fish cake, grilled beef or pork salad, and sticky rice with mango. Most of the food was cooked from home. We spent two hours selling them every morning before I went to school. I liked to see many people and talk to them. There were many Thai dialects at the market and also foriegn

languages like Vietnamese, Chinese, and Laos. The way people talked sounded like music to me. After the selling time ended, I helped my mom organize all the coins and banknotes by putting them in a group and counting them. I think I learned math while helping my mom at the market because I was able to do math in school fast. The market was one of my favorite places that gave me joy, and I learned many things at the same time.

Seangchan "Sunshine" Gudim is 71 and originally from Thailand.

My First Home

TEIDY OCHOA, MINNEAPOLIS, MN

I lived in Mexico with my mom, dad, sisters, and brothers. I slept with my sisters. I remember our home smelled delicious in the morning. My mom cooked eggs, beans, tortillas, and hot chocolate.

My favorite rooms were the living room and the kitchen. Every morning, I saw the trees and animals in the windows. It was a beautiful ranch. My life was wonderful with my family. My mom and dad worked hard on the ranch with the animals and planted beans, corn, pumpkins, and many other things. I helped my parents and also my sisters. It is wonderful to work on a ranch with your whole family.

Teidy Ochoa is 37 and originally from Mexico.

Memories from My Childhood

GABRIELA CELLERI, ROCKFORD, MN

During my childhood, in a little mud house in front of a mountain and near a river, I liked to play on our mountain where the wind blows. I found broken clay plates and pots to play with. I had the cactus plants with their red flowers and delicious fruits, which we called "tuna," to eat. I loved to collect flowers in the countryside to decorate my cakes and little houses made from mud. Here, I would play with my sister and cousins for hours and hours.

On sunny days, we liked to go to the river to wash our dirty clothes, and we would take all day to do it because we also played in the water and completely drenched the clothes we were wearing. We returned home happy, and our mom would be waiting with a warm meal and dry clothes for us.

Gabriela Celleri is 32 and originally from Ecuador.

My Childhood

PI LA MU, ST. PAUL, MN

When I was little, I lived with my parents and my sibling. My parents were growing rice and raising some animals. They also made rum. When I turned ten or eleven, I really wanted to go to school, and my parents could afford it, so I started going to school. While I was going to school, I needed to work at the farm, too. But I was always happy to work with my parents. Sometimes, when I was at the farm with my mom, if we saw some snakes, worms, or leeches, we ran away. That was a fun and memorable time in my life. Now, I want to say to my mom, "I miss you so much."

Pi La Mu is 34 and originally from Myanmar.

My Life in Honduras

VICTOR MANUEL RAMOS CHACON, HOWARD LAKE, MN

I am from Honduras and am currently living in Minnesota. When I was a child, I used to walk about half an hour or forty minutes to get to school. It depended on if I walked fast or if I was playing with friends along the way.

I liked school because I spent sixth grade with my favorite teacher. She was my favorite because she taught patiently, and she was very strict when she had to be. There were two rooms for the grades. The first, third, and fifth grades were in one room, and the second, fourth, and sixth grades were in the other room.

I have nine siblings: four sisters and five brothers. When I left school, I helped my brothers harvest the basic grains like corn, beans, coffee beans, et cetera. My favorite memory is when I rode my horse to get to work in agriculture. I owned a horse from the age of fifteen until I left my country at the age of twenty. I sold it because none of my siblings wanted to take care of him because it is a big responsibility. I miss my horse a lot.

Victor Manuel Ramos Chacon is 28 and originally from Honduras.

My Life

MAUNG NA, ST. PAUL, MN

I was born in the Mae La refugee camp in Thailand. My parents are from Burma. I have two sisters and four brothers. When I was six years old, I started primary school. I continued to go to school until grade eleven at the Mission High School. I did not graduate. All but one brother is still in Thailand. My brother came to the U.S. after I did.

I came here in September 2015. I was so happy when I saw snow for the first time. I like swimming and fishing in the summer. I studied at VSS School for three months before I got a full-time job at Bailey Nursery in March 2016. I did planting, pulling weeds, growing plants, cutting plants, et cetera. Many people worked there, so I had friends from many places, such as Karen, white, black, Hmong, Mexican, and Somali. They were my lovely friends, so I was happy to go to work. I learned a little Spanish from them.

In July 2019, I had to quit this job because I had a new baby, and I had to take care of my children. In September 2019, I started attending school at the Hubbs Center. Before COVID-19, I went to school, and after school, I went to work. I had a class in the afternoon and a part-time job in the evening. During COVID-19, I got laid off from this job, and I needed to start online classes. I really like online classes because I want to improve my English and get a diploma. I have a dream that one day I will become an engineer or a barber.

Maung Na is 28 and originally from Thailand and Burma.

Memory

MONE'T SPAULDING, ST. PAUL, MN

I remember when I was younger, my dad and I lived in Chicago with my grandma. Every year around Christmas Eve, we would bake chocolate chip cookies for Santa and build gingerbread houses. I loved this time of year. My grandma would tell my cousins and me a story about Santa Claus. How he would come down the chimney and drop our Christmas gifts off under the tree and eat some of the cookies from his long night of dropping presents off to different kids' houses, who were good for the year.

After she told us stories, we watched Christmas movies for most of the night. She would tuck us into bed, so we could wake up and open our presents from Santa and see that he ate some of the cookies.

Being the sneaky one, I stayed up all night so I could catch Santa eating the cookies we baked for him. And who do I see when I sneak a peek around the corner? My grandma and dad eating the cookies, laughing and saying, "We hope the kids don't catch us eating these cookies. They would be so disappointed if they found out Santa isn't real." Then I jumped out and said, "I caught you guys and I am disappointed, but if you let me stay up and eat a few cookies then I won't tell my cousins that Santa Claus isn't real." They let me do just that. I was happy. I didn't even care if Santa was real or not.

Mone't Spaulding is 24 and originally from the U.S..

My Father

WEI LIAO, LAKEVILLE, MN

My father is the most influential person in my life. My father is usually very strict with me, but sometimes he is gentle.

I remember the year near the university entrance examination. There was a midterm exam. I did poorly on the exam. It's true that I only got eighty-seven points on the math paper that had 120 points! How I wish it wasn't true, but it was true. After the mathematics score came, my heart was very sad, but I didn't cry out, my eyes quietly wept only.

I went home dejected, and I didn't lift my head until I got home. I was willing to tell my father about my poor score because he understands me better than my mother. He had a better idea of the educational process, and he would understand my situation. So this time, I explained the examination to my father as usual.

I stood in front of my father like a log and said, "Dad, this test…" I choked and didn't know how to say it. "My grades are not good…" I can't help the tears in my eyes.

But my father said to me with kind eyes, "It's okay. As long as you are willing to work hard, you can do well next time. I believe my daughter can do it."

Although my father's words were very short, they lightened the burden in my heart. I responded by deeply reflecting on myself. I put away my tears, and I felt thankful for my father. When I went to bed that night, my father's words lingered in my mind.

My father's love is deeply branded in my heart. My father gave me everything. I can not use words to thank him. The only way to show my gratitude is through my heart.

Wei Liao is 39 and originally from China.

We Persevere: Overcoming Challenges

Featured Author

Sue Jansen

CRYSTAL, MN

I have been creating at least since age three, and trading, selling, and sharing my works since age seven and a half. I create tangible items as a means of learning, healing, and understanding, for expressing love, gratitude, and resolution, and for telling stories, making statements, and creating interconnectedness with all beings, with mother/father life. I experience my medium as the world, as all materials hold promise, as each speaks to me, informs, and inspires me. I lived a great portion of my life in nature, where beauty and love abound, where the trees, rocks, plants, and waters loved, cared for, and sheltered me.

I have experienced dozens of brain injuries, along with other physical traumas, and currently walk with a cane or walker. I liken my brain and body functioning to the detours of Minnesota road construction; finding new ways amidst ever-changing pathways—new routes when faced with changing/changed routes. I am enrolled in Robbinsdale Adult Academic Program classes for people with stroke and/or traumatic brain injury. It is the most positive, welcoming, and kind educational experience I have experienced. While I have experienced hurt, I endeavor not to be a hurt person, nor to hurt others. This is where being a creatrix of works of art is especially beneficial—for self and others—with its power of voice and transformative healing, learning, and understanding.

Rainbow Skinned

I am the confluence of many rivers of peoples, and as with the waters of nature's mingling rivers, I cannot be separated into parts—a quarter this, a quarter that. I am solidly, evenly, all me, without choosing which part to acknowledge, respect, and identify myself as being. I am. And, as with all persons, I am rainbow skinned—skin containing all colors of the rainbow—differing proportions and intensities. I came to this process, developing over many decades, first found as a young child in dance with spirit and nature.

In my crayon pack, there were only the basic eight colors, but in my family, there were persons with very light skin, very dark skin, and shades and hues in between, nonlinearly. In school, we learned of the primary colors, and how all colors come from these. So when my curious and active mind tried to color each and all persons accurately, it was—and not so successfully—to attend to each person using multiple, separate crayons. Then, in frustration, I began melting, mixing, making my own crayons. From observing and coloring people and rainbows, I came to this knowledge. Every person is rainbow skinned.

At home, I was repeatedly bleached/scrubbed raw, being judged "too dark," and this treatment purported to fix "the problem." My friend Ronnie, diagnosed as albino, had been hurt and shamed for being "too light." We became simpatico, as he embraced my rainbow skinned concept, then new to him.

I first met Ronnie on a day after I had been brutally scrubbed, my skin bleeding. Ronnie came up out of the valley with others staying in the hobo camp, looking for food. My mother was known to feed them, but I was the interceptor. I was terribly ashamed, but Ronnie looked at me with compassion, rather than the horror seen on the other faces. I would learn that—then age twelve—Ronnie was on the run from home, and had blended himself in with these hobos. I invited him to share my fort and art materials, then to color on his shirt "Rainbow Skinned." One day, I went down to find his note: "Sue, they have found me, I must run. Thank you for loving your rainbow skinned friend, Ronnie."

Sue Jansen is 72 and originally from Robbinsdale, MN.

How I Survived Ten Strokes

DARRELL RAVITZ, BROOKLYN CENTER, MN

I am eighty-three years old, and if you saw me, you would say, "He looks like a man who is eighty-three years old." But, that is not the whole story. Physically, you can't see what has happened to my body. But there's a lot more going on inside of me that tells the tale of my strokes.

I have suffered ten strokes, both minor strokes, or TIAs (Transient Ischemic Attacks), and major strokes.

These strokes challenged me in many ways. One of the significant effects is prosopagnosia, known as "face blindness." Brad Pitt also suffers with this. It means I cannot recognize people's faces. I can see a general outline of a face, but I cannot recognize who the person is. I have to study hard and listen to the voice to know who that person is. I can't even recognize my own image! One time, at the hospital, my wife, Sue, was waiting for me. Five blondes were sitting in the waiting room, but I couldn't recognize my own wife! She had to call my name to get my attention.

Another effect of the strokes is aphasia. That is when I want to say something, but I cannot get my brain to form the words. It is like hitting a dead end, and I have to find another way to get the words out. I know what I want to say, but I keep trying words until I get at least close to the one I want.

I had to learn how to read again. I have to break each word into syllables, and three is the most I can handle. My eyesight is seventy-five percent of what it used to be. Colors are very muted, almost like a sepia or earth tone. Once, at a stoplight, I asked Sue why we weren't going. She replied that the light was red. I couldn't tell.

To overcome these challenges, I've had to find new ways to adapt. I've had speech therapy, and for eight years, I've attended Stroke and Brain Injury classes at the Robbinsdale Adult Academic Program in the Crystal Learning Center. This has helped me significantly.

But, most importantly, I don't give up!

Darrell Ravitz is 83 and originally from Minneapolis, MN.

My Beautiful Year 2020

AURA OLIVARES, BROOKLYN PARK, MN

My name is Aura, and I'm from Guatemala. I want to tell you, I can see a beautiful 2020 year.

I know everyone around us said, "What in the world is happening," but I can see it is a wonderful year because we are alive, we have food on our table, and we have a roof over our head. Thank you to God for everything you give to us. He has a plan for our lives. If everything is dark, you can see a light at the end of the street.

Aura Olivares is 32 and originally from Guatemala.

My Life

IFRAH AADAN, NEW HOPE, MN

Growing up in Mogadishu, I lived with my dad's family and my aunt. When I was born, my father first thought I was a boy. After he came to the hospital and saw I was a girl, he said, "She is the same as a boy! She is strong!" My mother passed away when I was one year old.

I came to the United States on July 17, 2012. At first, life was so hard. I did not speak English or drive a car. My husband worked a lot. I walked everywhere with my two kids. My son was four years old. My daughter was three years old. Now they are grown up. My oldest son is twelve years old and my daughter is eleven years old.

After I came here, I gave birth to two more boys. One was born May 2013. While I was pregnant, I was so sick. We were new to the United States. My husband worked in a warehouse. He brought me to two hospitals. They said he had to pay money before they would help me. We didn't have insurance. Five years later, my fourth child was born December 2018.

I started school at Winnetka Learning Center on October 17, 2012. Miriam was my teacher in Level One. I did not understand anything! I did not speak English! Next, I went to Level Two, and Katie was my second teacher. My third teacher was Colleen. I went to her class in 2016. After almost two years there, I stayed home for a couple of years.

Now, I have returned to school and am in Colleen's class again. I like to be strong and do it myself! I believe in myself. I will never give up until I reach my goals. I thank all of my teachers for their support and for teaching me English and how to read everything I need.

Ifrah Aadan is 32 and originally from Somalia.

Giving Birth

FATOUMA ABDI, ST. PAUL, MN

It is not easy to give birth. Giving birth and motherhood are a long journey. The day of the birth is a very hard day and stressful for the moms. The pain of birth is extremely unbearable, but the moms are very strong and focus only on their babies. The moms suffer pain and sacrifice their lives just to give another person life. The pain of some births last longer until delivery. You can not imagine the experience of delivering the baby if you haven't been through it. Moms are the only people who can live with this pain. The moms are strong, reliable, amazing, and gorgeous. The moms forget all the pain and stress as soon as they see or hear their babies crying. Moms are indispensable because through them a new soul comes into this world. Even though this experience is hard, the mom challenges herself and chooses to give birth.

Fatouma Abdi is 25 and originally from Djibouti.

My Pandemic Baby

ZEYNAB MOHAMED, ST. PAUL, MN

In March 2020, I left my job for a maternity leave. After three weeks I gave birth to my baby girl. I had a lot of dreams before the pandemic. I dreamed of going back to work, school, and taking my baby to daycare. At that time, I lived with my dear aunt who I really adore. As usual, my baby didn't allow for enough sleep for the first few weeks, so it was not easy for me, even though my aunt was helping a lot to care for the baby at night.

In my beautiful Somali culture, when a lady gives birth, friends and relatives visit with gifts for the baby and the mother, too. They also help with caring for the baby during the first weeks. I missed all of that as a result of the pandemic. That made me feel homesick. I missed everyone and everything back home. Sad! All I can do is pray to Allah, the Almighty, who can heal the world from this pandemic.

Zeynab Mohamed is 34 and originally from Somalia.

How the Pandemic Has Changed Our Lives

RAGHAD SHAREEF DHAHAD, NORTH ST. PAUL, MN

How has pandemic changed our lives? The COVID-19 pandemic has changed my daily life to some extent as I am stuck in my house, like many others during the lockdown. This global pandemic has affected various lives in different countries. Many of us are taking online classes, but some people in other countries do not use the internet to study or to order what they need. That is the reason why poor countries have had a lot of COVID cases.

The pandemic is big problem for kids who don't speak English. It is hard for them to study at home. They need to have contact with others and do some activities outside. This helps them to learn new things. My kids now study at home, and if we take them outside to play, we don't allow them to play with other kids so that my kids will stay safe from others, but this makes me sad. I feel that life is over and every person lives in a world alone.

I have a question to the scholars. Why and how did you name scholars of the past? The scientists of the past discovered many, many things but today's scientists are nothing when we need them. We are suffering from this pandemic for the whole year, and we are in an era of development and progress. But this small virus has changed the course of life in all countries, and our scientists now have a vaccine, but not all people trust this vaccine. Despite all of this, we must maintain our commitment, and pray to my God to save us from this pandemic. Finally, I hope that everyone stays safe.

Raghad Shareef Dhahad is 38 and originally from Iraq.

Arguing with Myself

CHRISTOPHER DRIFT, ST. CLOUD, MN

What can I say to make you understand my madness

the way I feel?

Nothing, not a damn thing

self-destruction becomes a normal meal

Stomaching the self-hatred self-made

the unteachable unreachable

I feel and act like a ghost

shy at times

hiding disguising myself

They can't handle me

unexplainable an understatement see

I do what I like what I want regardless of the
consequence or benefit

Don't know how to quit trying to be respectful and
understanding

Supply and demanding

protection on my hip not the man standing

Yearning for a different thrill

a different meal

still hungry as ever

Smart acting dumb

strong acting weak

quiet at times won't even speak

Underestimated to the fullest meaning of the word

I don't mind

I'd rather be unknown anyway I'm confused
sensitive as hell

Where did these feelings turning into emotions
come from?

I'm human

A little different from most what's normal anyway?
Are you? Am I?

Standup guy hard to swallow my pride

or stand down stubborn

A simple man the only son of a struggling broken
strongest woman

The ones who really know this remastered careful
bastard will

Miss but love the old me cherish

and still follow the new me unruly

I always wondered why I am one of the ones a topic
of discussion

I'm a nobody

a glimpse, a breath in freezing air mist who will be
truly

missed and dismissed as one of the greatest don't
cry I LIVED!!!!!

Christopher Drift is 36 and originally from St. Cloud, MN.

Push Yourself

SADIYO HASSAN, MINNEAPOLIS, MN

I came from East Africa in 2014. Since that time, I have lived in Minnesota. When I came to America for the first time, it was very challenging for me because I was a single parent with my four-year-old son and pregnant with my second son. I left my husband in Africa and I didn't come with any family. Everyone I met felt sorry for me and asked me why I left my husband. It made me scared, so I decided not to be scared anymore. I started ESL classes, and also I got part time work.

After four months, I bought a small car, and I started to practice driving, and I got my license. Coming to America is not easy, but what you need is to push yourself. You can achieve your goals, if you set up any goal in your life. First when I came, I realized that the language is very important because every job you apply to, the first questions are, "Do you drive? Do you speak English?"

When I got my license, I was so happy, but still I had a lack of English. I decided not to look for a job but go to school. After six months, I was level five, so this time I looked for a better job because I understood English and I drove. I attended a class, and I became certified for a Child Development Assistant. Then, I got a good-paying new job. I was so proud of myself, and I felt I was a good mom who can change her life and her kids' lives.

Again, I decided to change my work for more pay. I decided to become a school bus driver. I practiced for the Commercial Driver's License and got my license and got a big raise. I felt proud though COVID-19 came, and there is no work. I feel good, and I am wishing I will go back when schools open again. If you are willing to change your life, don't give up, just try it. There are many challenges in life, especially if you are a mama, and still you couldn't get any backup from your family. Although I have many friends, still we know the family is a big part in life. I wish I could have my family here in America. My family tree is more than sixty people, and none of them are here.

Sadiyo Hassan is 38 and originally from Somalia.

The Pandemic
ROSARIO CORTES, MINNEAPOLIS, MN

This pandemic has really changed my life and those of many more. I wonder when we will return to normal? Before the pandemic, I used to complain because my husband worked a lot and now that he only has one job, I tell him jokingly, "Hey, when will you be going back to your second job?!" and we start laughing.

In this time, I have put everything into practice that I have learned in school. I have become my children's personal assistant because they take classes at home, and when they have questions, I know what to answer and how to help them.

Taking math classes has helped me a lot. Thanks for the 1,000 ways that Bryce uses to teach us so that we can learn. I always put his advice into practice. He tells me that if I practice and practice, my brain becomes stronger.

Thanks to my other math teacher, René, for always being available to help clarify doubts.

Thank you, Jill, my English teacher, for your patience because sometimes I do not understand the words. You are looking for a way to teach me so that I understand. I always look forward to Tuesday to see what will happen in the next e-chapter of the book we are reading. Thank you all for your great work.

Rosario Cortes is 39 and originally from Mexico.

School Challenge
FEYISA BATI, ST. PAUL, MN

I was ten years old the year of 2009. The country was Ethiopia, the city of Assasa. My school had a dirt floor, and I sat on the floor. There were kids of all ages in my classroom. We were learning four languages in school: English, Afan, Oromo, and Amharic. I was nervous, and it was so scary to stand in the front of my class, the students. It was really a hard time. When I speak to the students, they laugh at me. After, I'm so mad at the students, and I go back to sit in my chair. I was crying that time my teacher was mean. My teacher would hit me five to ten times on the hand with a stick if I was wrong.

Feyisa Bati is 22 and originally from Ethiopia.

The World According to Simon: Simon's Life Story
SIMON ORTEGA, NORTH BRANCH, MN

My life has been trials and tribulations, but I fought through and made something of myself. I was born into poverty and the chaos of the seventies. My mom, stepdad, and biological dad were shoplifters, drug dealers, and violent. Sometimes, they got busted with us with them. The cops just took the man and figured the lady had to raise the kids.

My mom took care of her own and my dad's children, seven total. My sister and I raised them, making sure they were eating, and getting ready for school. For long stretches, we would not even know our mother's whereabouts.

In 1980, I was running wild. Mom sent me to live with my dad who was out of prison but still shoplifting and dealing drugs. I got special help in Mahtomedi Middle School and did really good there. Mahtomedi was my start in track and field.

Then my father sent me back to my mom. Living with my alcoholic, bipolar mom was chaotic. I tried to be a good kid, but even little things would lead to me being thrown out every other day. I wasn't doing very well at school. I liked running, so I ran and did sports. I slept underneath the Lafayette Bridge or at different friends' houses. I called it the "couch motel." But wherever I was, I would run for hours. It was my release. I didn't finish high school.

I went into the army drunk and on drugs, but they sobered me up. That's when I went to AA and found the Lord for the first time. It was a good thing.

After the army, I tried to do positive things. I got married and had a son. I worked as a roofer, truck driver, custodian, and in maintenance.

By my late forties, I realized it's possible to be who you want to be in this life. I started working for my adult diploma. I didn't give up. Finally, in 2019, I finished the work and earned my high school diploma through North Branch Adult Basic Education. Now I'm working on getting my associate's degree in tool-making.

Here's what I would say to others: don't sell yourself short in life. Believe in your dreams and go after them. Don't let your past choose for you. Be true to yourself, get a good education. That's where it counts in this world.

Simon Ortega is 55 and originally from St. Paul, MN.

A Challenge

MUSE DINI, WAITE PARK, MN

I was born in Somalia. I came to the United States in 2016. I like living here, but ever since then, I have been struggling with one problem. I wanted an artificial leg, but the doctor made a mistake. He put the bandage strongly on my leg. I've felt pain in my leg ever since then. Right now, I can't work because of my leg. It still hurts, and I can't put on an artificial leg. I'm waiting for an operation now.

Muse Dini is 47 and originally from Somalia.

My Challenges

SUPHATTRA (NENG) MCLEOD, BROOKLYN PARK, MN

Each day is a great opportunity to try something new and push myself into areas that test my capabilities as well as widen my horizons. I like to test myself on how brave I am. For example, July 2018, I tested myself with skydiving at Skydive Twin Cities. That was scary because it was really high, over 13,000 feet of altitude, and that is the biggest thing I've ever tried before. Another challenge is exercising my brain, such as learning to speak a new language or learning to play a musical instrument. I am trying to learn some of the programming that is called Python. Although I am not an expert English language learner, I still want to challenge myself.

Suphattra (Neng) McLeod is 34 and originally from Thailand.

My Work History

AYAN D., RICHFIELD, MN

I came here in 2007, the only one from my family who came here. I lived with my aunty from my dad's cousin for one and a half years in Ohio. I was looking for a job and a school to learn English. Every job I applied for they said, "You don't know English, we are not going to give you work." I had trouble finding a job, but after three months, I got a job in housekeeping. Those three months, I was going to school in the morning. The school was an ESL school. I did go to the housekeeping job for one year and half. I came home from my job at 4:30 p.m., and then I was home for a half hour, and then the English started at 6:00 p.m. This school was two days a week. My off days were Monday and Thursday.

When you are coming to America, you need to have a car to go to school or go to work. I don't have a car or a driver's license, and then I had a lot of people helping me. One of my friends came to my house every morning and picked me up, and every evening, somebody gave me a ride to school and back those two days a week. When I found a job, I stopped the morning school but I still go two days at night. I learn a little bit of English at work and school.

After that, I moved out of Ohio and came to Minnesota. The first time I came, my uncle lived here. He called me and said, "Come here and stay with me. It is a better life." And I say, "Okay." And I find a job when I came here. He is helping me with so many things.

I find a job in daycare. I start in distance school. Sometimes I work in the morning, so I go to school in the evening. If I work in the evening, I go to school in the morning. I never never go without school. The school is important, and you learn a lot. English is not my first language. It is my second language. Sometimes I need help at groceries. Sometimes I need help at the appointments with doctors or my kids have appointments. A lot of things you don't know. So I wanted to learn English and have a better education. Learning is good.

Ayan D. is 34 and originally from Somalia.

"Brown Eyes" and "February"
HEATHER RILEY, PLYMOUTH, MN

Beautiful brown eyes

Deep love and lasting passion

sing to lonely hearts

The month moves slowly

as I'm counting down the days

February tenth

Heather Riley is 32 and originally from Utica, NY.

When I Came to the USA
HALIMA DUALEH, MINNEAPOLIS, MN

I came from Somalia on July 14, 1999, a very hot and humid day. Since then, I have been happily living in exciting Minnesota.

I worked for different companies, like the post office and the Hilton Hotel in Minneapolis. I had to try very hard to understand because I didn't speak English.

I tried to understand my coworkers. I watched their body language and actions. So, all managers and coworkers were my friends. I was never late to my work. I was always on time or early, because I am a hard worker. Also, I was always finishing my work on time.

I am a friendly person and happy. I come from a big family. I have thirteen brothers and seven sisters. Also, I am a mother of four smart children. Two are girls, they are the first and the last born. My sons are in the middle. I like Minnesota.

Halima Dualeh is 43 and originally from Somalia.

My Challenge
ANONYMOUS, MINNEAPOLIS, MN

I am a mother of four children. I live in Minneapolis with my kids. My first year in Minneapolis is not easy. But I never give up.

My Greatest Challenge
SHAYMAA JAKJOOK, MINNEAPOLIS, MN

My name is Shaymaa. I am from Iraq.

I was working as a teacher in my country for eight years teaching social studies. After that, I decided to take a master's degree in the same specialty but that needs a lot of hard work and study. Because I have many responsibilities to my family in different ways, like cleaning, cooking, helping my three children with their homework, and taking care of them. And the last thing I think about is how to make time to read with all of the chores I have. I decided to go the hard way. First, I enrolled in a college and then studied hard. After that, I took the test, and I passed the second time.

This hard period was when I started to study after I left college fourteen years ago, and many facts changed and required me to study ten hours a day with my huge chores. Finally, I achieved this success after two years of studying hard and searching for references and resources in the library and internet. After one year of writing about two hundred pages and two months of paperwork, fnally, the last moment in my race that was the most difficult was the three hours in which I defended my thesis. This event occurred during Ramadan and I was fasting, so I needed to talk for about three hours and argue with my committee without a sip of water. I think that was the toughest event in my whole life.

Shaymaa Jakjook is 42 and originally from Iraq.

COVID-19 and Me

HALIMA ADEM, MINNEAPOLIS, MN

I first heard about COVID-19 on the news. Then teacher Lloyd told me that Open Door Learning Center was closing because of COVID-19. I worked in downtown Minneapolis as a lobby attendant. COVID-19 shut down the hotel, and I lost my job because people weren't traveling or coming from the airport. I got unemployment for one month, but then I found a new job pretty easily. Now I work in St. Louis Park and do packaging. I work forty hours a week. I wear a mask at work. They check our temperature every day.

COVID has changed everything. I can't go to visit my friends. Ibrahim, my son, can't play with other kids because everybody is scared. I do not know anyone who has had COVID-19.

Halima Adem is 29 and originally from Oromia.

A New Job

BRENDA ROMERO, MINNEAPOLIS, MN

Three years ago, when I was working in a factory, my sister told me about how the two of us could become school bus drivers. I said, "No, no, I don't want to do it" because I was afraid about my English and driving a big bus.

But, when I found out about the pay, I changed my mind. I would earn more and have insurance.

I had to take training, read a book, and take a test for a certificate. And then I trained behind the wheel of a big yellow school bus. Because I had never ridden on a school bus as a child, I didn't know anything about how busses worked, like turning on the lights before a stop and putting out the stop arm.

Now that I have confidence, I enjoy the kids. I like the little kids because they are creative. When we do the evacuation drill, they say "Oh, cool," and they get excited about learning how the bus works. They hug me, and they say, "Oh, Ms. Bus Driver, I love you."

Brenda Romero is 43 and originally from Mexico.

Football

SAHMAD NAKUMBE, MAPLE GROVE, MN

When I was twelve years old, I wasn't good at football. I was teased for not being strong.

When I was in eigth grade, I hurt my right kneecap in a football scrimmage. I had to sit out for the whole season. In ninth grade, I begged my mom to play again. I got better and improved myself! I was a part of the starting team. During high school, I was the starting quarterback. I got a scholarship to St. Olaf College! In college, I took the scholarship to St. Olaf. I was no longer the starting quarterback. I was the starting fullback! After college, I played semi-pro for four different teams! I was back to being the quarterback.

I stopped playing semi-pro when I had my stroke in May of 2018. I still love football! It will forever be a passion of mine!

Sahmad Nakumbe is 29 and originally from Minneapolis, MN.

Life in a Refugee Camp

FADUMO ABDULLAHI, ST. CLOUD, MN

I am sharing my life as a refugee in a camp in 1992. It was very difficult. People died because they didn't get medicine. The young people also did not have vaccinations for diseases like measles, polio, et cetera. At that time, it was very hard for people to live and that's my story.

Fadumo Abdullahi is 34 and originally from Somalia.

The Most Difficult Day of My Life

SHAMSO OMAR, MINNEAPOLIS, MN

You know, in Somalia, men like to have boys. But my father had five daughters and loved them very much. "If you had a son," I asked my dad, "what would you like your son to be in the future?"

"I would like my son to be a doctor," he said. I wanted to make my dad happy because he was close with me like a friend.

My mother worked very hard in the house all day. She never went to school, never learned to write. "Don't be like me," she said to me. "My father died when I was young. You have to learn for the future." My mother was proud of me, and she told me to keep going.

One morning when I was in eighth grade, I woke up at 6 a.m. and put on my school uniform, an orange shirt and tan pants. I loved school. My dream was to go to school and then to go to medical school.

I went to the living room where we ate. For breakfast my mother made tea and *lahoh*, Somali pancakes. We put many things in *lahoh*—honey, or meat, or sugar, and tea together. My father sat with us at breakfast. He was very tall and thin, and he had light skin like me. He was a policeman.

My sister Sahra might say, "Mama, Fatima tells me, 'You're ugly. You are not in this family.'"

"Don't tell your sister that because she is feeling sad," my mother might say.

"Listen to your mom," my father always told us. "Don't make your mom angry." I never saw my father angry or sad.

After breakfast, I went to school with my little sister, Ubah. At school, we got in two lines, boys and girls. We sang the Somali national anthem and did exercises. Suddenly I heard guns shooting! At the start, a few shots. Later, automatic guns. The principal told all the children to sit down. Everybody was crying. "Go home," the principal and the teacher said. "And don't play outside."

I went home. My mom was not home. My father was not home. I cried and cried. My two younger sisters cried. "Don't cry," my older sister said. "Mama will come back. She went to find you."

After about an hour, my mother came back. "I was scared I would never see you!" she said, crying.

My father never came home. Soldiers were killing policemen, so he went to Kismayo. This was the beginning of the civil war in Somalia. Soon thieves took everything in our house. Soon my school was bombed. My dream was gone. I never saw my dad again.

Shamso Omar is 43 and originally from Somalia.

Overcoming Challenges

GUTEMA ALIKO, ST. PAUL, MN

Coming to the United States made me feel excited and anxious about going to a new country. I came on June 22, 2018 with my wife and two kids (four years old and one year old). The U.S. is very different than how I thought it would be. I thought life would be easy. I didn't know how hard I would have to work. I arrived at my sponsor's house in Washington DC. The next day was a black day for my wife and me because we didn't know what to do and where to go. We stayed there for one month. Then, we came to Minnesota.

In Minnesota, we started a new life with our friends. We rented one bedroom in the basement of a personal town house. I was happy, but still afraid about a lot of things. I didn't have a job, and I did not drive, so I couldn't go shopping. It was such a difficult time for my family.

In July 2018, I got my work permit and started working at Sky Chief doing assembly, but it was still difficult for me because I couldn't drive and didn't have a car. Also, I couldn't speak English well and was dependent on the person who gave me a ride to work. After three months, I got my driver's license, but I still didn't have a car. After a couple of months, my friend lent me money to get a used car. Then I started driving and got another job as a machine operator at Seagate Technology.

Finally, in January 2020, I was blessed with a third baby girl, and my family became happier. I started working at the University of Minnesota. Also, my wife got her driver's license and started working the morning shift as a machine operator at Boston Scientific. I work afternoons. I thank

God for everything. Nowadays, all the darkness has passed. I am busy taking care of my three kids at home. The oldest one is learning at home. I help her and take care of the others. I continue studying online to improve my English skills at the Hubbs Center. This is the busiest time of my life, but I am living the best life. I am so happy. I love living in the USA. God bless America.

Gutema Aliko is 38 and originally from Oromia.

Goodbye 2020! Hello 2021!

ARACELI RAYA HERNANDEZ, NEW HOPE, MN

Goodbye, 2020! I would like to share my highs and lows of 2020. We can start with the positive things that happened. One positive thing that happened to me was that a very nice lady paid for my groceries. I felt very bad because the place where I buy my food is all organic, so it's more expensive than other stores. At the same time, I was very thankful that there are still kind people in this world that help each other through hard times. Something else that I enjoyed in 2020 was that I could start learning English from my home. I prefer that way because now I don't have to tell my husband to come and pick me up.

Now, we can talk about the negative. Something that was negative about 2020 was that I couldn't work in my garden during the cold winter. I feel like this year went too fast. Therefore, I was bummed when summer came to an end. Now we have snow!

I know the world has been in a lockdown for a long time, but there will always be hope with us.

Hello, 2021!

Araceli Raya Hernandez is 43 and originally from Mexico.

Transitions

AZIZA AHMED, ST. PAUL, MN

I am from Oromia, which is a part of Ethiopia. I want to share my life with you. When I was in my home country, I sold things in our clothes and furniture store. I didn't know anything about Kenya before we went there as refugees because of the political problems in my country. Just thinking about it makes me feel very emotional.

Life in Kenya was very difficult. We could not work. So, we just sat in our one room tent for ten years. The United Nations gave us food every two weeks. We had our three children while there.

After a long, hard life in Kenya, the United Nations High Commissioner for Refugees (UNCR) made a move to the United States possible for us. The United States was also a difficult transition. We had no relatives and no friends to help us. Everything was different than the countries we had come from. We did not know how to take a bus. We did not know how to register for school. We did not know how to get a job. So, we just stayed home for months, looking out the window. A church from the Minnesota Council of Churches helped us apply for jobs and get some clothes.

This is a funny story about learning American culture. When the church helped us get some clothes, I picked out the size that fit, not thinking about colors. When we went to daycare, they asked, "What is your daughter's name?" I said, "He is not my daughter. He is a boy." She said, "Oh sorry, in this country, pink is for girls, blue is for boys."

There was no alternative. We had to go through all of these challenges to get to the comfortable life we now have, thanks to my Allah. I want to say thank you to all the Hubbs Center teachers and staff. Thank you for helping me get opportunities in Minnesota.

Aziza Ahmed is 41 and originally from Oromia.

A Different Time: Before and after Coronavirus

HANAD MOHAMED, MINNEAPOLIS, MN

I liked going to school every day. In March, I learned that school was closed because of the coronavirus when my friend Sara called me. I felt sad then. I have felt sad when I watch TV and see a lot of people have died. But I feel like my family is together and safe. My family in Germany and Somalia is safe, but the coronavirus is there, too.

I am happy to have my school now online. I like to talk English online and do math and English with my teachers. I say thank you to Teacher Bryce and Teacher Sallie. I like typing on the computer and reading a book that my teacher sent. My children are happy studying in school online.

Every morning, we drink lemon in water to help keep us healthy. I also put garlic in the water, and my husband and I take two small tastes every day and the children once a week. It's good for us. I wear a mask when we go to the store, and people stay six feet apart.

Eid was different in this time. Every family stayed home. We had our special meal only for our family. We talked to our other family by phone and our family in Africa on WhatsApp.

When it is over and I think about the coronavirus time, I will remember how I ate more often, every two hours! I will remember listening to music while I cleaned at home. I will remember everyone was wearing masks.

When the coronavirus is over, I will be happy to go back to school, and I will learn to drive a car and get my license. We will see all of our family and be together again.

Hanad Mohamed is 43 and originally from Somalia.

A Year of Unexpected Changes
CARMEN ROA MAIRENA, GOLDEN VALLEY, MN

In this year, we have been going through many drastic changes to contain the spread of COVID-19. All of these changes altered many things: government, citizens, lives, economic growth, health fields, education, jobs, families, coexistence, and the practice of cultural and religious traditions.

I had changes, too. I hadn't considered early retirement, but after l had been stressed for several months by the fear of the pandemic and the kind of essential job that I was doing, I had to take the option of retirement to protect myself and other people. This difficult decision of my retirement was unexpected and the greatest change of the year 2020 and in my life.

I liked and enjoyed the work that I had been

doing for thirty-five and a half years since I came from Nicaragua in 1985 when I was forty-eight years old. In my country, I was a high school teacher, but here in Minnesota, I studied to be a nursing aide. I got my license and, thereafter, a job in a healthcare facility that had all levels of care. Since then, and until November 2020, working as a nurse's aide in a retirement home gave me the opportunity to know, treat, and understand many persons and help them with their individual needs.

At the beginning of the year, I had to confront all the changes and consequences of COVID-19. In my job, every day there were strict measures of safety that I had to follow for the safety of the persons under my care and myself. I didn't want to leave the job in this difficult time with the shortage of staff and all the extra work caused by the pandemic.

Little by little and month by month, my stress and fears of COVID-19 increased, and I ended up making the difficult decision to retire. It was a hard decision to make. l didn't want the residents to know that I was leaving. I wanted them to remember me as glad and happy, and I wanted to keep those memories for myself.

I miss my job, the personal contacts, and communication with all the persons that were around me. It has been a little hard to adjust to the new life changes, but I feel very satisfied with accomplishing the mission of my life: to help others with their needs and provide them with peace of mind and joy.

I thank God for letting me go through all those work years with His blessing and without any difficulty.

Carmen Roa Mairena is 83 and originally from Nicaragua.

The Driving Test
FATHI IBRAHIM, ST. CLOUD, MN

When I was nineteen years old, I came to America. I started to go to school, but I didn't have a car. Me and my sister walked together to school. It was hard for me to walk to school. One day, I met my cousin at the park. I asked him if he could pick me up and take me to school. I told him that

I didn't have a car and didn't know how to drive. He said to me, "I will pick you up every day." One day I waited for him, but he didn't come to pick me up. That day it was very cold, so I couldn't walk to school.

I went online and learned the answers to the questions for the driving test. Then I went to the DMV to take the test. I passed the test, and then I had to take the behind-the-wheel test. My brother taught me how to drive. I didn't have a car for the test, but my brother let me use his.

When I was taking the behind-the-wheel test, I made some mistakes. I forgot to turn on my turn signal. I also forgot the handbrake. When my tires went up and over the island in the road, the DMV instructor yelled at me. After all these things, I still passed the test and got my license. I was so surprised!

Fathi Ibrahim is 23 and originally from Kenya.

Adapting to Change

MARTRELL JACKSON, GARY, IN

Can adapting to change be hard for some people?

Adapting to change is not easy for some people. How do I know that? Well, let me enlighten you. Very soon, I will be being released into society from doing my second bid in Stillwater prison. Being released into society can be difficult for multiple reasons that include change of routine, surrounding yourself with old individuals, and most importantly staying out of trouble. To make it easier to adapt to society, you should try to maintain a schedule to keep yourself busy or involve yourself in doing structured activities.

For some people, adapting to change is easy, but for most it's not because a lot of people don't have flexibility as a characteristic, so having a strong support system can help with that. In the near future, for those who have a chance of being released into society, I encourage you to take it one day at a time and wish you the best of luck!

Martrell Jackson is 22 and originally from Gary, IN.

How My Life Is Different Because of COVID-19

KAWSAR MUSE, MINNEAPOLIS, MN

COVID-19 has made life harder for me because I cannot go to see my friends. I hate masks and gloves. You're scared when you sit next to people or open the door and if people sneeze. Then I hurry away. I have allergies. If I get COVID-19, it would be hard for me.

Many things have changed since COVID-19. Before, we washed our hands to stay clean, but now I wash my hands a lot, more than before. If my friends come to my house, they use masks. If I go to a friend's house, I use a mask to be safe. Now, I clean where the key fits into the door of my apartment and my sinks with Clorox. I learn at home with my computer which is hard for me and for my teacher. I speak some words, but my teacher doesn't understand them clearly. I miss my school, all my teachers, and all my classmates.

All over the world, families have lost mothers and fathers or even children to COVID-19. Many people have lost their jobs. COVID-19 changed my life and changed the lives of other people.

Kawsar Muse is 43 and originally from Somalia.

Life with Coronavirus

RUKIYA OMAR, MINNEAPOLIS, MN

The coronavirus is spreading all over the world. This pandemic is prevalent over the whole country. It is a killer. Many people die from Covid-19, but some people survive. And also, businesses shut down and people lock down everywhere: they stay home, they do not do anything, and they are so bored! But students are learning technology and taking class online. Sometimes the technology is crazy. It has problems like slow internet or a poor network connection. Then the students cannot learn well. Some students make YouTube shows and play games because they do not do anything else. So they are stuck at home. Some parents are confused about what to do with their children. Many people despair over the coronavirus.

This year, I made face masks because people want to cover their mouths. The face mask is crucial because Covid-19 spreads to other people through breathing. That is why I made face masks, which were homemade. Then I gave them to people for safety because Covid-19 is dangerous to people. I help my community to stay safe, particularly older people. I like to help people. People need to social distance, to wash their hands, and to cover their mouths because everyone needs to stay alive. Life is important!

Rukiya Omar is 35 and originally from Somalia.

Challenges in America
SEDJIRO DOSSA GOUBIYI, ST. PAUL, MN

My first day in the United States was difficult because I could not hear or say anything when people talked to me. I always said, "Can you repeat again, please?" This embarrassed me a lot, but people were very nice and repeated themselves slowly for me.

This prompted me to start English classes, which are helping me. After a few months, my vocabulary increased. I can now respond easily when people speak to me. I speak better, and everybody at work notices my improvement.

My next goal is to start nursing classes, so I can have a better life. However, the pandemic is a challenge. I keep my fingers crossed, while I wait for better days.

Sedjiro Dossa Goubiyi is 39 and originally from Benin.

This Is My Life
KATHERINE KASL, ST. PAUL, MN

People are always trying to act like they know me
    when they have no idea.

They haven't seen what I've seen,

heard what I've heard,

been through my pain, struggles and fears.

They haven't cried as many tears as I've cried
    throughout these years.

Getting beaten, pushed and shoved around,

every single day I fall to the ground.

It's hard to get up when you have no one there to
    help you get up because nobody cares.

I've been through it all. I ran the streets. I sold
    myself because I didn't want to get beat.

It's a tough world out there, so I play it like a game.
    My goal is to survive.

I know it shouldn't be this way. I smoke to relax. I
    like the way it feels. Some people try to judge
    me or speak on how they feel.

Most of them are faker than a three dollar bill,

which doesn't exist so you know they're not real.

I've heard so many lies I don't know what to believe.

It's like saying you didn't steal when it's right up
    your sleeve.

No matter where I go, I will never be free,

because I belong to a man and he'll find me.

Every single day I fear for my life.

I never know what could happen, that's why I carry
    a knife.

I know the way I'm living isn't right,

But I have no other choice so I guess this is my life.

Katherine Kasl is 27 and originally from St. Paul, MN.

Technology Use in the COVID-19 Pandemic Era
NALINI ELUMALAI, CORCORAN, MN

Even in the Covid-19 pandemic situation, we can make progress in our studies because of technology. In the pandemic, I lost my job, so I decided to change my career path to IT, and I started to learn about computer networks and cyber security.

The Minnesota unemployment welfare program offered free online courses for unemployed people, so I enrolled in courses through them. These courses help me to learn new things and be more confident.

Simultaneously, I am doing my English classes

through the Crystal Learning Center, and I am learning even better than before through Zoom. The teachers can focus on each and every student, and our teacher is sending daily updates through email and WhatsApp messages. The learning program keeps us keep up to date on current affairs.

I have learned more new vocabulary words using technology like Google Translate as it complements our learning programs. The WhatsApp communication application helps me stay connected with my parents and friends residing on another side of the world. Therefore, I am excited to say that the current technology facilities have reduced the impact of the Covid-19 pandemic isolation and also helped the education programs to stay on track.

Nalini Elumalai is 36 and originally from India.

"Strength" and "Red Roses"
QUINN ROBINSON, PLYMOUTH, MN

Strength

for dark lonely nights

a beautiful

sunny

heart

Roses bloom bright red

under beautiful blue skies

thorns, droplets of blood

Quinn Robinson is 36 and originally
from Minneapolis, MN.

Learning to Drive
QIN SUN, WAITE PARK, MN

When I first learned to drive, I was thirty-two years old. I used to use the company's transportation. Now, the company has cancelled the transportation, so I had to learn to drive by myself to get to work. When the driving school teacher took me to the street for driving practice, I was very nervous when I saw people, but when I got used to it, I relaxed a lot. I took the exam after a month's practice.

The first time I didn't pass because I backed into the simulated garage. I had so much tension. I passed the exam the second time. I'm happy to have my driver's license and drive to work by myself.

Qin Sun is 49 and originally from China.

My Life as a Mom Distant Apart
SHELLY BRESNAHAN, ST. PAUL, MN

Here I am

There u are

We sit far apart

U know me

My life as a mom distant apart

So as I go on

U tell me never go wrong

We come together

And sing that song

We travel them roads but it seems so long

I look up in the sky

I never want to say good bye

So please don't ever cry

My life as a mom distant apart

We sit here and analyze

We realize and finalize

God put me here

My life as a mom distant apart

Thank u for listening

Do u really see that?

It is me and I do agree

I am the key

As a mom distant apart.

Shelly Bresnahan is 54 and originally from St. Paul, MN.

Prison Changes Lives

RAMEY OLSON, ALEXANDRIA, MN

There are lots of ways prison changes lives. It may make life difficult or strengthen it depending on the circumstances. There are lots of changes in attitudes and appearances. Health and exercise may have a big part in life changes in prison.

I believe a person can make lots of benefitable changes with their lives because of prison.

Ramey Olson is 33 and originally from Alexandria, MN.

Believe in Yourself

FARTUN MOHAMED, MINNEAPOLIS, MN

When I was in middle school, math and reading were hard for me. When something is difficult at school, I feel anxious. I didn't give up because I pushed myself forward. I wanted my life to be successful.

Early high school was challenging, too. I didn't focus in the class. I felt that I was going to give up because sometimes I didn't want to do my homework. Sometimes, I felt sad at school because I knew I didn't work hard, but I also knew that I was going to do better. One day, I saw a flyer on the bulletin board that said, "You can change yourself to be a better person." I said, "This will help me focus in the class." I was lazy in school, but when I looked at people who worked hard, I told myself that I needed to stop and change to become a better student.

When I came to the USA, I used to be afraid of asking for help because I thought my English was poor. I didn't understand what was going on in the classroom. Therefore, it was difficult to learn. My mom told me, "Never be afraid of asking for help because if you don't, you will fall behind." My mom is right. I learned how to stand on my own feet with other people's help. Today I'm not afraid of asking for help.

When I went to high school, it was difficult because the classes were harder than what I thought they would be. Math was especially challenging. After school, I signed up for tutoring that helped me understand math problems. After that, I showed my teacher that I could do it on my own.

Now I believe in myself. I didn't give up so easily because no matter how difficult things can be, I remember what my mom and my grandmother told me: Keep pushing hard and you will get there someday. I learned to become persistent, not only in my studies, but also in other areas of life. I feel strong, confident, and happy knowing that I can do whatever I would like to do with my life. One day I will teach my own kids to fight for their dreams and never give up on themselves. I will also teach them other things such as my culture, my religion, and how to respect people, and behave properly. I learned from my mother not to let anyone put you down. Hold your head high and walk away. That way you won't get hurt.

Fartun Mohamed is 24 and originally from Somalia.

What Challenges Are Facing You Today?

UEL OLIVIER, BURNSVILLE, MN

Today I am facing a big challenge about English. It is a real challenge for me because I did not know anything about the English language (especially about speaking and listening). At school, I had some grammar lessons, but I could not speak and listen and have English conversations.

I have spent the past two years in France, studying for my master's in Business Law. When I left France to move to the U.S., it was so difficult for me to understand American people. Before moving to the U.S., I did not know anything about American culture. For this reason, I make many sacrifices to learn and improve my English and experience American culture to compare with my other experiences in Haiti and France. So, to reach my goal, I watch TV and videos in English, I read some books, study vocabulary, and speak with people in English.

Today, I have some success in English. I can think of preparing for my professional career in law. Indeed, according to my last experiences, when someone speaks English, there are many opportunities to get some good jobs. In Haiti, English represents good skills for working at good places or offices.

I hope that I will have opportunities to learn English like a native person. And I will say: I reached one of my best goals and accomplished a good challenge.

English represents more for my professional career and my integration in the U.S.

Uel Olivier is 32 and originally from Haiti.

Challenges of Moving to a New Country

FADUMO ABDI, ST. PAUL, MN

I was excited and also nervous about moving to the USA, a country I had never been to before. I came in November 2013. The picture I had of the U.S. before arriving was all wrong. I thought it would be easy to make money. I didn't realize how hard you had to work to pay bills.

In December, I got my work permit and started searching for a job. It was difficult to find a job because I didn't have job experience, didn't speak English, and didn't have a car. Additionally, most warehouses require females to wear pants. My religion does not allow women to wear pants. Finally, at the end of January I found a job.

I was a contract worker. If the company ran out of product, they sent me home. Furthermore, I was dependent on the person who gave me a ride to and from work. So, if he had to go home, I had to leave also. Sometimes I had to leave work after only being there for three hours.

Sadly, in February I broke my wrist. That was a bad day for me. I lost my job. However, that didn't stop me. I continued with the rest of my life. I continued to attend school. The school was far from my home. I walked about four miles because I didn't have money for the bus. It was winter, so the walk was very cold. At school, I improved my basic English. Then, I got a permit to drive. However, I could not practice driving because of my broken wrist.

In June, my doctor told me I could go back to work. I called my temporary agency, and they found a job for me. I also started learning to drive.

Then, I got my license.

In 2015, my whole shift got laid off. Luckily, I found a better job easily because I had experience, could speak English, and had a car.

In 2018, I got married. In 2019, I got the best gift from Allah. I had my beautiful baby, Ahmed. I am living the best life. I am very happy. I love living in the USA.

Fadumo Abdi is 32 and originally from Somalia.

My Scary Day

SAFIYA MAHAMED, MINNEAPOLIS, MN

I heard knocking on the door. "Who are you?" I said. No answer.

I was in my three-bedroom house in Port Elizabeth, South Africa. I lived with my three children and my husband. Sometimes family visited.

"Safiya, it's Asad," a voice said. "Please, could you open the door?" Asad was an employee at our store. I opened the door.

There were five men. Asad and a customer from the store had their hands tied behind their backs. The other men pushed me back and pointed a gun at my head. "Give me money!" the leader said.

"We don't have money," I told them.

"Where is your husband?" the leader asked.

"He is out," I said. I was happy that my children were with him in the backyard.

They pointed at a closed door. "Open this door."

"People are sleeping," I said. "Abda, Abda, open the door," I said to my husband's visiting brother. "Robbers are in the house. Allah will help you."

The men knocked the door down. They punched my brother, and the leader said, "I need money!"

One man looked at the hot water on my stove. "I will put boiling water on you!" he said.

"It's not for me," I told him. "It is for you robbers!"

For fifteen minutes, the men were looking for money in all rooms of the house. Then the leader went to my brother's wife. "Young lady," he said, "you have to talk to your husband."

I said to my brother's wife, "Be quiet. Be like you have no ears."

The leader said, "If you don't find money, I will take your baby." The baby was three months old and was asleep.

"Hey leader," I said, "this mother is young. Also she is deaf. Please leave her alone."

The leader said to me, "You have information about this family. You have to find their money."

"Yes," I said. "I have information and I know they have no money."

He said, "I will take this baby."

"Okay. Go ahead," I said. To the mother, I said, "Ask Allah to give you back your baby." The robber took the baby from the house to our store next door.

After two or three minutes, the leader came back with the baby. He said to me, "Take your baby." They put all of my family, Asad, and the customer in one room. They took all our phones, and they left.

When my neighbors heard what happened, they said, "Safiya, you are a hero!"

Safiya Mahamed is 46 and originally from Somalia.

The Year of 2020

KHADRA ABDI, ST. PAUL, MN

This year has been a very challenging year because of COVID-19, the problems with the police, and the presidential election. Life is all about facing challenges and improving ourselves. These difficulties are what makes us who we are today.

Each day the COVID-19 cases are increasing. The rate of people dying is also increasing. I hear a lot of people testing positive each day, and it scares me that the numbers seem to keep going up and never coming down. I really hope that the vaccination can help.

Ever since the incident with George Floyd, people don't seem to give the police the same respect they used to give them. Every day, we hear about people getting attacked or people getting their cars stolen. This is mostly happening to women and some are Somali women, too. I have some close friends who have been attacked, and some even got their cars stolen. Some of the people who were attacked were lucky enough to get away without getting beaten.

The presidential election was also a big event that happened this year. The results were a bit shocking, but not so surprising. The elections are now over, and the results are out. I really hope our new president can make a difference and for 2021 to be a new start for us. We need someone who is true to their word and can get the job done.

In conclusion, we face many challenges but it's the way that we see them that makes us each different and special. We have many challenges before us, and we need to face them with confidence. These events are big, but there will always be something bigger, so we must prepare. I hope to have a good rest of the year and a fresh start next year.

Khadra Abdi is 36 and originally from Somalia.

A Sad Day

HABSA ALI, WAITE PARK, MN

When I had my first child, I felt healthy. I didn't have a doctor to check on my baby because I was in a refugee camp. When I had my baby, a midwife helped deliver the baby. I was in labor for three days. When he was born, he was dead. I felt sad and sick.

Habsa Ali is 38 and originally from Somalia.

My Better Life

RODA GULED, BROOKLYN PARK, MN

I came to the United States July 17, 2004. I came from Kenya in Africa, then went to London. When I got to the U.S. I didn't know how to speak English, drive, or work. I stayed home one month, then I became pregnant. My first daughter was born in May 2005. It was tough to provide for my daughter because I didn't work. Every day, I stayed home alone with my daughter so my husband could work.

After one year, I got a job, which was being a

personal care assistant in my neighborhood. It was a part time job. I liked it because I knew how to do everything, like clean house, wash clothes, and cook Somalian food. My husband and I were able to get our first apartment. Shortly after, we had our second daughter. I was able to raise four more children from our hard work. With my six children and my husband, we got a bigger house, and I learned more English. The future was turning brighter.

Roda Guled is 34 and originally from Somalia.

Repentance and Forgiveness
KIMBERLY LESETMOE, SOUTH HAVEN, MN

I hate the way I feel inside

counting heartbeats just to remember I'm still alive

lost inside, struggling to claw my way out.

Head in my hands, Satan standing near

Silent screams echoing inside

trapped inside without a way out

light fading away

Marks on the outside

leaving deep scars on the inside

I cried out with NO reply

I can't feel you

Falling to my sinful knees

I pray out to my Heavenly Father,

weeping, I ask to take this burden away.

Scripture fills my head

Seeing you die on the cross

from the scars on your beautiful hands

to the thorns wrapped around your head

looking up at you like a child in awe of her father.

I'm laying it all down at your feet,

Feels as the world stopped for a moment.

Love washes over me

the lightest voice fills my ears.

"Today you are forgiven, my daughter.

I will see you again, my child,

in the Kingdom of Heaven."

Kimberly Lesetmoe is 32 and originally from the U.S.

Meeting Me
JESSICA STREICH, WAVERLY, MN

Starts off feeling like HELL

Sitting in this cell, total ISOLATION

There is no COMMUNICATION

Nor any human INTERACTION

Just Me and my HEAD.

There's no doctor, nor street MEDICATION

No MANIPULATION

No TEMPTATION

REALITY HITS ME—I'M SOBER

Looking at my REFLECTION

I try to recognize myself.

But, this is my first formal INTRODUCTION

I AM ME for the first time.

Jessica Streich is 32 and originally from the U.S.

Social and Racial Justice

Featured Author

Danielle Miller

OAKDALE, MN

Hi, my name is Danielle M. Miller and I was born and raised in Chicago, Illinois. I had four kids and was a single parent raising them alone when I left Chicago to make a better life for me and my kids. A friend told me that Minnesota was a "women and children" state and that my kids and I would be supported. Currently, I am forty-seven years old and now have a total of six kids—two older boys and two older girls, as well as my two youngest that I am now raising with support from the state. I have worked many years as a grocery store cashier and now I am going to school so I can do more.

I have a big family and they reside in many different states. I was a young mother at the age of fourteen years old but maintained to be successful in getting an education. Times were hard but I pulled through. Though Minnesota has been good for my family I am getting ready to leave. I am taking myself and my family—two youngest—to Arizona, to a warm climate where the weather will always be warm in all four seasons. One of my older children already lives there and I am already making plans to continue my education.

Black Lives Matter

Black lives matter.

Black is being human

Being Black is an honor

To be Black is to be wise and strong.

Black is beauty.

Being Black...

Your life matters.

Danielle Miller is 47 and originally from Chicago, IL.

In God Our Trust Is Found

MATTHEW MILLER, ST. CLOUD, MN

This world is so confusing and it causes so much stress

With social media telling us what all we should possess

From our looks, to our bodies, our desires, and our hobbies

They make us feel like outcasts, so that we all become copies

They don't want someone unique, because that you can't control

So they try to find a way to kill the light inside your soul

They'll do anything it takes to keep us in a box

Like saying we have freedom, when all the doors are locked

Because if we were like them then they wouldn't be superior

It's vital to their way of life that we remain inferior

Because once we've reached their heights, we can no longer be controlled

So they keep us at the bottom, where we can only do what's told

We have to rise above them not forgetting what they've made us

If we cannot stand together then they will surely re-enslave us

We're a nation built on freedom and it's all we seem to preach

From the beginning of our nation it's been in every major speech

But, do you actually believe you're in a nation that is free?

We are shrouded by a fog that's impossible to see

It's something you can't hold, It's in our social construction

But if we keep building in this way, it will surely mean destruction

For divided you can conquer but united we remain

And though we're different on the outside, in our hearts we are the same

Yes, we are a single nation but one culture we are not

The Indians are the only natives, in case you had forgot

We all came to this nation so our families could be free

We've been fighting for these rights since we started dumping tea

We've been fighting for these rights since Rosa Parks first took a seat

We've been fight for these rights since George Floyd said "I can't breathe"

We aren't fighting against a race, we're fighting the government

To free ourselves of tyranny too many lives are spent

We live in a time though where no bullets need to fly

To change the way we're living we need only to rely

On the people who surround, us in our own communities

We will stand shoulder to shoulder, until all of us are free

For if one of us is shackled, then to their chains we're bound

We are a single nation and IN GOD OUR TRUST IS FOUND

Matthew Miller is 27 and originally from St. Cloud, MN.

Oromo Protest

FETIYA EBRO, FRIDLEY, MN

My name is Fetiya Ebro. I am from Ethiopia. The Oromo are a big ethinic group in Ethiopia. However, they have fought for their freedom, land, and equality for more than fifty years and still continue to struggle. In April 2015, the Oromo protest began peaceful demonstrations and a non-violent revolution by mostly young Oromo men (Qeer-roo). The revolution focused on boycotts and shut down roads. An anti-government protest was held by political analyst and activist, Jawar Mohammed. He has lived in Minnesota for the last ten years. He invented the first free media, OMN (Oromia Media

Network), in Minnesota in 2015. After 5,000 people died in 2018, big changes came for most people. It was very exciting. Prime Minister Abiy Ahmed took office.

He reforms a lot of laws. For instance, many political prisoners were released from jail, and many opposition parties, activists, singers, and religious leaders went back to their native country. Jawar is one of these people. Since he came back, he has been helping and teaching Oromo people and others. His political analysis and ideas are very clear. He fought and worked for everyone to live equally, equal power share and economy. He is such a pacifist and influenced person.

Suddenly, all those reforms changed to disaster. Including Jawar, a lot of people were put in jail, fled, and were killed. Nowadays, there are a lot of protests in diaspora to show solidarity with their people, family, and friends back home. Finally, I hope all this chaos will be over one day, and my people will live without worry and fear.

Fetiya Ebro is 34 and originally from Ethiopia.

Justice in Ethiopia

REHIMA KETI, ST. PAUL, MN

My name is Rehima. I was born in Oromia, Ethiopia. I am writing about justice and equality in Ethiopia. When I think about my country, I think about fairness and equality of people's rights. Everyone needs to be treated the same way in order to survive.

In Ethiopia, we have more than eighty-four languages and cultures. One group, from Northern Ethiopia, is superior to others, because they control the economy and have the political power. As a result, they impose their interest on the other people in Ethiopia. Not all people of Northern Ethiopia feel this way, but some do, and choose to control others. Because of this, war is still happening in Ethiopia.

I will now tell you about how I came to the USA. My husband was one of those in my family who came to the USA with a student visa. He couldn't move back to Ethiopia because the government was following him and would put him in jail.

Instead of going back to Ethiopia, he stayed in the USA. Two years later, my daughter and I joined him in the USA.

I know that living far away from family and learning to live in a new environment is very hard, but you can learn even though it is challenging.

In short, this is my story. Thank you for reading.

Rehima Keti is 29 and originally from Ethiopia.

Teaching and Learning in the Pandemic

Teaching and Learning in the Pandemic:
Journeys 2021 Special Feature

By Maya Garcia Fisher, *Journeys* Copyeditor Intern

The COVID-19 pandemic has upended so many aspects of our daily lives, education being among the most important. Yet despite the huge hurdles that COVID has presented, Adult Basic Education teachers, learners and volunteers have shown great resilience, creativity, and dedication to their work. In this special *Journeys* chapter, "Teaching and Learning in the Pandemic," we invited anyone affiliated with Minnesota Adult Basic Education—learners, teachers, tutors, support professionals, volunteers, and interns alike—to submit pieces. We are excited to share the stories of challenges, lessons learned, and unexpected surprises experienced this year.

One program that has adapted to COVID-related changes is Open Door Learning Center Northside in Minneapolis, Minnesota. Since the pandemic, one-to-one tutoring has become a popular way for learners and volunteer tutors to connect remotely and work on English, citizenship, GED—or writing pieces for *Journeys*.

Open Door Northside volunteer Pat Strandness wrote her own piece for this special *Journeys* chapter, which you can find on page eighty-eight. Pat also has two learners, Safiya Mahamed and Shamso Omar, whose work is featured in *Journeys* on pages seventy-seven and seventy, respectively.

Pat spoke with *Journeys* Copyeditor Intern Maya Garcia Fisher about how teaching and learning has changed during the pandemic. Pat has been teaching adult ESL since 2000, and a popular activity in her classroom had always been dictation, because it "provides good writing practice for students," Pat notes. However, this is something that has become harder to do digitally—while Pat asks students to write down her dictations and then show them to the camera, it's harder to see and give feedback than in person.

Yet, Pat mentions that there are some advantages to teaching virtually, including accessibility. As she points out, students have busy lives outside of the classroom, often leading to students being unable to attend in-person classes. The increase in one-to-one and small group tutoring has also meant that tutors have more time for each student. When she taught in person, Pat's classrooms would have about twenty students, whereas this past year, she has only been teaching two. Having such a small class gives Pat the ability to really focus on her students and make their learning more individualized. She even mentioned that one of her students prefers virtual over in-person learning!

Over the years, Pat has noticed that many students choose to write about their own experiences for their *Journeys* submissions, and that has never been more true than in this past year. Her students Safiya and Shamso have also recently been studying time periods, which led them to hone in on one specific day for their pieces, "My Scary Day" and "The Most Difficult Day of My Life."

We hope you enjoy these stories of the challenges, lessons learned, and unexpected surprises of teaching and learning during the pandemic. Perhaps you'll find inspiration in the resilience, creativity, and dedication of Adult Basic Education teachers, learners, and volunteers in the face of many challenges and changes.

Featured Author

Faytu Gemeda

ST. PAUL, MN

My name is Faytu Gameda. I was born in Ethiopia, in a small and beautiful town called Hasasa. I went to many schools when I was young, but there was one school, Mujema Talem, that I loved and had a good childhood experience. My childhood didn't last long as I had to get married at a very young age. I was only eighteen years old when I got married. In our culture parents decide who the daughter marries. So, my arranged marriage was in February 2012. Now I'm a mother of three beautiful children and beyond happy to have them in my life.

But unfortunately, my marriage didn't last long. I was in an abusive relationship for almost seven years. By God's grace, I'm finally out of that relationship and living life with my kids. Life has taught me so much at a young age and I'm extremely grateful for that. Now, I'm able to stand on my own two feet and face anything life throws at me. The experience I have had with my marriage was bad, but I work hard every day to be a good role model for my kids and empower them. I will also help them in every step of their lives. The biggest lesson I have learned is don't let anyone break you, and never give up, no matter what.

The Pandemic

The coronavirus is a pandemic that has affected so many lives in both negative and positive ways. Not only has it made so many changes in the world, it has also affected so many individuals. This virus has had an impact on students, healthcare workers, small business owners, all countries, and all economies.

These are some of the struggles people have had to face during the pandemic. One is the school system. Most schools have changed to online classes. Second, people are losing their jobs, struggling financially, and are not able to pay for their expenses.

One of the biggest struggles that I have had to face every day is helping myself and my daughter with school. It is like I am becoming her teacher, since she is only six and not able to complete her activities by herself. She always runs and plays around with her siblings, which is very understandable because she is still a kid. It is very challenging for me when I have to chase her around to help her do her homework. On top of that, I have two other children that I have to take care of. Because of this pandemic, my school has also decided to switch everything to online, and that makes it even harder for me with the life that I have.

On May 3, I lost my job due to COVID-19. I live with my mom and my three kids, who are all minors. My mom is sixty-three, so her immune system is very weak. I worry about her, since older people with underlying health conditions have more difficulties fighting the virus. All the responsibility is on my shoulders, since I'm the only one working and taking care of my family. It has been a really hard, challenging time for me. There are so many bills that I have to pay such as insurance, rent, internet, phone bill, and my children's expenses. I get no help for the finances of my family.

Even though it has been a very stressful and challenging time for me, at the same time there is a good side to this pandemic, which lots of people are not paying attention to. One of the positive sides of this pandemic is spending quality time with family. Due to our busy life, most of us don't get to spend much time with each other. Now that we are in lockdown, we are able to spend time together, doing different activities as a family.

Faytu Gemeda is 27 and originally from Ethiopia.

The Pandemic

THANTHAN BO, ST. PAUL, MN

This has been a very unusual year. COVID-19 is in every country, all over the world. Millions of families have suffered loss. Some have lost a family member. Many people cannot work. Some businesses, schools, movie theaters, beaches, casinos, et cetera, are shut down. Most schools have online classes only. Students are not having as much fun as usual because they stay home all day.

I feel like I am trapped in a jail cell because I can't go anywhere except to work. I can't go on a trip. Fortunately, the government is helping families who have to stay home and cannot work with unemployment. I am so lucky. I have a job at Lyngblomsten Care Center.

Unfortunately, my mother, husband, and I all got COVID-19. My mother was in the hospital for four days. My family was isolated at home for fourteen days. Now, we are all feeling better, but still tired. We are happy there is now a vaccine, so people can be protected from the virus. Hopefully, life will get back to normal.

ThanThan Bo is 44 and originally from Myanmar.

Teaching during the Pandemic

PAT STRANDNESS, MINNEAPOLIS, MN

When time has passed and we all reminisce about the 2020 pandemic year, my clearest and warmest memories will be of the two Somali women who, through Zoom, welcomed me into their homes every Tuesday and Thursday afternoon. I have always been grateful that my intermediate ESL students include Muslims, offering me regular exposure to their kindness, humor, resilience, wisdom, and individuality, making me immune to stereotypes. I have often been touched by their expressions of affection and gratitude.

During the past year, my relationship with my two assigned students became still closer. I glimpsed their homes and their children. We laughed together and, when one lost her father, we grieved together. In our conversations, we shared personal experiences with ease. When I saw how their colorful scarves enhanced their Zoom images, I took to draping a scarf around my own neck some days so we could then exchange compliments. When one broke her glasses and was unable to leave her children to replace them, she was grateful that I delivered a pair of readers to her door.

In short, these women became my friends. Our bond of trust magnified their attention. One once remarked, "My son says, 'Mom, your English is getting better!'" This trust also made possible the best writing they have done. For their *Journeys* submissions, written by dictating to me, their "humble scribe," both offered detailed accounts of harrowing past experiences. These writings, I told them, will someday be treasured by their American-born children and will become part of their family histories. I hope you will read them. Their names are in the index: Safiya Mahamed and Shamso Omar. I am proud of them!

Pat Strandness is originally from the U.S.

Muchas Gracias Open Door Learning Center!

RUTH ZHANAY, PLYMOUTH, MN

I was furloughed from my job last June of 2020, "the year that we will never forget." My brain, after many days, remembered that I was an ESL student at Open Door Learning Center in 2018, and I was welcomed again to brush up my English. It is online through today's famous Zoom, from the comfort of my home, in a safe way with an awesome teacher, Nikki, her assistant, Mohamed, and the CNA teacher, Aggie.

Volunteer Sheila greeted me by my name, and after some days, I realized she was my dear friend that I already knew, I think since 2015. Also, we have the help of other wonderful volunteers, Margaret, Peter, and Miriam.

The classes are so well structured, following a planned schedule. I am also learning about American culture with readings about laws, like Title IX. We have readings and discussions of general interest such as advertising, prescription drugs, renting, pets, teen curfews, when someone should be considered an adult, recycling, and other topics.

In addition, we have access to many websites to keep practicing English. I enjoy my classes with my nice multicultural classmates, who have the same objective: to improve our English. My classmates are great and fun team players, showing their skills especially on Thursdays, which is Bamboozle Day. It's really the "synonyms, antonyms, or different from" vocabulary day. Sometimes the winner is the lucky team; sometimes life is not fair in this game.

Through Sunday Book Club, I had the opportunity to listen to my first audiobook, *Far from the Tree*. It was free of charge.

A million gracias!

Ruth Zhanay is 65 and originally from Ecuador.

The Pandemic Has Changed My Life

ELIZABETH ESTRADA, RICHFIELD, MN

In 2020, my life has changed due to the pandemic. We have lived through difficult times because my husband got COVID-19. It was a very difficult situation. My son cried, asking when he would see his dad again since he had to isolate himself. There were moments of economic crisis and mentally, everything has changed for my children having them locked up at home.

My son has many questions about when COVID-19 will end. It is very stressful for him to be at home and take classes online. He had the idea that Santa Claus would do magic so that the COVID-19 would end and everything would return to normal.

Due to COVID-19, we have stopped sharing with family and friends, but I had a happy Christmas with my husband and children.

Thanks to the technology, I had video calls with my family and knew that they were fine.

The COVID-19 changed my plans completely. My son had swimming, soccer, and karate classes, and everything had to be canceled. My husband had work hours cut back. It has been a stressful year, not only for me and my children. Hearing that every day there are deaths and more infections is scary for me.

I hope that 2021 will be much better and that we do not lack health. Now, my son is very happy because he can return to classes. I am excited to see him so happy that he will see his friends and teachers again. I do not lose hope that everything will be as before, taking my children to parks, enjoying the pool, and enjoying their birthdays with the family, but the most important thing is that my family and I are well and healthy.

Elizabeth Estrada is 33 and originally from Mexico.

Learning and Teaching in a Pandemic

MARION ANGELICA, MINNEAPOLIS, MN

Hayicho is a proud, devout, older Oromo man, learned in the Koran, but born too long ago to have ever gone to school as a child. He is learning to read both Oromo and English for the first time. During face-to-face classes at Northside, he diligently attended classes, but rarely spoke English and made slow progress in his reading.

I began working with him in March 2020 over WhatsApp on our cell phones. He was living with his adult children and their families, and they were the people who went out into the community. Many of the pre-literate materials, which appropriately focus on terms and situations out in the community, did not relate to his current life experience. So, with advice from his daughter, who learned English through Literacy Minnesota, I developed stories that pertain to his life. He reads stories about his family, time, food, and peace. He now recognizes many sight words and has mastered several of our stories. We even have a short chat in English before each lesson.

I have asked Hayicho to teach me Oromo, and he likes to be my teacher. Doing this lets me learn a new language (which is good for my old brain), and it enables me to assess whether he comprehends the English words we are studying. Over the past months, because the family with whom he lived all caught COVID, they moved him to an apartment with a grandson as a roommate. So now, we read stories about the rooms in an apartment and their contents, the seasons, and a visit to the zoo (in the future) with his grandchildren. He loves animals and specifically asked to learn about them.

Lloyd Brown's "magic touch" procured him a computer, and now he spends a large part of each day learning English, on his own, through his computer. He and I meet on Zoom or WhatsApp, twice weekly and, if I could, I would meet with him more often. We have a lot of fun learning together, and I am so proud of his work ethic and the progress he has made, both on his own on the computer and through our tutoring sessions.

Individual tutoring really fosters personal attention for each student, creates an environment in which one can "make mistakes" without embarrassment, and allows a tutor to tailor learning to the individual's needs and preferences. I hope we continue to offer it in addition to returning to meeting together face-to-face when we have finally conquered this pandemic.

Marion Angelica is originally from Minneapolis, MN.

I Love Online Teaching

MARILYN GJERDE, ST. PAUL, MN

I love teaching online. It took time to become comfortable with this new method of teaching. However, now that I have arrived at a satisfactory level of teaching, I prefer it. The students are speaking English, unlike in the classroom where they speak their native language with people from their home country. The students and I are both happy with the way online classes are going.

I have the good fortune to have five excellent volunteers. They make it easy to make small reading groups in break-out rooms. Readworks.org has interesting articles for us to read. It has become our online textbook. Additionally, we are doing Conversation Circles, which students find interesting and fun.

In addition to teaching online, I am doing mother care for my ninety-four year-old mother in Willmar, Minnesota. She broke her left hip in 2018, and in 2019, she fractured the other one. Conse-

quently, she walks with a walker and needs help. Therefore, this pandemic has been a blessing. I have been able to help my mother and teach classes from two hours away from my students.

Marilyn Gjerde is 73 and originally from Willmar, MN.

Don't Put It Off!

JUDY KIM, PLYMOUTH, MN

I've lived in the U.S. for one and a half years. There was no coronavirus in the summer of 2019, when I first came here. I could go anywhere and meet anyone if I wanted. But at the time, I just put it off for later because of my English, and sometimes because of my laziness and fear of a new country. If I were back then, I would have moved around more, traveled more, and met more friends.

So I would say, first of all, we have to keep ourselves healthy, and also, we should do what we can do right now. It could be something you can enjoy at your home, or it could be doing something that interests you, or it could be taking care of something.

Do not put it off for another day! Nobody knows what will happen!

Judy Kim is 41 and originally from South Korea.

The Pandemic of 2020

IGNACIO SANDOVAL, FRIDLEY, MN

COVID-19 started in late 2019, in Wuhan, China. They called it an epidemic in the beginning, but in March 2020, they named it a pandemic because it extended all over the world.

The pandemic affected more than 225 countries. The European continent was affected very fast; Spain, France, and Italy were the most affected early in the pandemic. Many people died.

In the USA, it began in New York, the epicenter of the pandemic. All the country was terrified, and all the hospitals were overfilled and didn't have enough rooms or equipment to control the virus.

A lot of people died, and the illness spread rapidly. Doctors and nurses got sick and couldn't work. The medical demands were crazy. A lot of retired doctors and nurses helped to take care of the sick people; even some medical students also supported them. Even though they felt unsafe, they fought against the pandemic, risking their lives to save others.

They decided to shut down the world to stop the pandemic, but the virus didn't stop. It continued and still gets worse.

Millions of people died all over the world, but we figured out how to live during the pandemic, following health protocols and practicing social distancing.

Living with the pandemic is not easy. It's a big challenge because it's difficult to stay away from our families and friends. We learned about helping each other to survive. We learned to wash our hands, wear a face mask, and stay six feet away from each other. We are now used to hand sanitizer, even with the bad smell and how it burns and hurts my hands.

Finally, the scientists have made two vaccines. It wasn't easy for them, but they worked hard, and it took less than a year.

I hope soon it will return to normal, and we can continue with daily life. I want to go to school, go to the parks, and spend time with friends again. I want to travel far again. I want to be happy and not worry about getting sick or making others sick.

Ignacio Sandoval is 37 and originally from Mexico.

Volunteering before and during the Pandemic

ALYSSA BOLLENSON, ST. PAUL, MN

Volunteering at the Hubbs Center has been quite different since the start of the COVID-19 pandemic. I'm happy to see students online, but I wish I could see them in person again. I feel that the connections we made in class helped us all be more comfortable with each other. There was also more time for a variety of activities in class to help students improve their English skills.

I'm grateful for the online resources we have during this difficult time because without them, I'm not sure when I would see the students or my teacher again. I'm also glad that we are able to connect online but be apart so everyone can stay healthy while continuing to learn. After more people are vaccinated and the virus is more under control, I hope that we can start having in-class sessions again, even if it's only part time.

Alyssa Bollenson is 24 and originally from St. Paul, MN.

Volunteering at the Hubbs Center

STEVE GEHEREN, LAKELAND, FL

I am a volunteer at the Hubbs Center with Marilyn Gjerde's ELL 6 afternoon class. I am retired and living in Central Florida. Marilyn and I have known each other most of our lives, since we both grew up in Willmar, Minnesota.

Marilyn and I were reacquainted at a funeral several years ago, and she fascinated me with her career in Japan and the United Arab Emirates. I was also intrigued with her current position, teaching English to adult immigrants in St. Paul.

At some point last summer, Marilyn suggested I become a volunteer. Although I have a bachelor's degree in English and a BST in Elementary Education, I have to admit that I was concerned about whether I could actually be of value in an online program, especially working from Florida.

I have been volunteering now for about a month and enjoy the daily interaction with a marvelous group of students from all corners of the globe. Unbelievably, to me, I am becoming versed in Vocabulary A-Z, Readworks, Zoom, breakout groups, and even Jamboard, with the aid of our math teacher, Kris. Right now, I am struggling to teach my group to make a colored pie chart that provides the percentage of immigrants to America by areas of geographical orientation.

Finally, it has been a fascinating journey that has probably had more value to me than the students. I am learning again, I have a new purpose in life, and a new group of acquaintances, from all over this world.

Steve Geheren is 76 and originally from Willmar, MN.

Zooming Along

BARBARA BEYSTROM, PLYMOUTH, MN

Never underestimate an adult student's passion for learning! In March, when our school canceled in-person classes and we had one week to prepare for virtual classes, I had never even heard of Zoom. I had no idea what to do, nor what to expect. Fortunately, I had an assistant and two volunteers who were willing to jump right in and help me forge ahead.

We had impressively high attendance on that first Monday and, as a class, we learned to navigate the new world of online learning together. We spent a lot of time practicing and perfecting our use of the new technology, and students helped other students in a myriad of ways to achieve success and encourage participation in the class. It required a lot of patience, but we persevered because we shared a powerful common goal.

Eventually, we established a comfortable routine. Our class grew in size, and the students were bonding with their classmates and learning English! There were some tears and occasional frustrations, but Zoom classes were working well. Some students admitted that they liked the new format even better than traditional face-to-face classes.

During a class in December, I had a remarkable experience. We had been working on a particularly vexing grammar concept, and I asked the students to practice by writing some examples in their notebooks. I put up my virtual whiteboard and asked them to put up their sentences. While they were dutifully showing me their work, I unexpectedly lost my internet connection. I was booted out of my own class!

After a long five minutes of panic, I was able to reconnect to the class but was nervous about what I might find. Would the students still be there? What would they be doing? To my surprise, not only were the students still there, they were actively engaged in the grammar lesson! One of the students had shared her whiteboard with the class, and it was filled with student work, and a lively discussion was in progress. I was welcomed back to the group and learned that they had never doubted that I would return to finish the lesson, which we did. It was at that point that I knew we had become a well-oiled machine, and I'm not sure I've ever been more proud of a group of students. Despite the pandemic, technology challenges, and other hardships over the past year, I consider myself fortunate to be part of such an amazing group of people who are so motivated to learn.

Barbara Beystrom is 57 and originally from Wayzata, MN.

Learning during a Pandemic

HAMEED JARALLA, BLAINE, MN

People have different experiences with learning during a pandemic. For those who enjoy online classes rather than in-person classes, they are more likely to enjoy learning more. Those who enjoy in-person classes have a harder time enjoying online learning. Many experience difficulties with adapting to online classes. For someone who was already at home most of the time before the pandemic hit, it did not make much of a difference, so I kept doing what I was doing before. I have been learning online for a long time, so it has not caused any changes considering my past experiences. Yet it still makes you work more on your time management, as doing things from home can be an unusual experience, and it will take time to get used to.

Hameed Jaralla is 47 and originally from Iraq.

Online Nursing Aide Class

FARTUN OMAR, ST. LOUIS PARK, MN

On April 6, it was my first class online. My program was for a nursing aide certification. The first three weeks were exciting and fun. After one month, I had to take a test, but I failed. That morning, I was so sad and felt bad. I went to work, and all day I was thinking about my test. After I finished my shift and went home, I emailed Principal Julie. I requested a copy of the book because they told the students they have a nursing aide book, but nobody gave it to us. Mrs. Julie replied and told me, "Sorry, there is no book to give students. Just go to the online class and read." I understood and I know Julie is very nice and kind, but the pandemic changed everything.

There were not any libraries open, and I did not have anyone to help me, because I was highly at risk to get COVID-19, as I am a healthcare worker. Anytime I needed to review or read my lessons, I had to use a computer and even attend classes online, which gave me a headache. I felt uncomfortable. I learned a lesson from stressful pandemic days: starting at the hardest point makes easy things seem like difficult things. I was the one who got an excellent score and had good attendance, had good communication, and shared all my opinions.

Finally, I had a test on December 11, 2020. That day I was very happy and felt very confident in myself before I took the test, because I was ready. Students asked me, "Fartun, why do you look so happy?" The stressful pandemic days were ending happily, and I was going to enjoy my new CNA career.

Fartun Omar is 29 and originally from Somalia.

Bye 2020, Horrible Year, and Thanks

NAW PAW HTEE LAH, ST. PAUL, MN

The whole world was cracked in 2020 because of the COVID-19. In January 2019, WHO declared to the public that it started in Wuhan, China. Many families lost their loved ones. We lost lots of health workers, and it is so scary.

In the whole year of 2020, almost two million people died worldwide. During the outbreak of COVID-19, schools were closed. When people were in public, they had to wear masks and face shields to protect themselves from it. And sometimes when cities had many cases, they even had to go into lockdown.

Meanwhile, hotels were turned to hospitals because they were overcrowded with sickness from that disease. Health workers and patients were not in balance, and hundreds of countries couldn't get enough food.

The impact of coronavirus has cracked economies around the world. Workers lost their jobs, and I was one of them. My boys and I couldn't go anywhere. We just stayed at home for almost a year and only went outside if it was an emergency.

But there were holy worlds in the darkness. There were things for which I want to say thanks. Thanks for a chance to spend more time with my family and talk to my family and friends back home. Thanks to COVID, I got time to help the Mon community as much as I need to. I am especially thankful for it teaching me not to want more than I need.

Now, I can say goodbye to horrible 2020 because scientists have found the vaccine to end it. I wrote this story on January 1, 2021 and believe that there will be a beautiful brightness again this year.

Naw Paw Htee Lah is 37 and originally from Myanmar.

I Never Signed Up to Be an Online Teacher

EMILY RICHARDSON, MINNEAPOLIS, MN

I have been teaching adult students of English as a Second Language at the International Institute of Minnesota since 2016. Most of my students are refugees or immigrants. Some of my students have also been spouses of scholars or researchers at the University of Minnesota. I love teaching these students. They come from so many different places around the world. One of my favorite things is for students to share their cultural knowledge with each other and with me.

Like everyone else, I was not prepared for all the changes that came with the pandemic. The last day we were open for classes was March 16, 2020, and I had stayed home that day because my younger daughter had a fever. I really didn't get to say goodbye to my students in person, and there was no way to know when I would be able to see them again. Indeed, some of those students have since returned to their countries, so I never got to see them again at all.

For about two weeks, my coworkers figured out how we could start having classes on Zoom. It has been a very long journey since then, with all the social distancing and remote teaching. During the summer months, I struggled with depression and anxiety. For a long time, I felt like I not only didn't know *how* to teach online, but I didn't know *what* to teach, either. I didn't believe I had anything to say that would be of value to my students.

In September or October, I finally started to feel better, like I could cope with virtual teaching and all the other aspects of pandemic life. One thing that helped me a lot was going back to my workplace. Of course, the students stayed at their homes, and we met every day on Zoom. But even though I was alone in my classroom, it helped me to feel more like a teacher again.

The pandemic isn't over, and we are still teaching at a distance. I have gained enough tech skills and regained enough of my confidence to be comfortable teaching online, for now. I was even able to connect emotionally with one or two students who went through pandemic depression like I had done. But like most everyone else, I can't wait for things to return to something closer to normal again. How amazing it will feel to meet face-to-face with students in my classroom again!

Emily Richardson is 44 and originally from Wauwatosa, WI.

Life in Minnesota

ESTER AYE, ST. PAUL, MN

My name is Ester Aye. My family moved to the USA last year. I am very happy here because health care is working very well. Most importantly, every school is very good with students. I see all the teachers are very interested in the students. In Minnesota, all four seasons are colorful and very beautiful.

Due to the coronavirus, we are unable to travel to natural places. Most children want to go to school, but they cannot go to school. Studying at home and studying at school is not the same because at school they have a lot of friends. More importantly, they have good teachers. I hope we can get rid of this disease everywhere. May everyone be safe from this disease. Goodbye from Ester.

Ester Aye is 33 and originally from Burma.

Thanks to All of You

EDWIN DESINTONIO, MINNEAPOLIS, MN

Classes are great, teachers are awesome and they inspired us/me to continue with my journey. Minnesota is my new home, and I am probably going to stay here the rest of my life.

COVID-19 times have put the whole world under pressure. I am thankful the International Institute of Minnesota is still helping people like me. Classes are helping me to improve my English skills, no doubts about it; but you know what…it also has helped me to deal better with depression, anxiety, and loneliness during these horrible times. Zoom classes make me feel connected again and now that I am waiting for my papers, those classes give me a purpose…a reason to wake up in the morning. Thank you!

Can you imagine that I have no idea what the Institute looks like? I also have no idea who those people are behind Zoom; all the people that make Zoom classes possible. I have no idea who they are, but I do want to say thank you so much for being the heart of the Institute. I also want to say thank you to all members of the board. I wanted to send a gratitude letter, but who should get it?

Our teachers are awesome, thoughtful, and charismatic. Emily L encourages us to speak, write, and improve. She has such an amount of energy, I can compare that energy with the Energizer bunny. Emily R worries about how to make her classes better. Well, tell her that her classes are great. She is so humble, saying, "I don't know much about it." We all know she knows everything.

I am still a bit confused about volunteers. They seem like teachers too. Maybe they are. Anyway, I want to say thank you to all of them: Julie, Carrie, Bill, Dale, Lisa, Marie Ellen, and more.

Finally, keeping in mind that the International Institute of Minnesota is located in the best state of all fifty states, I want to say thank you to the State of Minnesota. It might sound stupid, but Minnesota has given me more than what I have given back. I wonder, if people wanna say thank you to Minnesota, how we can do that…No idea! I pretty much wake up every day thinking about a way to pay back all the support that I have received from the state. For now, I just want to be an exemplary resident, and as soon as we are back to normal, I want to contribute to Minnesota in any possible way.

Thank you to all of you!

Edwin Desintonio is 33 and originally from Ecuador.

Our Changing World

MARK WRIGHT, PLYMOUTH, MN

I didn't realize my wife was changing the world. It took a global pandemic and months of working from home for me to finally understand what she does teaching ESL to adults.

After COVID hit, we both found ourselves camped in different corners of the house, doing our best to do our jobs online. I work for a global company that has been holding virtual meetings for years, so adapting to doing it one hundred percent of the time was not a struggle. My wife, however, has always been teaching in-person to a classroom full of students and needed to chart an entirely new path to teaching.

During our virtual workdays, we were able to see each other a lot more and often took walks when we needed a break. I listened to how her class quickly and cooperatively learned how to be in a virtual class. Many of her students had their own home challenges for their children's classes, sharing computers, and not having enough internet bandwidth to get it all done. Despite all of this, they were passionately committed to attending her class to improve their English skills.

As our walk breaks continued through the school year, I started to learn more about her class: the number of students that were attending, the countries they were from, the new things they were learning, and how much they really, really wanted to stay involved with the class and their fellow students. They had become an online family.

I was soon listening to stories about the fears and hardships that some students were enduring and hearing unbelievable stories of compassion and support that they were all doing for each other. Most of all, I heard how her students were so thankful for all that they were learning, and how

they tried to never miss a class. This was confirmed many times during the year when students would still dial in even when they were eight time zones away in another country, visiting their families.

By the end of the year, I could see that my wife was literally changing the lives of many of her students. What she does as a teacher is far beyond just helping them learn English. Her classroom is a place where adults from all over the world can feel safe to express their fears and talk about their dreams with a group of people that they trust. She's changing the world one student at a time, and for that I will always be amazed.

Mark Wright is 60 and originally from the U.S.

"Follow Your Dream"

ANONYMOUS, MAPLE GROVE, MN

"Follow your dream." An inspirational expression that encourages a person to never be content but to make the leap, to follow a passion. I think I understand the concept...but why is the story title in quotes? A little background first.

I am a staff member at the Crystal Learning Center. Our adult student learners are mostly immigrants from many different countries, cultures, languages, and backgrounds. They gratefully and enthusiastically come to our school with a variety of educational and work skills. Students are placed in one of four levels of ESL classrooms. At all levels, we encourage active group conversation on a variety of subjects.

During conversation groups in December, we asked students to discuss two questions: what was the best year in your life, and do you have a New Year's resolution? In many cases, our students answered, "The best year of my life was when I came to the United States." To encourage additional conversation, I always ask the student to give us more information. Many students answer, "My dream was to come to the United States. I had to follow my dream." Or they say, "My number one goal for 2021 is to learn English so I can achieve my dream." But do I really understand what they mean? And even more important, do I still have a dream?

The student conversations remind me of similar discussions I had with my parents about our own immigration history from as far back as 1624 to the early 1900s. Were things really different for them as they followed their dream? Our students have shared their stories and perhaps, I am able to better understand what challenges and successes my immigrant family had when they followed their dream.

I am in awe of our immigrant students. They are striving for the unimaginable goal of being successful in the United States, just as my ancestors were. They are overcoming barriers that we probably don't fully understand. Most of our students have come with virtually nothing but the desire to fulfill their dream. I am honored that I can share in their dream in some small way and perhaps rekindle the dreams in my own life.

Learning during the Pandemic

HOLALI AMEKOUDJI, MINNEAPOLIS, MN

During the pandemic, I learn English on Zoom. Zoom is the same as being at school, but the only thing that is different is that we cannot see each other in person and work together. I like it as much as being at school. In my opinion, it is easier to stay in my home and learn with my tablet. I don't need to wake up so early, take a shower, and run to school. Other things have changed for me as well as school. At work, I do not see as many people, and we need to stay socially distanced. I do not like that because sometimes, it's difficult to recognize someone in a mask. At my braiding station, I like to talk to people, but sometimes I can't understand them because of the mask. Also, after every client, I must clean everything well. I wipe the chairs and the door handles with Lysol.

Holali Amekoudji is 36 and originally from Togo.

Finding Zoom

VICKI VIALLE LARSON, INDEPENDENCE, MN

Zoom? What's that?

I didn't receive an invite.

Whoops. I'll send the invite now.

No entiendo. I don't understand.

Microphone? We can't hear you.

Video? I see the top of your head.

Sorry, my cat did that.

I can only see the speaker.

Change the view. Upper right. No, not there.

Ich verstehe nicht. I don't understand.

We've missed you. My phone broke.

Is that the doorbell? Please mute.

We can't hear you. Unmute yourself.

Play video again. There's no sound.

Je ne comprends pas. I don't understand.

Sharing my screen. We don't see anything.

Chat? Oh, that went to everybody?

Bad connection. Please repeat.

Bad connection. Please repeat.

Non capisco. I don't understand.

Pants? What pants?

Whose dog is that? Please mute.

Shh...I'm on a Zoom call.

Just a minute, my son needs me.

Ana, your turn. Ana? Where'd Ana go?

Successful Zoom class.

I understand, I understand!

See you in person next week.

Vicki Vialle Larson is 48 and originally from Independence, MN.

Maybe Next Year

MONICA ESPINOZA, ST. PAUL, MN

Today is Friday, December 4, 2020. My daughter and I just woke up at 8:30 a.m., and there is no school for her, and no work for me because we are in quarantine once again. The first one was because my coworker got COVID-19, and now a child in my daughter's classroom got the virus. All of the second grade was sent home for fourteen days.

We are going to get the COVID-19 test again. I'm so very tired of this, and I know my daughter is, too. I hope all people can have a normal life next year.

Monica Espinoza is 40 and originally from Mexico.

The Pandemic Teacher

KAREN ANN LOE, ST. PAUL, MN

The Pandemic teacher

Like Dr. Seuss,

Balancing fish bowls.

My monitor and mouse have declared a truce,

Directing traffic in a cyber-forest of this ways and
    that ways.

Of hybrid trees, grammar studies and

science lessons on honey bees.

This way?

That way?

Blue fish or green?

Streaming in a new stream.

Feeling like Horton too large for the room.

Only one girl hears me in that place we call Zoom!

This way.

That way.

Back and forth.

One week they are there.

The other they are not.

Creating the lesson is like becoming Sam,

Convincing my students to try the green eggs and
    ham.

Some student like it.

Some students do not.

Some students are Suzy, they hear what I say.

Some students are this ways or that ways,

and will not budge

even if offered a big piece of virtual fudge!

Some students are Horton, big as the room.

Learning so much from this platform named Zoom.

Just like the Grinch, they all have a heart.

We teach them and guide them for that is our part.

And when this is all over,

The Pandemic no more,

I will turn OFF that Zoom and

Open my door!

Karen Ann Loe is originally from St. Paul, MN.

The Restrain in My Brain

ADAM TRAVIS, ZUMBROTA, MN

I'm going to step up and make things right and do
    my best,

to be honest I'm not going to lie there's a lot on my
    chest,

I want to make it out, I'm going to put it to the test,

I want to ball and own it all instead of fall just like
    the rest,

my mind is yelling at me like this is a game of chess,

it has me thinking some thoughts with no filter that
    I confess,

my heart beats are screaming at me not to be
    depressed,

I'm thankful that I'm living so I'll keep my life
    suppressed,

I feel like there's something missing,

they tell me but I don't listen,

I'm trying to see division but it's a multiplied decision,

It's like going on a mission that's a suicide incision,

so this is what I've learned from my incarceration in prison,

I'll start my conversation with important information,

beginning my operation with starting my occupation,

presentation is motivation it's giving me inspiration,

I'm showing cooperation improving my communication,

inside my current location this covid investigation has limitation to our rotation,

we have a critical situation while living in isolation,

so I'm using imagination instead of retaliation,

increasing my recreation to succeed my education,

so I'm showing participation until I show resignation,

I'll be keeping my meditation it's a form of medication,

this is my reputation to get to my destination.

Adam Travis is 23 and originally from the U.S.

My COVID-19 Life

RAHMA AHMED, ST. PAUL, MN

I lost my job after COVID-19 started. Then my kids had to stay home from school. The school gave us all the materials needed for the school year. But it was a hard time for me because I have seven kids who all need to use the internet at the same time. Since this was all new to my family and me, it was hard to attend school on the internet.

The thing that was hardest for me was not going to work. I had been at that job for twenty years. It was a good job. I was a supervisor. I really miss it. I was happy to be not working for two weeks. Then, I started missing my job. Although I lost my job, the pandemic gave me a new one. I am a teacher for my kids in our home. The first week was difficult, but after the first week, it became easier.

I will remember COVID-19 forever because I lost my cousin, my best friend. COVID-19 has affected everyone in the world, but we will try to recover and get better.

Rahma Ahmed is 44 and originally from St. Paul, MN.

Sketches and Snapshots

Buck Fever

JOHN HIGGENS

John Higgens is originally from the U.S.

Doin' Time

KARL HENDRICKSON

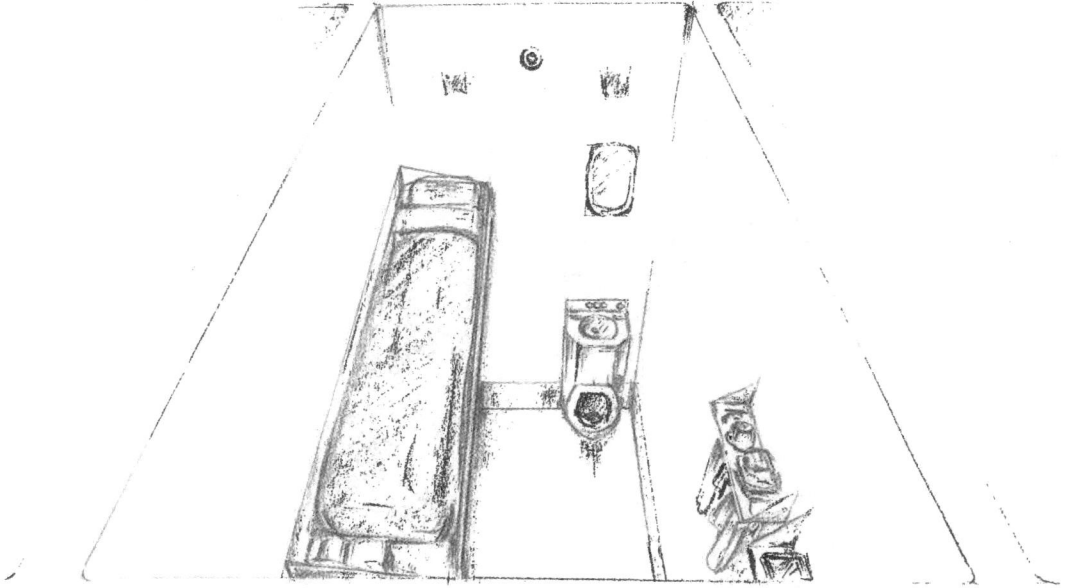

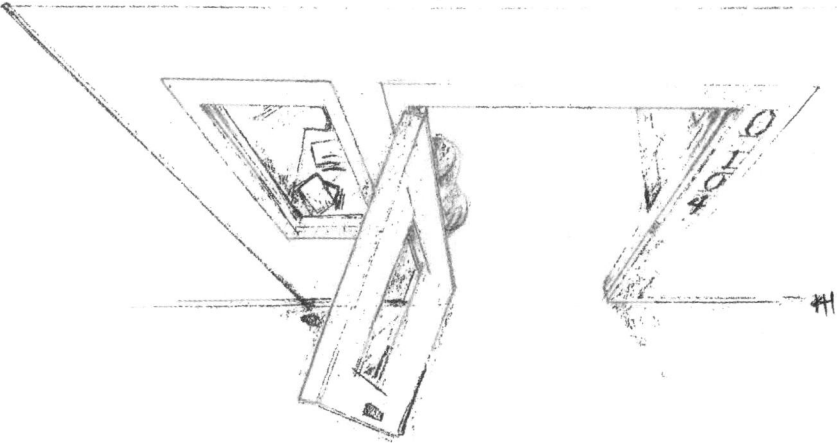

Karl Hendrickson is originally from the U.S.

Flying Bird

ALMAS ATTAR

Almas Attar is 27 and originally from India.

Girl in Wind

CLARE SIERRA

Clare Sierra is 65 and originally from Savage, MN.

On Route 66

TOU BEE XIONG

Tou Bee Xiong is originally from the U.S.

Leader of the Pack

DEVIN VU

Devin Vu is originally from the U.S.

We the People

CHRISTIAN PORTER

Christian Porter is originally from the U.S.

Exploring Culture and History

Featured Author

Hawi Jarso

ST. PAUL, MN

I am standing with my Oromo leaders. They lead us and show us what freedom can look like. My name is Hawi Kasim Jarso. I am the mother of an eight-year-old daughter. I left my country, Oromia, because I got an opportunity to immigrate through the lottery system. I wanted to leave because there is a lot of violence and I never felt safe there.

When my husband and I immigrated here, I was only twenty-one. It was a terrible time for me because I didn't speak English, didn't know how to find a job, didn't have experience, couldn't drive, had little money, and no family and friends here. However, I was persistent. I went to school, learned English, got a job, got a driver's license, made friends, became a citizen, and brought my mother and siblings here.

Now, thanks to God, I am in a better place with my family, friends, and a good job. I am grateful to all of my teachers, who believed in me and helped me a lot, especially Marilyn Gjerde. I continue to worry about the Oromo leaders and my people back home being mistreated. I miss my country, hope for peace, and would love to return, but not until there is peace. I am proud to be an Oromo living in the USA. God bless American people for giving me hope and inspiration. I hope the U.S. government can help my country get peace.

My Dream of Freedom and Peace for Oromia

I'm writing with anxiety, as I tell you how my country was colonized by Menelik. For 150 years, he led by force in Oromia. He caused the genocide of ten million Oromo people. Also, our ethnic identity, culture, and religion were dominated by him. But Oromia was discovered before Ethiopia.

For many centuries, there has been conflict between the Ethiopian government and the Oromian political leadership and Oromo people. The Ethiopian government never allowed fair and free elections. Instead, Oromians were being brutally beaten, raped, murdered, and jailed for many reasons just because they were Oromo, and Menelik wanted Oromo land. Oromo people deserve democracy, freedom of speech, civil rights, and justice. The Oromo people are persistent in their struggle for freedom and their desire for Oromo leaders.

Unfortunately, for these reasons we lost the popular activist and artist, Hachalu Hundessa, who was assassinated after he spoke in public in June last year. He spoke about how Menelik came to Oromia riding a donkey, killing our people, and stealing our horses. After his death, many innocent Oromo youth are still being murdered and many more put in prison. Oromo high profile political leaders, like Jawar Mohammed and others, are in prison today.

The conflict still exists. We still are struggling. We deserve our leaders to be free. Eventually, activist Jawar Mohammed, artist Hachalu Hundessa, and our youth will be treated with civility. There were peace protests by the civil rights movement from December 2014 to 2018 seeking freedom. We lost more than 5,000 people, and we were overcome by the Ethiopian government. Abiy Ahmed was selected to be the leader of Ethiopia. He was previously involved in violence toward Oromo people. Therefore, Oromo people are not happy. We fear things will get worse than before, and he will still be murdering, and we will be suffering from the empire system.

We deserve freedom and justice for Hachalu Hundessa. The Oromo people should have an Oromo leader, and Oromia should be free of Ethiopia.

Hawi Jarso is 36 and originally from Oromia.

New Year in Ethiopia

YENEWORK WOLDEYOHANNES, ST. PAUL, MN

Ethiopian New Year is on September 11. In this month everything is new. Winter is gone, the sky is blue, the rivers are clear, waterfalls sound like music, and the grass and trees are so green.

On New Year's Eve, the girls go to the river to pick special grass and shiny yellow flowers. This flower is amazing and grows only in September. The boys draw flowers on cards.

At night, all neighbors bring sticks to make a fire in the green area. We sing New Year songs and wish each other good luck.

On New Year's morning, the boys go door to door to give their neighbors cards, and neighbors give them money. The girls go around the neighborhood singing and giving the neighbors yellow flowers, and they receive money from their neighbors.

Parents make a big meal for lunch and dinner, and we eat together and celebrate all day.

Yenework Woldeyohannes is 50 and originally from Ethiopia.

My Favorite Holiday

MUNIRA RASHID, BROOKLYN PARK, MN

My favorite holiday is Ramadan. Ramadan is a month of fasting and is when our sins are removed. In this month, we give money to poor people based on the amount of money we have. At the end of Ramadan, we celebrate the day of Eid. We go to pray with the community. We eat breakfast with our family. Then, we give money to any children that we see. Next, we go to the park and celebrate with the community. The men cook the food and serve everybody. First, they serve the children. Then, they serve the older people. Then, they serve everybody else. The children enjoy playing inside the big balloon castle. Everyone enjoys the delicious foods, drinks, and sweets.

Munira Rashid is 60 and originally from Ethiopia.

Christmas in Mexico and the United States

MIRIAM OMANA CONTRERAS, ST. PAUL, MN

In my town Teotlaco, Puebla on December 24, people celebrate the son of God's birth. It is a tradition that someone offers his house for the celebration. Each year, it is in a different house. That family makes and shares food and drinks. They make tamales (with pork or chicken, corn flour, and mole enrolled in leaves of corn) and drink *atole champurrado* (made with water, cinnamon, chocolate, corn flour, and sugar). All food is shared with people who come to the celebration which starts at 7 p.m. and continues until midnight. During this time, the teenagers dance and sing in honor of Jesus. At midnight, people go to church for mass to pray and thank God for everything. This tradition is amazing, because we remember each person with kindness and love.

In the U.S., the majority of people celebrate Christmas on Christmas Eve, December 24. It is common for Americans to get gifts which are put under the tree by friends and family. Santa leaves gifts on Christmas morning, December 25, for children. Families gather together to eat and enjoy Christmas together. There are more people in Christian churches on Christmas than any other time of the year.

Miriam Omana Contreras is 36 and originally from Mexico.

Venezuelan Christmas Food

GLADYS DEL VALLE BRINK, ST. CLOUD, MN

Christmas is a time to share, enjoy, and celebrate. Every Venezuelan would say food is an important part of that enjoyment. I will describe two of the most common things we eat. *Hallaca* is prepared with corn flour to form a dough. It is filled with a delicious stew of beef, pork, bacon, green olives, capers, raisins, and dressed with different seasonings (onion, garlic, chives, chiles, parsley, coriander, oregano, salt, pepper, and paprika oil). All of this is wrapped in a banana leaf and tied with a white thread. Then, it is put in a pot of boiling water for forty minutes. Depending on the region of Venezuela, the *hallaca* can also have slices of green pepper, potatoes, egg, and chicken. The preparation of this food requires the help of several people. Therefore, *hallaca* is usually prepared with family and friends.

A second common food is *pan de jamón* which is prepared with wheat flour. It is a rolled into a bread dough, to which ham, bacon, green olives, and raisins are added. After the bread is rolled, it is coated with egg yolk and baked for thirty minutes at a temperature of 350 degrees Fahrenheit. Other foods we also have for Christmas include pork leg, chicken salad, papaya, black cake or Christmas cake, *panetton*, nougat, and cream punch. These foods contribute much to our happiness at Christmas.

Gladys Del Valle Brink is 51 and originally from Venezuela.

Cambodian New Year
SOKLIM TOU, FARMINGTON, MN

The biggest celebration in Cambodia is New Year. Usually, the New Year is in April, and it lasts for three days. People return to their parents' or grandparents' house. Before the New Year, people clean their houses.

When we arrive at my grandparents' house, we have a lunch together of smoked fish with green tamarind sauce, rice, cucumbers, lettuce, and bamboo soup. After we eat, we relax and enjoy each other's company.

The first day of the Khmer New Year is called Maha Songkran. The people make an altar with candles, flowers, fruit, and lights in front of the house. They believe that the New Year angel will come to take nourishment from the altar, and she will bless the people of the house. On the first day, we wake up and prepare the fruit on the altar for the new angel of the New Year. Sometimes during the day, we watch TV to see the angel of the old year transfer her position to the new angel of the year. Then, we light the candles and incense to welcome the new angel and pray for health, happiness, and wealth.

The second day is called Virak Vanabat. People spend time with their families and enjoy eating together.

The third day, Vearak Loeng Sak, is a day of honoring tradition. In the morning, my grandma always brings food to the temple for the monks and our ancestors. We give the statue of Buddha a bath. When we return to the house, we bathe my grandparents, wishing them a long life and good health and ask them for forgiveness for anything we might have done to offend them.

All three nights we play traditional games and dance. Usually, we play and dance in open space in the middle of the temple and sometimes on the street. We have a lot of different kinds of dancing such as a circle dance, a line dance, and couples dancing. Vendors sell food and drink for the revelers. Some people, like my uncles, stay home and have alcohol and play cards.

Khmer New Year's Day is a wonderful time for Cambodians. It shows our tradition and culture for the next generation. After a whole year of being busy with our jobs and school, it is a nice time for gathering with family and relatives, relaxing, and enjoying the happy moments on New Year's Day.

Soklim Tou is 29 and originally from Cambodia.

What I Like about Minnesota
LUM NAW CHYAU HPA, ST. PAUL, MN

Minnesota is my first state in the U.S. What I like about Minnesota is the weather, and there are a lot of lakes. It has good weather, and it has many places to visit for relaxation and exercise. Many parks have a lake, and I like to walk around Lake Phalen with my family and friends.

But there is one thing I don't like. I am concerned about driving in the snow. When there is snow, I don't like to go outside or do anything. But the children like to play in the snow. They play and slide on the snow, and they build a snowman.

When the snow is gone, Minnesota is the best state in the country.

Lum Naw Chyau Hpa is 24 and originally from Burma.

Chinese Culture

RONGYUN RUAN, COON RAPIDS, MN

Chinese culture has its own unique characteristics. Among its many traditions, we can find special Chinese New Year celebrations, exceptional food, and a conservative concept of marriage.

Chinese New Year happens every spring and marks the end of winter and the beginning of spring. It is celebrated for sixteen days, which starts from Chinese New Year's Eve to the Lantern Festival. To welcome the new year, people decorate their houses with red lanterns, red couplets, paper cutouts, and New Year's paintings. They think these decorations can keep evil away and pray for blessing, longevity, and health. On New Year's Eve, people make a sumptuous dinner for all family members reuniting to enjoy food and times together. After dinner, parents usually give their children lucky money, which is in red envelopes to wish them health, growth, and good studies in the coming year. At midnight, every family lights very bright and colorful fireworks. On the first day of the new year, people wear new clothes and wish "Happy New Year" to everyone they meet.

Chinese cuisine focuses on color, smell, and taste of food. Most chefs pay attention to the ingredients used in seasoning, knifework, and cooking time. For example, Buddha Jumps Over the Wall is a well-known Chinese dish all over the world because of its delicious taste and special manner of cooking. The two or three day cooking process for this superb soup is complicated and contains more than thirty ingredients, such as shark fin, abalone, tendons, chicken, tripe, ham, gizzards, sea cucumber, pigeon eggs, mushrooms, scallops, and bamboo shoots. Different ingredients are cooked for separate times; they are layered in a clay jar with soup and wine, which is placed on the fire to cook for a couple hours.

Chinese people are very serious about their marriage. They are still very traditional and have a low divorce rate. Some of them think they can only marry once in their whole life. To have sex or have a baby before the marriage is not acceptable, especially in rural areas. This may still be discussed behind the scenes. Chinese couples usually marry people who have similar social status and economic standing. They marry not only for love, but also for their families. Marriage is under the control of family elders and is considered an important part of a family's success. Chinese people remain faithful to their marriage.

China has different traditional cultures which have their own way to celebrate the New Year, enjoy unique food, and live a conservative marriage life.

Rongyun Ruan is 37 and originally from China.

What I Like about Minnesota

MUMINA KOCHI, ST. PAUL, MN

My name is Mumina. I have lived in Minnesota for two years. I like Minnesota because Minnesota has a lot of lakes and beautiful parks and also a lot of places for shopping. It has a lot of different cultures, and people are also friendly. There are also a lot of local restaurants from around different countries. In Minnesota, there is great education if you want to learn, too.

Mumina Kochi is 48 and originally from Ethiopia.

Arranged Marriages

ANONYMOUS, MINNEAPOLIS, MN

An arranged marriage has positive and negative consequences. My point of view is that arranged marriage has more negative consequences. First, an arranged marriage is against someone's choice. It is a decision made by your parents. Second, an arranged marriage is sometimes done for the wrong reasons. Third, young people find it hard to believe in.

An arranged marriage is against personal freedom. An arranged marriage is not your own choice. It's your parents' choice. It may cause you depression and dissatisfaction. It may cause conflicts with your family, and sometimes it could lead to hatred. It is not smart to marry someone you don't really know. Before the marriage is arranged, at least introduce them to each other. Spending time with the other person and getting to know each other can help you to see if they're compatible. An arranged marriage takes away your child's decision making, but parents should at least give their advice.

An arranged marriage is sometimes done for the wrong reason. Some parents want their children to marry into a wealthy family, so that they can come out of poverty themselves. Some cultures arrange for young teenagers, especially girls, to be married in order to prevent shame because pregnancy outside marriage is very shameful for that culture. Some cultures are very tribal cultures. They only want to marry within their own tribe. This is not necessary and promotes selfishness. Some people marry to keep the bloodline pure.

Arranged marriages are traditional practices. It is hard to convince the younger generation to embrace such traditions. Young people are more exposed to different cultures and ways of thinking. They're not afraid to challenge traditions. They want to make their own choices. This generation will create their own culture, one that is blended with the many other cultures of origin, which will result in an increasingly diverse culture in America. I want to be someone who embraces that diversity and change for the future.

Finally, an arranged marriage is your parents' choice. It is against your personal freedom. When people marry for the wrong reason, it may cause family conflicts and drama. An arranged marriage is a tradition young people don't want to follow. Today, many countries still practice it. The countries that arranged marriage is common in are India, Pakistan, Japan, China, Israel, and some parts of Africa. I think some old traditions like arranged marriage should be abolished.

Culture and History

CHAITANYA GUNDU, MAPLE GROVE, MN

India is a country that is divided into various cultures and languages but united by various types of festivals. Being a part of the festivals in India brings you closer to understanding the rich tradition that they have been following for generations. I am going to explain to you today about one grand festival Diwali (Festival of Lights). Diwali literally means a "row of lights." It is the story of King Rama's return to Ayodhya after he defeated Ravana by lighting rows of clay lamps. Southern India celebrates it as the day that Lord Krishna defeated the Narakasura. Diwali is a five day festival celebrated with music, lights, fireworks, and traditional sweets. Many people prepare for festivals by cleaning and decorating their home and wearing new clothes to take part in the family puja, in which prayers of devotion are offered to goddess Lakshmi to make a fresh start and new beginning. India celebrates thirty-six festivals in the whole year.

Chaitanya Gundu is 32 and originally from India.

The U.S.: Then and Now

CHRISTELLE BAISSAT, PLYMOUTH, MN

Pennsylvania Station, Manhattan, December 1999: I remember the high-energy crowd, the breathtaking skyscrapers. Everything was exactly like in the movies. As a twenty-five-year-old, I spent one year living in Plainsboro, New Jersey with my fiancé, then I went back to France, convinced that in the United States, everything was possible for anyone. That's why, twenty years later, we came over and settled in Plymouth, Minnesota for at least three years with our family. We thought it would be a fantastic adventure. However, here I am, one year later, asking myself, "Is the atmosphere quite different from the one during my first experience in the U.S.? Does the American Dream still exist? Was the American Dream ever real?"

I concede that some issues existed twenty years ago.

I was shocked that the poorest parts of the big cities stood next to the richest ones. We didn't have such huge differences in France. The different communities lived separated from each other. When I went to the New Jersey state capital, Trenton, I felt stranded being the only white person surrounded by African American people. I had the feeling that people were staring at me. I never had this experience in France, even when I used to work in poorer suburbs.

President Clinton was impeached because he lied to the public about his personal behavior. In France, infidelity was not a topic that could remove a politician from his office. In the eighties, one of our presidents used to host his mistress and his illegitimate child in the Élysée Palace. When this situation was revealed by the press, the public disapproved. However, nobody asked him to resign because of that scandal; what was private remained private.

According to the CDC, in 1998, eighteen percent of the U.S. population was obese. There were a lot more fast-food chains than in my country, and the chips shelf was bigger. Food was everywhere: on the streets, at malls, at sightseeing places, even on the boat to the Ellis Island Museum.

Despite these problems, I had a positive feeling about the American way of life. In September 1999, a category four hurricane named Floyd struck Florida. Immediately after this disaster, I watched the news on TV that showed Floyd victims trying to save what was left of their houses. They didn't complain; they simply said, "We will rebuild our homes!" Coming from a country where people always asked for some help from the government when they experienced hardship, this reaction was incredibly striking. I was impressed by the resilience of the American people.

Christelle Baissat is 47 and originally from France.

My Favorite Holidays

ROMAN TESEMA, ST. PAUL, MN

I love Eid al-Fitr and Eid al-Arafah! They are the best holidays. Here are some reasons why I love Eid.

First, I can celebrate with my family. I have two kids, and they love to dress up in fancy clothes on this holiday. While the kids are getting ready, my husband goes out and buys cake and goat. I wake up early and make lunch!

The second reason is that Eid al-Fitr is all about our Prophet Muhammad. This is when the Prophet got the first revelation of the Quran! We also celebrate and thank Allah (God) for giving us strength

and the will during the many days of fasting during Ramadan.

Lastly, I love it when my family is happy and all together! It's a great time, and everyone is happy, which I love. All of the aunts, uncles, and cousins gather together to celebrate. It's a time I will always hold dear in my heart.

Roman Tesema is 40 and originally from Ethiopia.

Folklorama Festival

BONTU ALI, WAITE PARK, MN

The Winnipeg Folklorama is a very interesting annual festival. It brings together over 400,000 visitors each August. The Folklorama Festival is Manitoba's most popular event and the largest and longest running festival. It's the world's largest multicultural celebration. For two weeks, people wear traditional clothes and celebrate ethnic diversity through games, music, food, and fun. It is an important festival in Winnipeg, Manitoba. The festival takes place at The Winnipeg Convention Center. It happens in August. Folklorama Festival is a fun event.

Bontu Ali is 35 and originally from Ethiopia.

Living in Nature Has Many Advantages

BET SI PAW, ST. PAUL, MN

I was born in a village around the mountains. I would like to share my ideas about nature because I love nature. Nature gives me a major benefit in my life. For example, I get fresh air when I go to the forest, and it gives me shelter for living. When I don't have any vegetables to eat, then I go to the forest and get some vegetables and fruits to eat. When I don't have any meat for my family, we go to the river and catch fish to complete our meal. Sometimes, if I am in a bad mood, then I walk near the river and breathe the air and listen to the birds singing or a different kind of creature whisper in the forest. Creatures in the forest can also grow the plants for humans. For example, when I lived in my country, in the village around mountains, I couldn't plant mango trees, but we could eat mangoes because some creatures in the forest carried mango seeds from other places to my area.

Also, nature gives humans oxygen to breathe. If we look at the trees, they distribute a lot of things to humans. For example, buildings also need the trees and some furniture requires trees. Another important part of nature is water. For example, when I go to the forest, I don't need to carry water because in the forest I can consume the water that comes out of rocks and caves, and it is fresh water for villagers.

So these are some of the ways that nature is important for me and for people and animals all over the world.

Bet Si Paw is 29 and originally from Myanmar.

Fishing in Laos

YAXENG VUE, ST. PAUL, MN

I was born in Dounsamphan village of Laos in June 1988 and grew up there. It is full of memories. Some are sad, happy, and scary. When I was young, I remember my cousin with my friends. We always played together.

I was born near a lake which is the biggest lake in Laos. The lake is Nam Ngum Dam and is the main source of meat. Catching fish is a big part of how we get food to the table. In Laos, we are hunting and fishing and do not need to have a license. You can go fishing anytime you want.

The best and worst memory I remember is when I was twelve. I went to catch fish with my older brother and a cousin. That was my first time catching fish with a casting net. The water is kind of rough and the waves are sort of scary, but I grew up there, and it is just like every day, so I was not scared until I experienced something that changed my life.

One day, I beg my older brother and cousin to teach me how to cast a net from our canoe. I follow them. The net is heavy with some steel chain so it can fall down to the bottom of the lake. My first time casting, I fall outside of the canoe because I do not have the stability in the canoe, and I almost drown. Luckily, my brother got my hand. I could not swim that good, and plus the waves are kind of rough. I remember when I fell, I felt like I could not swim, and I felt like my body is so heavy. I did swallow water because I need to breathe. When my brother pulls me back inside the canoe, I felt shaky, and I was coughing. I told them, "Let's go home," but they told me to sit steady and let them catch some more fishes. When we get home, we are scared to tell my mom because we will get yelled at for it. So, we act like nothing happened, but I did learn that water is not something to play with.

Still, since the lake is part of our food source, I started to learn how to swim to prevent that happening to me again. This memory is scary and makes me a better swimmer because I trained hard to swim after that event.

Yaxeng Vue is 23 and originally from Laos.

My Beautiful Country

FATOUMATA DIAKITE, BROOKLYN CENTER, MN

I'm going to talk about my beautiful West Africa, especially my nice country, Guinea. Guinea is a country of West Africa. There are many amazing things such as mountains, forests, and rivers. The mountains are beautiful and tall.

We have Mount Nimba (1,752m) and Mount Loura, the Lady of Mali (1,500m). They are tall and nice.

My Guinea has beautiful forests and rivers too. The beautiful forests are the High Forest Guinea and the Sacred Forest. They are all green, and the trees are big and tall. Guinea has many nice rivers: River Niger (2,597 miles), River Gambia (9,696 miles), Cavalla River (320 miles), and Mao River (264 miles).

My Guinea is a beautiful and amazing country. It has a lot of potential. That's why we call Guinea the water tower of West Africa. It has mineral resources like diamonds, gold, silver, and iron. It also has tourist places.

Fatoumata Diakite is 22 and originally from Guinea.

All about My Country

KEMERIYA JARA, ST. PAUL, MN

What I really like about my culture is the tea that me and my mom and my sisters make. It smells good, and you put sugar in and a little salt and milk. We don't have enough milk in my country, so we just put a little milk in, like one cup. Milk is very expensive in my country. My country mostly has tea which is made in Kenya. It is a country in Africa, if you are wondering to know.

Sometimes, we make coffee in my country. Some people have it on their farm. They bring and sell it to us. Then, we buy it and put it on the fire and make it black. We don't have a machine, so we just do it by hand.

I have a little something else to tell you. My favorite food is injera and soup. It is delicious. I really like the injera with soup. I really like sauce too.

This year, I am going back to my country! When I visit my country, I am going to visit my grandma and aunt. I used to live with my aunt since I was a baby. My aunt is the nicest, but I know my mother and father are much more loving and caring, and they really care about me. My mom is the nicest I have ever seen.

When I go to Africa, I am going to visit my aunt that used to take care of me and my cousin that I always used to play with and hangout with. Then, I am going to meet some of my old friends.

Kemeriya Jara is 22 and originally from Ethiopia.

Beautiful Beaches

MORAIMA DEL CARMEN CASTRO, ST. PAUL, MN

Amazing Beaches!

I want to tell you about the amazing beaches in Venezuela.

Venezuela is a country in South America, specifically in the north. It has 2,485 miles of Caribbean Sea coastline. The sea is warm and crystalline. The sand has different colors: orange, white, light brown, light gray, and it can even be rose. In addition, at these beaches you can find several species of flora and fauna, corals, et cetera. The beaches are mostly surrounded by coconut trees and palm trees that will make you feel like you are in a paradise.

There are two National Parks, Morrocoy and Mochima, which have beaches. They have many islands which you can only reach in a boat. Some of the beaches you should not miss if you visit Venezuela are: Isla de Coche, Bahia de Cata, Playa el Yaque, and many more. Visit them because they are very fun.

You can go to any island, and in the afternoon when you return, if you get lucky, you can see and swim with the dolphins.

Moraima del Carmen Castro is 52 and originally from Venezuela.

About Minnesota

EH SAY WAH, ST. PAUL, MN

I like many things about Minnesota. One thing I like is my children study English. This is good for them. Another thing I like is when my family is sick, the hospital takes good care of my family. I like that it is easy here to wash clothes. It is easy for me. In my country, when I washed clothes, I washed them by hand. Here I do not wash the clothes by hand. I go to the laundromat and the machine washes the clothes.

I like the summer because sometimes, I go to the park with my family. My children go to the playground. In the summertime, I have a garden. I go to the garden. In the garden, I plant vegetables like cabbage, eggplant, cilantro, cucumbers, tomatoes, chilies, onion, and garlic.

I don't like wintertime because I see a lot of snow, and it is so cold. I stay home. Sometimes, I go to my uncle's home or my sister's home. Sometimes in the winter, I go to the store, but I want to stay home.

I like many things about Minnesota, but I don't know how to say them in the English language.

Eh Say Wah is 37 and originally from Burma.

Eritrean Holiday "Nigdet"

ELSA AMARA, ST. PAUL, MN

I was born in Eritrea, which is located by the Red Sea on the horn of Africa. I want to tell you about our special holiday, Nigdet. It is a holiday in which all family members in all parts of the country get together in one village or county. Nigdet is celebrated once a year in one village. However, the holiday is celebrated every month in different villages. During the holiday, we prepare a lot of cultural food depending on the season. For example, at the time of Easter, we prepare food without meat such as *hilbet, timtino,* and *alcher.* Hilbet is a vegan Eritrean food and is made of sprouted fava beans and sprouted fenugreekk. In addition, we prepare a local fermented drink called *siwa.* All family and friends dress in traditional clothes, and women braid their hair in traditional styles.

Elsa Amara is 40 and originally from Eritrea.

Mexican Traditions

KARIANA REYES, RICHFIELD, MN

Mexico is a country with many traditions in all year. On January 1, it is very common to celebrate the New Year with all family, and everyone has dinner together. A typical dinner is pozole. Also, on January 6 is the sale of many toys in the marketplace at night because on January 7 the children wait for the Reyes Magos. At night the same day, the families get together to break the Rosca de Reyes, which is a typical Kings Day bread. It's very delicious to eat it with hot chocolate.

On February 2 in Mexico is the Candelaria day, also know as the day of the tamales, because all people eat tamales with *champirrado* that day. The *champirrado* is a typical hot drink in Mexico. It's made with cocoa and corn flour. On February 14, it's the day of lovers, more common as the day of love and friendship. On that day, you can see many giant stuffed animals, balloons, roses, candies and chocolates, and many, many hearts everywhere.

March 20 is the date commemorating the day of spring. Therefore, in many preschools, the children dress up as flowers, butterflies, ladybugs, trees, et cetera. In March, Holy Week begins. Since this date, the churches have various activities and sometimes processions. Holy Week ends the first week of April, and many people have the costumes of visiting watering place those dates.

September is "the patriotic month." This month in Mexico, we celebrate the Mexican Revolution and Independence Day, and at all the markets you can see many national ornaments and flags everywhere. Also, on the 15 at night, the president makes "Grito de Independencia." On the 16 the schools do a carry out parade in the center of each municipality.

In October is the Day of the Dead. The last days of this month, the people make *ofrendas* for relatives who have died. These *ofrendas* have fruit (oranges, bananas, mandarins, and apples), mole, bread, rice with milk, *tejocote,* sweet pumpkin, and cempasuchil flowers.

The first days of November also celebrate the Day of the Dead, and on this date the children go to the all houses asking for *calaverita,* similar to candy or trick.

December is my favorite month, because in this month in Mexico we celebrate posadas, break piñatas, and also eat dinner with all my family on the last days of the year.

Kariana Reyes is 25 and originally from Mexico.

My Favorite Food

PAW TA YAUNG, ST. PAUL, MN

Fish paste is made out of fish. First, people put fish in jars, and then they put water over it. They leave the jar and the fish inside together for days or weeks. Later on, they take out the fish. They only take out the fish paste when they want to cook it.

Fish paste is salty. To cook a fish paste, you need to boil the water, and then you put down the fish paste. If you want spicy fish paste, then you will need to add pepper.

Paw Ta Yaung is 21 and originally from Burma.

What I Miss about My Country

KIFAH MOHAMED, ST. PAUL, MN

My name is Kifah. One thing I miss the most about my country is my friends. I miss playing together with my friends. I also miss my dad and step-siblings. I used to have a lot of fun in my country. I still do, but it's not the same. Now it's different because I go to work and school, and it's not the same as in Africa.

The weather was actually nice back home. It was always like summer. There was no snow, but sometimes it was raining. I also miss the place called Dugsi where I learned the Quran. I went together there with my friends and my sisters. I miss everything about my home.

Kifah Mohamed is 24 and originally from Somalia.

Fall

JOEUN LEE, PLYMOUTH, MN

I like fall weather. Fall weather is good for exercise, like walking, riding, and jogging. Also, I like fall colors. Fall has many different colors. Especially, Minnesota's fall is very beautiful.

Korea's fall is various. First, it has lots of fruits, for example persimmon, pear, and chestnut. Second, people go to see the fall colors. It is famous for Naejang Mountain and Changgyeong Palace. Last, there is the Korean holiday, Chuseok. In Chuseok, every family meets each other.

Joeun Lee is 40 and originally from South Korea.

Eid

FAISO JAMA, MINNEAPOLIS, MN

There are many things to do for people to celebrate Eid. First, people are wearing new clothes and new shoes. Also, that day has a set time. It is always at the end of Ramadan. That day, they fix their homes because they visit all their families. People celebrate the festival Eid. Second, people go to the mosque to pray. After that, they go out, and they eat different food. People visit relatives and go togeth-er to tourist attractions. Third, people make gifts that day because they are happy on Eid. They give to their relatives and friends. Also, they give their children some money. Children buy something with that money. They are interested in toys to play with. Finally, some people do the Hajj pilgrimage. The day is very special for many people. Eid day is a day of rejoicing and celebrating.

Faiso Jama is 25 and originally from Somalia.

A Ukranian Wedding Feast

LULIYA LAVRIV, VADNAIS HEIGHTS, MN

If you ever find yourself at a traditional Ukrainian wedding, you will be surprised by the pantophagous of the menu. The tables are just full of dishes! It all starts with cold appetizers, after which they move on to hot appetizers, followed by hot soup—borscht or broth, then the entree, and everything ends with sweets. In the city, food preparation falls on the shoulders of the restaurant's chef. In the villages, this is done by mothers and relatives of the young couple. Very often in the villages the celebration lasts for two days. The first day is at the bride's house, and the second is at the groom's house. At the end of the party, when the guests begin to leave, each of them is presented with a small box of sweets.

Luliya Lavriv is 44 and originally from Ukraine.

Eid – A Muslim Holiday

IFRAH WARSAME, ST. PAUL, MN

I want to tell you about two of our Muslim holidays. One is Eid al-Fitr, and the other is Eid al-Adha. Eid al-Fitr is after Ramadan. We fast for twenty-nine or thirty days. We use the moon to see if we fast for one more day or celebrate Eid. To celebrate, we decorate our house and buy new clothes. Before we pray, we give money to the poor. We get together or call our family. We eat many kinds of food and sweets. We are very happy that day. We have fireworks and an amazing time with our family and friends.

Eid al-Adha is the second Eid in our religion. Eid al-Adha is the Eid where you go to Hajj, which is in Saudi Arabia. We fast for Eid al-Adha, except for one day called Arafah. It is not an obligation like Ramadan is, but it is highly recommended because the Prophet (peace be upon him) did it. If a person is healthy and has money, they are obligated to go once in their life. Women can only go with their husband, son, dad, or brother. In the last few days of Hajj, men must shave their heads, and women trim their hair. Nails must be cut short. Then, a lamb is slaughtered as part of the ritual. If Allah accepts the person's Hajj, all their sins get erased, and they go back home as if they are a newborn baby with no sins and a clean slate.

Ifrah Warsame is 43 and originally from Somalia.

My Traditional Somali Wedding

BAHJA MOHAMUD, WAITE PARK, MN

My wedding was a traditional wedding that happened in the Kakuma refugee camp in 2013. The Somali traditional wedding has two different days. In the first wedding, everyone can come and eat and make *dua* for the new wedding. The second one happens after seven days from the first wedding that only women can come to. The groom can't come because the women are dancing and bringing gifts. After the second wedding, the bride will be taken to her new house to start her new family.

Bahja Mohamud is 27 and originally from Somalia.

Al-Shahaniya Camel Racing Festival

ELMI BARE, WAITE PARK, MN

The Al-Shahaniya Camel Racing Festival is a very popular festival in Qatar. It happens from November to February every year. The camels are clothed in colorful silk. An activity that happens during these months is camel racing. It happens five miles from downtown Doha. People stay there for about two months. During the months of the festival, camel racing is a very exciting activity to watch.

People watch the race and eat delicious foods such as sweets and meat. In conclusion, this festival is a big event in Qatar and about 6,000 camels participate in it every year.

Elmi Bare is 44 and originally from Somalia.

My Favorite Festival

SUMEYA MOHAMED, ST. CLOUD, MN

One of my favorite and most important festivals in my religion is called Eid. This festival lasts three days or more. People get excited and ready before it even comes. They buy their kids a lot of toys that they can play with and new clothes. It takes place all over the world every year. During this festival, people do many activities, but the first and most important thing people do is wake up early in the morning around 5:00 a.m. or 6:00 a.m., wear new clothes, and then go to the prayer. After the prayer, people come back home and cook a lot of different kinds of food. They help little kids to get ready for a fun and long day. Little kids go around the neighborhood and get money and food. They also go places where they can play and take pictures. Some people also go to the zoo with their kids or visit family and friends. On this day, people also help homeless people by giving them food, money, and clothes too. This festival is the best festival for me, and I have a lot of memories that I can't forget.

Sumeya Mohamed is 25 and originally from Somalia.

My Country Nepal

MANOJ YADAV, ST. PAUL, MN

My country is Nepal. It is a small country. Nepal is a beautiful country. It is known for its natural beauty. Nepal is the second richest country in hydropower resources. Its total population is 29 million. My language is Nepali. The national animal is the cow. The national bird is the Himalayan Monal.

Nepal is a good country. Nepalese people are hard workers. They have a lot of peaks in Nepal, like Mount Everest, Annapurna, and Kanchanjunga. They have a lot of forests in Nepal. Nepal is an agricultural country. Its main income is farming. Nepal has a good education system. However, it's very political in Nepal. They have different parties in Nepal, as it's a democracy. Nepal is the largest Hindu majority country in the world. Nepal has a good climate. The three state divisions have different climates. Nepal is a difficult place to survive. Nepal has a lot of corruption. Nepal's unemployment rate is high. Nepal has a lot of people who are foreign workers.

Nepal has three state divisions: Teria, Hill, and Himalayan. Teria is to the south. It has a hot climate. It is a good area for farming. Teria is a plain land. Teria's most famous festivals are Diwali and Chaite. Most people work in farming and industry. Teria does not have a good water resource. In Teria, farmers depend on the natural resources. Most of Nepal's agricultural products are produced in Teria. My favorite place is Teria.

Hill is such a beautiful place. It has a lot of forests. It has a moderate climate. It is a good place for new trees. Transportation is difficult because the area is hilly. Himalayan has a cold climate. It has snow fall. Himalayan people have a difficult life because of the cold and snow.

Nepal is a democratic country. Nepal is a naturally beautiful country. It has a diverse climate and people. Despite this, Nepali people live in peace.

Manoj Yadav is 23 and originally from Nepal.

Irrechaa (Thanksgiving in Oromia)

HANA BORENA, ST. PAUL, MN

Irreecha is a unique Thanksgiving holiday for the Oromo people. The Oromo people celebrate Irreecha to thank God for the blessings they have received.

The Irrecha festival is celebrated every year at the beginning of spring, the new season after the dark and rainy winter season. They celebrate this festival from the middle of September to the end of October to thank their God for the harvest.

They throw grass and flowers into a lake to thank God for the blessing of the past year and to wish prosperity for the coming year. They wear colorful cultural clothes.

Hana Borena is 38 and originally from Oromia.

Diwali before and after COVID-19

RASHMI JHA, RICHFIELD, MN

From Diwali as a child, I have my own wonderful memories. My mom used to cook so many sweets, even a month before Diwali, and we all used to get new clothes, toys, and gifts. Although, this year being a pandemic, we tried to keep the tradition with my kids to giving gifts and celebrating at home just with family.

We used to help our parents with cleaning our house even a month before the day of Diwali.

Just two days before Diwali on the day of Dhanteras, my mom used to get gold or silver coins. Every year, she used to get household things or kitchen items, which is a tradition of the Dhanteras Day, but this year that would have affected many families due to the rise in unemployment rates, but we tried to get something for our kids just to keep the tradition of my childhood.

On the day of Diwali, we used to decorate home by putting garlands at the front door of the house, light up *deeyas* (candles) made with clay, and lighting up the cotton with oil and with lots of lights, candles at home, worshiping Goddess Lakshmi with lots of fruits and sweets in the evening, and festive meals and fireworks at night.

Diwali celebrations are even done here in Minnesota at Hindu Temple and SV Temple with the fireworks at night, but this year they limit the numbers of gatherings due to the pandemic, and we didn't go there.

Even being far from families, we all celebrate this festival wherever we are, with our families or at the temple with community members, and even in offices with team mates to share the joy of happiness and sweets. But this year, this also was not possible, whereas it used to be a wonderful celebration in Indian attire with fun games and special festive foods.

There are many historical and mythological reasons behind this great Indian festival which is celebrated by all Indians all over the world.

Even in the USA, during the time of Diwali, the White House celebrates Diwali by lighting up the candles and lights and decorating with flowers and issuing the stamps of Diwali.

May this new year, 2021, bring up the lights in our life with joy, and we will be able to celebrate Diwali and all other festivals with all our friends and families.

Rashmi Jha is 32 and originally from India.

Chinese New Year

YAN BARTEL, COLUMBIA HEIGHTS, MN

When I lived in China, my favorite holiday was the Chinese New Year. It includes a seven-day long celebration. Some celebrate traditionally, while others choose a more modern way of celebrating. Here are several and most popular ways that I like to celebrate the Chinese New Year.

Before New Year's Eve, I would try to rush back to my parents' home for a traditional reunion dinner with my family. This reunion dinner would be the most important event for me. It was where the whole family would gather together, no matter how far away we lived from each other. My parents would sometimes order various delicious food from restaurants in advance for the reunion dinner. Sometimes, my mother would make and add her own tasty food with festive tableware set around a round table, where our whole family would sit and greet one another.

After the reunion dinner, my family and I liked to watch the New Year's Gala together. This tradition we have done since 1983. There were always many wonderful programs to watch, including singing, dancing, sketches, magic, and more. Their background images were always quite colorful, which gave me a sense of pleasure. The Gala would begin at 8 p.m. and would end at midnight. Usually, the song "Unforgettable Tonight" would bring the New Year's Gala to an end.

On New Year's day, eating dumplings was another traditional part of celebrating the Chinese New Year. The dumpling is a symbol of reunion, harmony, and wealth in Chinese culture. I enjoy eating and making the dumplings. However, they take a long time to make. They include minced meat and vegetables wrapped in a round and elastic dumpling skin and formed in the shape of a Chinese silver ingot. Minced pork, fish, diced shrimp, tofu, and vegetables are the most popular stuffing for the dumplings. Generally, my family members all help to make the dumplings together. This is also a good time for us to talk and enjoy being together.

There are many other activities included in the Chinese New Year that people may choose to celebrate. I like more of the traditional celebrations. The Chinese New Year, also called the Spring Festival, is my favorite holiday and the grandest festival in China. I continue to celebrate the Chinese New Year in the United States, but I miss my family and celebrating in China.

Yan Bartel is 50 and originally from China.

Fiction and Folktales

Featured Author

Lorena Cruz Jiménez

MINNEAPOLIS, MN

Lorena G. Cruz Jiménez was born in Oaxaca, Mexico and she lived for a long time in Morelos, Mexico. She moved to Minnesota with her husband in May 2003. She has two amazing kids and a great husband. She enjoys being a mom every day because she waited almost ten years to have babies, and she is thankful with God. She has a part time job, and her goal is to get a GED diploma.

Mountains Iztaccíhuatl and Popocatépetl: A Love Story

The mountains Popocatépetl and Iztaccíhuatl are localized in Mexico between the states Morelos Puebla and Mexico State.

There are several versions of this legend. This is one that people count.

The story begins with Iztaccíhuatl, which means "white woman" or "sleeping woman," a princess who fell in love with a captain named Popocatépetl.

The princess' father told Popocatépetl that he could only marry her if he returned the head of the enemy boss.

After months of fighting, the father received the news that Popocatépetl had died, but this was false news.

When the princess heard of Popocatépetl's death, she refused to go outside the palace and stopped eating. Then in a few days, she died of sadness.

When Popocatépetl returned, the princess' father was preparing Iztaccíhuatl's funeral. Very sad, Popocatépetl took Iztaccíhuatl's body and went to the mountains where he built an altar, and Popocatépetl stayed with her until he died of pain and sadness.

The story ends when the gods were moved by their tragedy and converted them into mountains.

The people follow up by saying that the Popocatépetl (the smoking mountain) still emits smoke to confirm that he is with her and sleeps with her and throws fire with great courage and pain for the loss of his beloved.

Iztaccíhuatl mountain was called "the white woman" or "sleeping woman" because the mountain looks like a woman lying down. And, it always has been an inactive volcano.

She continues to sleep eternally with her beloved.

Lorena Cruz Jiménez is 44 and originally from Mexico.

The Two Monkeys

ABDIRIZAK ALI, MINNEAPOLIS, MN

Once upon a time, there were two monkeys. They found a piece of meat, and they fought about how to divide it equally. They decided to go to someone to divide it for them. They saw a cat, but the cat was very hungry. They asked her to divide the meat for them. The cat was excited, and she immediately said okay and grabbed a scale. She cut the meat into two pieces, one big and one small. She said that it was unequal, so she cut the big piece and ate it. She continued like this until she finished all of the meat. The moral of the story is how not trusting everything between two people can benefit everyone who has his own interests.

Abdirizak Ali is 22 and originally from Somalia.

Halloween

XOCHITL ITZEL DENIZ MYRILLO, ST. PAUL, MN

On Halloween day, a lot of people are dressed up in scary costumes. Some houses are decorated with a lot of scary ghosts and monsters. Some kids are frightened by these decorations and the sounds of fake ghosts. Little ones will not go to pick up the candy without their parents. They are afraid that a ghost will come after them if they take a piece of candy. If kids are brave, they will even go to these frightening places that have a real person dressed as a scary ghost and try to hurt or kill them. Some of the kids, they scream like crazy, and some act like nothing even happened. Many kids really like Halloween because they can get a lot of candy by the end of the night.

Xochitl Itzel Deniz Myrillo is 25 and originally from Mexico.

Dhegdheer (The Long Ear Ogre)

SAGAL IBRAHIM, HOPKINS, MN

Hargeysa was a beautiful valley in Somalia. Unfortunate events of climate change and land degradation changed the landscape, turning it into a desert wasteland.

Here, Dhegdheer found an opportunity to lure unsuspecting travellers, who were in need of shelter and water. Dhegdheer was a monstrous, cannibal woman endowed with incredible strength, speed, and hearing, thanks to her infamous long ears, where the nickname "Dhegdheer" was derived.

Dhegdheer lived with her daughter, Aisha, who was fortunate enough not to inherit the cannibalistic traits of her wicked mother. Aisha was caring and kind to travellers who sought water and food.

One day, along came a widow and her son. Worried that the oblivious travellers would turn into dinner, Aisha hid them while her cannibal mother was away to get firewood. To disguise the guests' scent, the daughter cooked a lamb. Aisha served the meat to her mother, which she ate to her fill and fell fast asleep.

Her daughter tiptoed outside to free the widow and her son, but as Aisha was turning back, the son hesitantly inquired whether Aisha wanted help in getting rid of her monstrous mother who had claimed many lives.

"Yes!" she replied doubtfully, and the brave young man started describing his plan to Dhegdeer's daughter.

Aisha went back to the hut and took a sleeping potion with her, which was part of the young man's plan. By the time the sun went down, Dhegdheer had eaten the remaining lamb, which had the sleeping potion in it. She was quickly drawn into a deep sleep when her daughter began to tightly secure Dhegdheer's arms with a rope.

They prepared some hot oil and a funnel, with which to pour into Dhegdheer's ear, and the brave young man approached the hut to commence with the plan while the widow and Aisha hid in a nearby bush.

A deafening sound came out from the hut. A fearful, trembling Aisha hurried out of hiding when suddenly the shrieking sound faded and a figure stepped out of the hut. It was the young brave man.

Aisha walked towards the hut and inside lay the lifeless body of Dhegdheer. Instantaneously, the heavens showered the valley with rain as if to declare a new era. The widow, Aisha, and the brave young man rejoiced with a song.

"Dhegdheer is dead with her evil ways. The

land is peaceful once again."

The valley of Hargeysa returned to its previous glory and became a booming, bustling town. Dhegdeer's daughter married the young man, and together, they lived happily ever after.

Sagal Ibrahim is 33 and originally from Somalia and Kenya.

Wishes and Wonderings

Featured Author

Luisana Mendez

ST. PAUL, MN

Luisana is originally from Venezuela and came to Minnesota three years ago. She is a Civil Engineer with more than ten years of construction experience in both the public and private sectors. Luisana has worked with multidisciplinary teams in the administration, execution, and inspection of public works. Additionally, Luisana has a master's degree in Urban Planning, with research focused on urban facilities and network service infrastructures. She has coordinated important projects of municipal regulations, updating of spatial planning plans, local urban development plans, as well as different special plans for urban intervention. Luisana has experience working directly with the community and in the media (radio and TV) with the dissemination of information. Luisana is innovative and enthusiastic; she is an excellent communicator and an entrepreneur with a great sense of responsibility, commitment, and loyalty. She is deeply committed to the empowerment of women, the emergence of new leaders, and the development of communities, which is why she has been closely linked with nonprofits in Minnesota. Currently, Luisana leads her own consultancy through which she provides digital marketing, outreach, and technology education services. She also volunteers on the boards of directors of the Society of Hispanic Professional Engineers Twin Cities and Mujeres Latinas Unidas MN. Additionally, she is an English student and a Spanish teacher at the International Institute of Minnesota. Luisana considers herself a multifaceted woman; in her spare time, she likes to read and write, and when the weather permits, she loves to hike and ride her motorcycle.

The Wishes of Our Souls

No human being is born wanting to be an immigrant. Social injustices have forced us to leave our countries because of wars, discriminatory mistreatment, or political persecution. Whatever the reason, many of us leave a lifetime behind searching for security, new opportunities, and fulfilled dreams. When I look back, I can see how lucky I have been. Most of my dreams have come true.

I obtained my bachelor's degree as a civil engineer and my master's degree as an urban planner. I had my own consulting company and my own nonprofit. However, there is a gap between dreams fulfilled in your own land and dreams to be fulfilled in another country when you are an immigrant.

In 2012, I visited Minnesota for the first time. I was impressed with the majesty of the city, the lakes, and the museums. At the time, I thought, "One day I would like to live in a city this beautiful and be able to ride my bike around the lake." I believe that the thoughts and desires of the heart have an enormous power of attraction.

Six years later, the political and social crisis worsened in my country, Venezuela. I suffered political persecution because, as a political activist, I spoke out against the government. As a result, I had to leave my country. Despite the sad reason why I left, I was lucky enough to move to this beautiful place, and I have ridden my bike around the lakes.

I am always chasing my dreams. However, my dreams have changed during my stay here. I have started to learn a new language, a new culture and traditions, how to not get lost on the bus, to make new friends, to get a good job, to be independent and, why not, to fall in love and have a family. Also, I've tried not to freeze to death. With each step, I feel safe and I feel like I belong in this place.

I would like to be able to close the gap between the dreams I had in Venezuela and the dreams I have here. One day, I can give my contributions for the development of cities in Latin America and especially my country.

I do not know how far or close I am to fulfilling my dream. All dreams take their own time. Having discipline, perseverance, and persistence is key to building one's dreams. There are no big dreams or small dreams, pretty dreams or ugly dreams. Dreams are simply the wishes of our souls that give meaning to life.

Luisana Mendez is 33 and originally from Venezuela.

The Day Trump Left Office

LEONARD MILES, MINNEAPOLIS, MN

The day that Trump left office, it was a feeling of better days to come. People had realized that we took a lot for granted. We didn't just want better for ourselves or to go back to the way it was before Trump, because the problem didn't start with him. We wanted better for our kids and their futures, better for our community and peers, better policing, better healthcare and schooling, and prison reform. More people are paying attention now and want better for themselves.

The day Trump left office, it was a feeling of better days to come.

Leonard Miles is 30 and originally from Minneapolis, MN.

Be Kind at All Times

TUFAH MUHUMED, MINNEAPOLIS, MN

Value yourself, if you want to know

the value of compassion

See your heart, how it feels

the suffering of others

The answer belongs to you

when you find your self worth

Time is of the essence, the past

will never return

Spend your time doing important

and worthwhile things

Tufah Muhumed is 27 and originally from Minneapolis, MN.

Education Is the Key of Life

ABDIRAHMAN DIRIYE, MINNEAPOLIS, MN

My name is Abdirahman. I would like to share my journey with other students and whoever reads about my educational history. I dropped out of my basic education when I was in the eighth grade because one of my teachers used to punish me without reason. After that, I got angry with him, and I decided to quit that school, and I never went back.

When I became an adult, I thought of getting the best education, even though at that time it was difficult because of the civil war in my country when I fled from where I grew up. I got another chance when I came to the United States. I went to an adult school when I arrived in San Diego, California. Unfortunately, I didn't attend that school for a long time because I moved from California to Tennessee.

When I arrived in Tennessee, I got a job. After a while, I went to school and started learning skills. When I finished learning those skills, I became a truck driver. After driving a truck for eleven years, I went back to school in Minneapolis, and I started at Open Door Learning Center from 2017 until now. When I get a GED, I will attend the university. I hope to achieve a doctorate.

Abdirahman Diriye is 48 and originally from Somalia.

Five Goals that I Would Like to Achieve

CORY ZERNA, COLUMBIA HEIGHTS, MN

I have five goals that I would like to achieve in my life.

My first goal, I already accomplished, which was getting my nursing degree in my country, Ecuador. To get my degree was difficult because I had to travel four hours daily to attend school for five years. After that five years, I had to do an internship for one year in another city far away from home, in a small town called El Empalme, and then I got my license.

My second goal I just achieved, and it was getting married in the USA. Before that, my husband and I were engaged for one year. It was a great time, when we know more about each other and spend time together. We got married in October 2020.

My third goal is to get my nursing license here in the U.S. I love my career, and I want to still do what I love, which is taking care of people. I don't see myself doing any other job.

My fourth goal is to buy a house with my husband. This goal is a dream for us. We want to buy a house in Florida because we like the hot weather. And my last goal is to have a baby. My husband and I already chose the name. If it is a girl, her name will be Charlize, and if it is a boy, his name will be Mauro.

I hope to complete all my goals in the next two or three years.

Cory Zerna is 27 and originally from Ecuador.

My Goals and Dreams
ANONYMOUS, COLUMBIA HEIGHTS, MN

I have been in the U.S. for more than five years. Now that I live in the U.S., my goals and dreams are to work towards a good job and future in the United States. I plan to work hard to improve my English. I hope to use my skills as an EKG technician and then someday get a nice house and travel.

In my five years in the U.S., I did not continuously learn English because sometimes I needed to work, so I missed the class. Language is very important for whatever you do. I am very envious of the people who can speak English fluently. When I would be talking with someone, I lacked confidence and worried that they didn't understand what I said. I think it was causing trouble in some situations.

My first job was a server at Old Country Buffet in the U.S. I could only say a few words in English. I remember one time, a customer put his dentures in a napkin. Then he left his seat to go get food. While I thought it was garbage, I put it in the trash can. The customer hurried to ask me, but I did not understand what he said. He was very angry. Finally my manager helped me and found the denture and returned it to him. I wanted to apologize to him but I could only say "sorry."

After studying for three months now, I feel that my English has improved. I like to communicate with people. If I watch movies, I can understand most of them. My goal is to have no obstacles when I am talking with the people in English.

I have experience as an EKG technician in China. In 2016, I successfully met the requirements set forth by the NHA as a Certified EKG Technician in the U.S. I hope I can find this job as I wish to.

If I can find it, my professional job, I think that someday I can get a little bigger house. I hope my family will be able to come to the U.S. to visit me, and I don't want them to sleep on the floor in the living room. I hope my one dream can come true within five years.

My other dream is to travel to different countries with my husband. I like to learn about different cultures, taste different foods, and enjoy different landscapes. But these are based on my language level and whether I can find a good job.

My Journey around the World
SVETLANA KARTAK, ST. PAUL, MN

I was born in the far eastern part of Russia, on the shore of the Pacific Ocean. Starting my life on the edge of the Western Hemisphere, I always felt like a part of me remained somewhere near America.

I was only one year old when my family went to the central part of Russia, near the famous Volga river. Then we moved close to the city of Leningrad (former and present St. Petersburg). I started reading books, and through them, traveled around the globe and throughout time and history. At only ten, I was drifting down the Mississippi, searching for diamonds in Pretoria, South Africa, surviving Polar expeditions, and walking on Mars!

In 1980, we moved to Leningrad. I then got married, had two children, divorced, and started my own career. No matter how poor we were, I managed to save some money to go on trips, even if it was just the nearest suburb. I was lucky enough to visit some European countries and the Asian and southern parts of Russia.

One day, I met an American man through my job. We corresponded for two years before he proposed to me and brought me to the Unites States. I had never planned on leaving my country but went off for new adventures and opportunities. I remember landing in New York and seeing the Statue of Liberty through the rain and darkness. I cried, probably like all new immigrants do.

I had to start my life over again one more time. My second marriage did not last long either. I did my best to settle down but still had a list of places that I dreamt of seeing. I started with getting a library card and reading kids' stories, as I needed to master English. In sixteen years, I visited twenty-two American states and drove through Canada.

Three years ago, my husband and I (yes, I found a true love after all) took a trip to Los Angeles. I wanted to see the Pacific Ocean, from where I would look west and imagine my birthplace. And I did.

There I was, standing on the very edge of the American continent, imagining that little girl who was born in poverty, now being able to observe my whole life from a geographical point of view. I had worked my way up to where I was happily inhaling the air of the Pacific.

P.S. My two daughters are now adults with college degrees and have their own families. They and their kids love reading and traveling.

Svetlana Kartak is 55 and originally from Russia.

My Journey
KAH HEH, FULDA, MN

My name is Kah Roh Heh. I was born in Thailand in 1985. I have one brother and two sisters who are all younger than I am. One sister lives in Thailand and my brother and other sister live in Minnesota. My mother also lives in Minnesota.

I came by myself to America in 2008. My mother, sister, and brother came one year before I did. I lived in St. Paul for two months before I moved to Worthington where I had friends. My friend helped me find a job, and we lived together. My job is very hard work. Now, I am learning enough English in an ESL class in Fulda to look for a better job. I hope for a better future. I hope to get a Commercial Driver's Lisence so I can drive a truck.

I have a wife, one son, and two daughters.

My wife and my children like Fulda because it is a small, safe, and quiet place to live. When I lived in Thailand, I couldn't have a car because I didn't have an opportunity. I have the freedom in America to buy anything I can pay for. I earn enough money to live in a house and buy everything my family needs. My wife likes our family to go to church each week, and we have many friends there. Everyone speaks Karen.

I am happy that I live in America. My children will have a good education and a better life. We thank you, America!

Kah Heh is 35 and originally from Thailand.

By the Grace of God
JARTU KENNEDY, NEW HOPE, MN

My coming to America was by the grace of God. America is where people come to make a life better for themselves. America is full of rules and regulations, which I had to understand. When I came to America, I was able to meet with good friends and family members. I came to America to improve my life and to help my friends and relatives. The first thing I did was to meet my new family at the Crystal Learning Center. By the almighty God, I am working to help my friends and family. Now I can move on my own and pay my rent and bills. Some good friends gave me a piece of advice on how to go with the rules and regulations, so I won't end up with problems. Behind every success, sometimes come difficulties. They can be solved if you have Jesus in your life. Nothing has to change if all you do is go by the rules and regulations in this country.

Jartu Kennedy is 49 and originally from Liberia.

My Education in the U.S.
LEYLA IMAN, ST. PAUL, MN

I arrived in the United States in 2004. I lived in St. Louis Park. I went to school from 9 a.m. to 2 p.m. I had to take two buses. I didn't always make the connection and had to wait for more than an hour for the second bus.

I moved to St. Paul and started school at the Hubbs Center in 2005. I started working on December 13, 2008. I continued going to classes because the Hubbs Center has classes from 8 a.m. to 8 p.m., so students can work and study. I love the Hubbs Center because I am increasing my skills and education. When I apply for jobs, the interviewer asks me about my education. I say, "I don't have a diploma, but I am studying English at the Hubbs Center and will work on my GED after I finish all English classes." I will decide what to study in college later. I am happy. After arriving here, I had many problems, but now my life is good.

Leyla Iman is 39 and originally from Somalia.

Dreams for My Life

LARMAY PAW, ST. PAUL, MN

When I was young, I had a dream for my life. I wanted to be married, have a nice family full of love and happiness, and be a businesswoman.

My parents died when I was young. So, a man who was a stranger brought me from Myanmar to the refugee camp in Thailand. Two times a year, he visited me. He said, "Tell me what you need." I told him what I needed, and he gave me everything. He fulfilled the duties of a father. He became my second father in my heart.

In the refugee camp, every school had only ten grades. After I finished tenth grade, he brought me to be near him and sent me to the Women's Internship. I stayed there and learned many things. I met my husband while I was living there, and we got married.

We came to the United States on September 20, 2011. We had many difficulties because of the language, no car, and no phone. We did not have any relatives to help us. We knew we had to learn English. So, we went to the Hubbs Center and learned English for six months. During those months, we went to school on foot. My apartment and school were forty minutes apart. In the snow it was very hard for us but we were happy. After six months, we both got jobs.

At that time, my life became very happy because we had money and could get the things we needed. First, we got one hundred dollar phones and after six months of working, we bought an old car. In 2015 and 2018, I had children. After I had them, I left my job to take care of our children, my husband, and our house.

I have a nice family full of love and happiness. My dream came true. Now, I have another dream. I want to become a businesswoman. In January, I will attend an Introduction to Small Business class at the Hubbs Center. One day this dream will also come true, and I will have my own business, such as a bakery.

I am thankful for my second father who supported me with everything I needed. I am thankful for my husband and my kids who give me a nice family. I am thankful for President Obama who welcomed refugee people to the USA. I am thankful to the American people who have given me a good life in this country.

LarMay Paw is 32 and originally from Myanmar.

About a Person's Dream

HANNA VOLKAVA, ANDOVER, MN

Every person should have their own dream. Often, as children, we come up with dreams. Some children dream about cool toys, others want to be like cartoon heroes.

As people grow up, their dreams become more realistic. Adults dream of a promising job, a strong family, or traveling the world. This is how a dream grows into a goal and often comes true. Sometimes children also bring their dreams into adulthood and accomplish them. Unfortunately, dreams may remain dreams because of the fear of failure, or dependence on public opinion, or even what they will do next if their dream comes true.

A dream is a goal, which after reaching, helps people find harmony with themselves. This is a secret desire, which is stored deep in the heart; in it is what they sincerely want to receive. A dream is what they think about before going to bed with their eyes closed. They are afraid to tell someone.

Thanks to dreams, a person becomes more purposeful. It encourages one to work on oneself and helps to overcome difficulties and hardships. Many people are not limited to one lifelong dream. Having realized one dream, there is more confidence and perseverance in oneself. One feels the excitement, then new dreams come and the thirst for their realization.

It is stupid to be afraid of your desires. Don't shut yourself up in public opinion. If you have a dream, do everything to make it come true. No one has the right to restrict you in your actions. A dream that comes true will bring happiness and joy. Naturally, you will encounter those who take your dream for delirium and say that it is doomed to failure. Don't take such words seriously. On the contrary, they should become motivation. Prove to such people that you can do anything. Often, they are discouraged by those who have not achieved what they want.

You need to make every effort to not become someone's negative opinion. Support your relatives and friends in the implementation of your goals, so that they too may become an example for other people. Listen only to yourself and your heart.

Everyone decides for himself to live a dream, feel pride and happiness, embody it, and come up with new desires. Children or adults can and should dream. Dreams do not need to be limited, because they motivate people to do great things.

Hanna Volkava is 36 and originally from Belarus.

Today I Want to Be Your Poet

ANDREA ORTEGA, NEW HOPE, MN

Today, I decided to be your poet. I want to be music
    to your ears.

For one minute, I want to become Pablo Neruda, so
    that my

perfect, sweet, passionate sounds, like a hurricane
    will catch you and make you vibrate. Then
    you want to live trapped in this magic, in this
    adventure.

Beauty is everywhere: in the seas, in the sky, on
    the earth, also in each letter, in each word.
    You are beauty, you are wisdom, you are my
    inspiration.

Birds fly and I want to fly, I want to go far, I want
    to discover what no one has seen before. For
    when that day comes, your poetry will be
    ready.

You will only wish to hear my words, my poetry.
    My poetry will be

Your addiction, you will cry out for a new
    composition, and of course!

I will be ready every day to tell you the most
    beautiful and delicate things that you deserve.

Andrea Ortega is 33 and originally from Ecuador.

Goals, Hopes, and Dreams

ZEINABOU MAIGA, MINNETONKA, MN

To succeed in life, you need to have dreams and goals. However, you must also give yourself the means to make them happen. I have four main goals, and I have the means to make them happen. First, I want to be fluent in English. Secondly, I would like to get a good job in an international organization. Thirdly, I want to open a business in my country, Mali. Finally, I want to support and care for my family.

I received my associate's degree in law in Tunisia. After Tunisia, I went to France to further my studies in law. I attended Nanterre University, and I spent six years in France. I have achieved one of my main goals in France, which was to have my master's degree in business law.

When I went back to my country, I applied to some international organizations, but I did not get a job because I was not fluent enough in English. However, I got a job in a bank for one year as a compliance analyst, and after that, I worked for another company as an assistant in human resources.

For me, learning English is very important. I would like to get a job in an international organization in the department of human resources or compliance. Getting those experiences will help me to acquire some business skills and eventually make it possible for me to open my own business in Mali. In the future, I would like to create a trade school in Mali for teenagers who do not have a chance to go to school. I really like to help people, especially children.

I met my husband in Mali in 2017, while he was vacationing. Although he lived in Minnesota for many years, he is originally from Mali also. We communicated over WhatsApp for a few months. He came back to visit me after one year. I got my visa in August 2019 and I came to Minnesota in September. We married in Minneapolis in October. We have a five-month-old baby girl who brings us happiness with her beautiful smile every day.

I have many hopes for my family. First, I would like to send my parents on the Muslim pilgrimage in Saudi Arabia. Secondly, out of love for my children, I have a responsibility to give them a good education, so that one day they can be a good person in the world. Finally, I hope to return to Mali, buy a house, and be close to my family.

Zeinabou Maiga is 32 and originally from Mali.

I Give My Daughter Advice about Her Future

SULEKA AHMED, ST. PAUL, MN

As you grow independent, I have a lot of advice for you as your mother. You should have a good time with mom and dad but also should soon become independent of them. When you grow up, you must have a job, car, and get married. After graduating high school, first look for a job so you can build up your life. Also, you should make friends—hopefully many. Secondly, you must have a bank account to keep your money and have credit. Thirdly, you must find a way to increase your life and marry your best friend. Then you will value your independence.

Suleka Ahmed is 39 and originally from Somalia.

My Goals for My Life and Family

MY VAN HUA, BROOKLYN CENTER, MN

When my family from Vietnam moved to the United States, I knew that everything would be different. Therefore, I have set goals for my family and my life.

In my family, I have two children. My son is eighteen years old and my daughter is eleven years old. And I have three goals for my family. First, I had to find a school for my children because my son was in twelfth grade at Brooklyn Center Middle and High School, and my daughter was in fifth grade at Brooklyn Elementary. Second, my husband and I had to learn to drive the car, and I never drove the car before, so I was scared of it. Third, my husband and I have plans in three years to buy a house. Since we have been in the United States for fifteen months, we don't have a house. We stay together in my sister's house.

In my goal for study and work, I will go to college and get an accounting certificate. That will help me get a better job, and I can earn more money, so I can achieve my goal to have our house. I will continue with my goal until I can get it. It is very important to set up my goals and achieve what I have started.

My Van Hua is 46 and originally from Vietnam.

The Day Is Wonderful

PAOLA VARGAS, WORTHINGTON, MN

Today is wonderful. Every day is every day. Today we have worries, but if we begin positive and finish positive, we won't. All one must do is activate the sense and avoid the negative. New ideas, positive people, but the negative always wants to enter. But what can we do? We have to stop and analyze our thinking. If we don't stop, this monster will increase worries and fear. The negative monster only goes out if we change our thinking with positive. Every day we can turn our caterpillar into a butterfly.

Paola Vargas is 35 and originally from Ecuador.

Dreams

KAMONPHAT (MAI) KERBEL, MAPLE GROVE, MN

I believe everyone has a dream, including me. I have four of my dreams that I really want to happen. One is that I hope that the virus will be gone before New Year's comes. Two, I dream of having a house in the USA, and this dream will come true when the virus is done. Three, I dream to have more kids before my daughter gets too old. I want her to have friends as siblings. And my last dream is that I will get a better job and get a GED. That is why I keep learning from Osseo Area school. Thank you to Nanny, my teacher, who always helps and teaches me very well.

I hope all my dreams will come true as soon as possible. Thank you.

Kamonphat (Mai) Kerbel is 28 and originally from Thailand.

My Hope

NATALIYA KRUPATKYKH, MAPLE GROVE, MN

Every country has its own traditions and customs. It is important for me and my family to save our Russian and Ukrainian traditions for my kids and grandkids. It helps connect the generations.

When we lived in Ukraine, we didn't often go to restaurants. They were expensive and not available to us. I am used to cooking at home. My family and my friends love to gather in our home for food and conversations.

As in most countries, food plays an important part in our daily lives, as well as in holidays. When I invite my friends to my house, it is my way to show my love to people who are important to me. I try to prepare varied food and entertainment for them. I have always dreamed of having a big table. It was my first purchase in America. The table occupies a central spot in my dining room. Usually, it is set for a meal with a linen cloth, silverware, plates, glasses, and fresh flowers.

I don't allow my kids or grandkids to turn on the TV or their phones during the meeting instead of having a conversation with parents or grandparents. I think it is impolite. They should participate: tell a story or news or share their problems and successes at work or school. Also, we listen to music or sing songs together and discuss books and movies. I would like to keep these traditions that unite our family.

I think good traditions and customs from many countries enrich the American culture and life with world values. I hope that our lives will change for the better soon. Covid-19 will go into the past. We will remember it like a nightmare. We can return to our normal lives. We will meet more often to celebrate holidays. It is my dream. I hope it will be so.

Nataliya Krupatkykh is 61 and originally from Ukraine.

Moving Forward

TRI DUC TRAN, BROOKLYN CENTER, MN

I grew up in a city of the Mekong Delta in Vietnam, called Cần Thơ. My two sisters and I helped my parents run their small business since we had been in high school. We lived there for twenty-five years. Life was so difficult due to high taxes on small businesses and high joblessness rates.

One day, my parents said we all had to move to Sài Gòn, a big city of Vietnam, for a new life. This journey changed my life. I did many different jobs for my life and study, such as a refrigeration technician, hand worker in a workshop, waiter, receptionist, and sales director for a life insurance company. Everything went smoothly with my own family. I got the best job ever, and my wife was in a good position in her multinational company.

That was not the last journey in my life. Last year, 2019, was the very year for my last change hopefully. We left behind everything that we built for over twenty years in Vietnam, moving forward to the USA.

At first, my family had arrived in California. We sought a chance for my two children to go to school. My wife and I knocked, school by school, but unfortunately, we got a problem with our son's study. He could not join high school as we planned due to some different reasons. That was the worst time. "Was it game over?" I sometimes thought.

Time for the new school year was passing. We did not reach the first goal.

Then one more time, we all moved to Minnesota for another chance. No job and no car, my wife and I walked together sometimes by bus to schools and government offices. We had to rush to catch the new school year to get the first goal done in time. Thank God, this time my son got a chance to study at high school; my daughter came to elementary school. They had a chance to study in the USA that I never dreamed of. My wife and I overcame the first race. Life challenges us and we never give up.

Here, we have help from Vietnamese communities, and Minnesota's government offices, and teachers from Metro North Adult Basic Education, and Anoka County's Job Training Center. I am so happy; now my wife has a job, and I have just passed the test for an IT course.

New life starts, moving forward.

Tri Duc Tran is 52 and originally from Vietnam.

The Biggest Failure Is Not Trying at All
TIANNA SALTZMAN, NORTH BRANCH, MN

Everyone thinks the only way to graduate is through high school, and if you don't graduate, your life is over, and you won't amount to anything. No one ever talks about other options. No one ever talks about what else you can do if you don't graduate.

When I was a kid, no one believed I'd graduate. When I was in high school, I had a very hard home life, and I was constantly told that I would never succeed, that I wasn't smart enough. I was afraid of trying because if I did try and fail, they would've all been right. I didn't see a future and didn't think I would get anywhere in life. Throughout high school, I was moved around a lot because of foster care. Due to moving to different schools often, I was failing all classes, but I didn't care because I didn't care about my future and didn't think I would have one.

My junior year, I found out I was pregnant. This fear washed over me because in that moment, I knew I'd actually have to try. I no longer had a

choice on if I wanted to succeed or not. The only choice from then on was to succeed. And because of that, I was terrified because trying meant I might fail, but I still had to try, and I still had to fight.

So, I got a job and started working full-time, but couldn't do high school work and raise a baby by myself all at the same time, so I dropped out of high school my senior year. I was then introduced to the GED program. The GED program gave me hope and gave me an opportunity I thought I'd never have. Without the GED program, I would have never graduated. I would never have gotten the opportunity to go to college and give my daughter the life she deserves.

It wasn't easy juggling a baby, work, and my education, but because of it, my daughter will live a happy, carefree, healthy life. I have now shown her that anything is possible, and it doesn't matter where you come from. I want to give her the life I never had. I want her to know she's loved, and she can do absolutely anything she sets her mind to and to never let other people make her afraid to try.

Tianna Saltzman is 17 and originally from North Branch, MN.

Why I Want to Learn English
SERGIO CHILEL, DELANO, MN

I need to learn English for three reasons. First, I need to get a better job. Second, I need to order food from restaurants. Third, I would like to make friends.

The reason that I want to find a better job is because I want to learn something new because I have been doing the same work for a long time, and I would like to gain some more money.

One more reason is I want to order food from restaurants because sometimes I have no time to cook. I like the food that I make better, but sometimes I have to eat food from restaurants.

The last reason is I'm feeling sad and alone. Well I'm not saying that I can't be by myself, but sometimes I need a friend to talk to about things. Speaking with someone makes me feel comfortable, especially if it is a woman, and that could help me practice English.

There are a lot of reasons why I want to learn English but here are the three most important that could help me while I'm living in the United States.

Sergio Chilel is 45 and originally from Guatemala.

Blessed

LYMAN LOWRY, DETROIT LAKES, MN

Blessed are the eyes that see what sees (Beauty)

My lips shower you with the joy of Angel kisses (Kisses)

Your heart will rejoice like a shooting star; Let
    my eyes overflow with tears of Love & Joy
    (Happiness)

She makes clouds Rise from the ends of the Earth.
    He sends Lightning with Rain & Brings out
    The winds from his storehouses (Gifts)

His Great Love—Your unfailing Love (Heart)

In the High hills & Tops of Mighty Mountains my
    Love for you will Burn forever (Zeal)

When you look up to the sky and see the sun the
    moon & All the Heavenly Array (Light)

AMEN FOR YOUR BEAUTY...

(ANGELS)...

Lyman Lowry is 37 and originally from Detroit Lakes, MN.

My Dream Home

ANIECE RENARD, BURNSVILLE, MN

I would like to live in Canada, especially Montreal, because they speak French and English. Because I speak French very well and now that I learned English, I think if I can speak both languages, life will go easy for me and my family. The second reason is usually my husband travels to Canada. He loves Montreal, and he tells me it is a good place to live.

I would like to have a beautiful house with four bedrooms, five bathrooms, and a large backyard. In the backyard, I want a playground for tennis and volleyball, a large garden to plant some vegetables like potatoes, spinach, and carrots, and a pool because I like swimming. I wish my two year old girl to grow up learning to swim. I also want a farm with different animals like ponies, ducks, chickens, and peacocks. A pony is a good animal. In my country, I learned to ride a horse as a child.

I am really so excited to share my dreams with you because if someone can share dreams with others, you will just start to live your dreams. My eyes shine, and I live when I talk about my dreams. I know by sharing it with you that I can do it.

Aniece Renard is 35 and originally from Haiti.

A Butterfly's Sting

JAMES LEE, ST. PAUL, MN

Eclipsed by none

I foresee the sun

Of sunshine this forecast must bring.

Cause lost and forgotten

Past true love turned rotten

Could this be a Butterfly's sting?

But you said I look like your dream

And what if I see the same things

Does this mean that we both could be sleeping?

No!

Wait!

These tingles are real

Awake pinch me to feel!

Plus there are no alarm clock Rings Beeping.

And yet as I write this I can

Picture the tightness we'd awaken inseparable!

So, if dreams could be distended let me

Hope I've not lessened that our fairytale can still be
    exceptional.

James Lee is 30 and originally from the U.S.

Journeys
ANTHONY RED HORSE, DETROIT LAKES, MN

Every "Journey" in life starts with a thought

Every thought turns into a dream

So dream, think, fulfill your fantasy

Turn what's wrong into right

Bring your every dream into light.

Fight or flight

Always stand on your own two feet

This "Journey" in life is everything.

"Journeys" in this beach of a world

We are merely footprints

Easily washed away.

Love more

Hate less

All and all stay fearless

Do yourself a favor and be like NIKE

"JUST DO IT!"

CHECK YOURSELF TO PREPARE YOURSELF!

So take your "Journey"

Take your step

Climb your ladder with no regrets

People come people go but the memory of your
    soul will grow.

Anthony Red Horse is 35 and originally from
Standing Rock Indian Reservation.

My Walking Stories
ELENA CHEREDOVA, LINDSTROM, MN

"After walking and swimming, I feel that I am getting younger, and most importantly, that with bodily movements I have massaged and refreshed my brain." –Konstantin Tsiolkovsky.

Minneapolis and the surrounding area are home to a myriad of parks, trails, and recreational facilities. I really like this opportunity for Minnesotans to pursue various hobbies. Walking tours in incredibly beautiful places can be done for free. For a little money, you can buy a parking pass and go on your little hiking adventures all day long. Various types of hiking can also be done with skis, special snow shoes, or simply using your feet for hiking. There are also many places for skiing and snowboarding. I also managed to try these sports and learned how to ski.

Still, my favorite is the simple walking tours of the local natural beauty spots. I especially like O'Brien Park. There are incredibly beautiful and picturesque paths leading from the St. Croix River up the mountain, crossing Highway 95 under the bridge. Once I climbed this winding road up the mountain and froze from the beauty that opened to my gaze into the distance. I looked into the blue sky and saw an eagle hovering above me. It was a white and large bird. Minnesota has very beautiful nature and animals. Nature has generously rewarded this land. People here treat their land with care and use the opportunities and resources of this country correctly and fairly.

Elena Cheredova is 54 and originally from Russia.

My Goals and Dreams
MARIAMA ANN, BROOKLYN PARK, MN

My goal and dream is to build a house in my country for my family and take my parents to Mecca and build schools for the children that don't have money to pay for their school fees. I would also like to build a community where elderly or retired people can help themselves with different trades and still get paid for their work. As for myself, I will graduate, open my own business, get married, and have wonderful kids. That's my goal and dreams.

Mariama Ann is 31 and originally from the Gambia.

Letters about Literature

Letters about Literature:
Journeys 2021 Special Feature

By Maya Garcia Fisher, *Journeys* Copyeditor Intern

In collaboration with the Friends of the Saint Paul Public Library (as the Minnesota Center for the Book), Literacy Minnesota is proud to feature Letters about Literature for a second year.

This fall, we invited *Journeys* authors to submit a written piece on this special Letters about Literature theme. The authors in this chapter took the opportunity to select and read a piece of literature, reflect on it, and write a personal letter to the author explaining how it changed their views of the world and/or themselves.

Letters about Literature helps students practice writing personal narratives, develop authentic written voices, and celebrate the power of reading written work. Educators statewide value the program because it gives students perspective on the ways stories can "bring us to a new understanding, touch our heart, and see ourselves and build empathy for others."

This spring, *Journeys* Copyeditor Intern Maya Garcia Fisher sat down with Christine Brunkhorst, teacher at Minneapolis Adult Basic Education program Learning in Style, to hear about her experience helping learners write stories in response to Kao Kalia Yang's *Somewhere in the Unknown World*.

Maya Garcia Fisher: How did you get started in Adult Basic Education?

Christine Brunkhorst: I started teaching because I love writing and literature, and because I think sto-ries are an essential part of being human. The most important lesson I've learned from my students is that everyone has a story to tell, and everyone has their own voice with which to tell it.

MGF: What was it about Kao Kalia Yang's *Somewhere in the Unknown World* that caught your attention?

CB: The book is wonderful. It describes the journeys of fifteen immigrants in their own words—how they left their countries and ended up in the Twin Cities. I knew it would resonate with my students because their lives are similar. As expected, the students loved it. Reading two of the stories from the collection, we discussed vocabulary, sentence structure, and genre, but more importantly, we talked about personal experiences. Having read the stories in the book, the students were moved to share their own. Hearing someone else's story and being inspired to give voice to your own—that's why we read literature.

MGF: How did your learners work on their *Journeys* pieces in the remote classroom environment?

CB: Since class is held remotely, it was a challenge getting printed materials to the students, and so I sent them out electronically. The students who were able to download the stories read them at home, but we also read them aloud in class over two weeks. The tales spurred a lot of personal memories and discussions, and the students crafted letters in which they acknowledged how much they enjoyed the stories and how deeply the stories resonated with them. To write the letters, we used the chat feature on Zoom or the students would read their writing out loud while I transcribed it using the screen sharing feature. This worked well because it engaged the students' listening and reading skills at the same time.

Featured Author

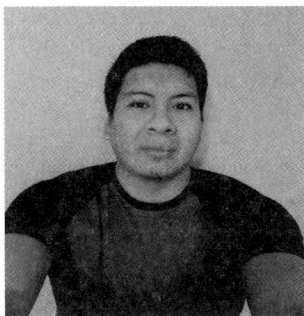

Angel Morocho

MINNEAPOLIS, MN

I am Angel Morocho from the city of Azogues in Ecuador. I was a student there, but I never worked there. I graduated in 2008, and after few months I decided to come to the United States. When I came to the USA, I knew only a few countries. For example, I knew Guatemala and Mexico. When I came to America, I knew Tampa, Florida. I didn't like Florida because there were snakes around. I lived there for one year, and then I came to Minnesota in 2010. I didn't find a job for six months.

In 2017 I started learning English at Learning in Style School because I needed to communicate with my coworkers and other people.

I am grateful for the teachers and volunteers at school, for the time and patience to teach us a new language. So far, I can understand a lot of English, and I can write and read. I just want to say thank you for everything, for being with us on this journey.

Crossing the Rio Grande

January 12, 2021

Dear Kao Kalia Yang,

I enjoyed Fong Lee's story, "Sisters on the Other Side of the River," from your collection, *Somewhere in the Unknown World*.

I felt a connection with Fong Lee when he and his family crossed the river because in my experience, I saw a lot of people with families crossing the Rio Grande. I saw children crying and parents worrying because the water had big waves. Some people died as they were carried away by the current. We couldn't help these people. I didn't know how to swim, so if I tried to help them, I would have drowned, too.

I wondered when I read the story why Fong Lee had to cross the river to immigrate to a new country, but now I understand it was because he needed better opportunities and a better life for his children.

The most vivid scene I remember from the story is when the refugees tried to find food. Some shared or exchanged their food. I remember when we had no food when we crossed.

The story made me feel worried and sad because their experience at the Mekong River made me remember my experience at the Rio Grande. I think a lot of people have crossed the Rio Grande and have stories that are difficult to tell because they are very hard.

Sincerely,

Angel Morocho

Angel Morocho is 33 and originally from Ecuador.

A Letter about *Left Behind*

JAY LI, ST. PAUL, MN

Dear Tim LaHaye and Jerry B. Jenkins,

Thank you for sharing your intriguing fiction and giving me invaluable time.

Currently, I am incarcerated in a jail facility and have been converted to a Christian. In the book, I found some resemblances of my own experience: "After Revelation began, all devout Christians and God-believing people disappeared from the Rapture; only the populace of the non-believers, the religion hypocrites, and the evils were left behind." I was once a guy in the midst of the three identities. An agnostic, who casually went to Sunday School, lived a restless life, and chased relentless craving of material satiety. Eventually, I woke up in the county jail.

One of protagonists, Rayford Steele, finally turned his mind to God and asked for repentance and redemption. Likewise, during the year of incarceration, I have converted to a pious Christian and put my faith and reverence in the Christ. I believe everything happens for a reason. And this predicament is somehow through God, to steer me back from the deviated route, to recognize my sinning deeds and register God's forgiveness, and to provide guidance in embracing God and a fresh start. Or, as simple and succinct as a Christian describes, "To be born again."

While others bound across life, my life has remained a stagnant pool, dull and getting foul. I was supposed to get married, to have a baby, to build up a promised family. But look at where I am now: in a confined cell less than fifty square feet.

The single access to the world outside is through a local daily newspaper, instead of pedestrian phones or ubiquitous internet; the chance to get in touch with family is solely left to a recorded landline. It is one thing to understand jail policy and the price to pay. It is another to truly struggle through such a life over a long period. However, not long before reading your book, my attitude turned 180 degrees. If people can glean hope and love from family, loss, social collapse, and the world on the brink of being pulverized, "a stark post-apocalypse

devastation," why would not I survive the subtle plight?

Again, I sincerely thank you both for choreographing such a wonderful story. It helps me to regain otherwise worn-out courage, to steadfastly grasp God's strength of faithfulness, to overcome the gloomy life suffering. Thank you all that take time to read this letter, and I wish it would contribute some help and comfort through your own struggle. Amen!

Jay Li

Jay Li is 32 and originally from St. Paul, MN.

Dear Kao Kalia Yang

EYA AZIADOUVO, MINNEAPOLIS, MN

January 14, 2021

Dear Kao Kalia Yang,

I have read Awo Ahmed's story, "The Strongest Love Story" in your collection, *Somewhere in the Unknown World*, and was reminded of when I came to the United States on March 16, 2018. The first months were very rough on me. Finally, however, I got used to my new life.

Sincerely,

Eya Aziadouvo

Eya Aziadouvo is 42 and originally from Togo.

Reading Kao Kalia Yang

HANA MOHAMED, MINNEAPOLIS, MN

January 13, 2021

Dear Kao Kalia Yang,

I read Awo Ahmed's story, "The Strongest Love Story," in your book of refugee stories, *Somewhere in the Unknown World*. Awo's mother came to America to escape war. I came to America to avoid marrying an old man in Syria.

When I came to the United States, it was November 29, 2005. When we were living in Syria, my mom promised an old man that I would marry him.

So I left Syria for Detroit, Michigan. I called my friends. We drove to Minneapolis. Then we went to a party. At the party, I met my future husband. My mom was angry about this and said, "Then don't come back to my home." I told her, "Mom, this will be my husband. I need to marry him." She said, "No." Then I called my uncle, and he told me it was okay. Now my home is in Minneapolis.

These days, I am like Awo's mother because I am separated from my husband. He was deported back to Africa in 2017. Like Awo's mother, I am now trying to get my family back together in Minnesota.

Sincerely,

Hana Mohamed

Hana Mohamed is 40 and originally from Somalia.

Letter to Stephen King

ROCHELLE ANDERSON, MINNETONKA, MN

Dear Steve (Stephen King),

How are you? What's new?

In 1975, before I had heard of you, I was in high school and read several works by Hemingway. That summer, somehow I found out about a book called *Carrie*. It was scary, but the book was written in a way I could relate to and seemed contemporary to me. Hemingway is the favorite author of a friend of mine, and she couldn't believe that I like reading your books better than Hemingway's.

About every five years, I travel to see the ocean and Acadia and think about you when I see signs for Bangor. When I am in Maine, I always shop at L.L. Bean and pretend to try to find Castle Rock.

You might not remember, but in 2019, my teacher and I wrote to you to see if you would donate copies of *Different Seasons* for use in our adult education class for people with aphasia and brain injury. You graciously provided twenty books. Thank you. We read *The Body* along with an audio version so we could better understand it.

The Body is one of my favorite stories of yours. After I read it, I thought about the time I was the age of the boys in the story. In 1971, I was twelve

and the youngest in my family. I biked and saw my friends, just like the boys in *The Body*.

The narrator's (is this autobiographical, Steve?) brother died before the actions occurred in *The Body*. I could relate to this because I was twelve during the Vietnam War, and my brother had several acquaintances killed in the war.

The Body takes place in 1960, and one of the memorable sections is the boys crossing the train trestle bridge near Castle Rock. There were train tracks near where I lived, and there was a trestle bridge that went across a creek. My friends worried a train would come as we were crossing, but we often went over the bridge anyway.

At the end of *The Body*, the other three buddies all died young. For me, I had a stroke and didn't die. My three friends and I get together at least once per month. We laugh and cry, as we remember being twelve years old.

Steve, I have read your stories for almost fifty years, and I still love them. Keep on writing! I hope that you will write a story where the main character has aphasia and how they are coping with life in Castle Rock.

Sincerely,

Rochelle

Rochelle Anderson is 61 and originally from St. Louis Park, MN.

Love and Courage

NGA NGUYEN, BLOOMINGTON, MN

Dear Kao Kalia Yang,

Fong Lee's story, "Sisters on the Other Side of the River," from your collection, *Somewhere in the Unknown World*, reminds me of a connection. I connected to Fong Lee when he left his country because of war because I, too, left Vietnam because of war. I learned a lesson. Love and courage are the driving force that helps us to overcome painful trials. I understand my future depends on my ability to learn how to be a good person and have the courage to face a situation.

The story makes me think a lot about facing

challenges and fulfilling promises. When we face challenges, we need to stay calm to solve the problem. Worry and confusion make things worse. Fong Lee faced challenges like jungle, heat, hunger, fear, and death. He acted calmly. The price of peace and freedom is expensive. When Fong Lee crossed the Mekong to find freedom and life for his family, he showed how expensive this price is. Lastly, when I make a promise, I try to fulfill it. The promise can stay with me for a lifetime.

Sincerely,

Nga Nguyen

Nga Nguyen is 68 and originally from Vietnam.

Letter to Kao Kalia Yang

FARTUN ISMAIL, MINNEAPOLIS, MN

January 14, 2021

Dear Kao Kalia Yang,

I have read Awo Ahmed's story, "The Strongest Love Story," from your collection, *Somewhere in the Unknown World*. Awo's story touched me because I, too, am a single mom living in the United States. Like Awo's mother, I don't own property such as a house, and I don't have any skill, but I have to work. I also started a new life in the United States. Awo's mom is a hard worker, so I am glad Awo has such a good mom.

Sincerely,

Fartun Ismail

Fartun Ismail is 39 and originally from Somalia.

Dear Cheryl Casone

MOUA XIONG, LINO LAKES, MN

Your book, *The Comeback,* is one of my favorite books. This book has lots of encouraging advice for me and all women. Its content basically supports women who have been delayed at home as a stay home mother like me and have had a hard time going back to the workplace. It also has a lot of

information that I found to be useful to women in helping them to become motivated, and what women can do to show the world that they are seriously involved in it and have been and will be a part of its development. We as women can also be an example and be a role model for the next generation like most men do. I have found a lot of good advice after reading many pages in the book. I felt that as I went through the pages, the more pages I read, the more encouraged I felt.

Moua Xiong is 24 and originally from Laos.

A Letter to Kao Kalia Yang

SAHRA AHMED, MINNEAPOLIS, MN

January 8, 2021

Dear Kao Kalia Yang,

Awo Ahmed's story, "The Strongest Love Story," in your book, *Somewhere in the Unknown World,* reminds me of a connection. Awo and her brother Hamed remind me of my friend and her child. They came from Somalia to Kenya. While they were waiting to come to America, my friend's child fell from the third floor balcony and cut open his forehead. They had to go to America the next day. They took him to the emergency clinic in Kenya and put stitches in his forehead. The next day, they flew to America.

Sincerely,

Sahra Ahmed

Sahra Ahmed is 38 and originally from Somalia.

Index

A

Abdinasir Osman 55

Abdirahman Diriye 127

Abdirizak Ali 123

Abena Pomaah 31

Abhini Vennikkal 49

Adam Travis 97

Ada Zepeda 56

Akossiwas Agossou 52

Ali Tussa 21

Almamy Sillah 32

Almas Attar 102

Alves Sesebi-Mupepe 45

Alyssa Bollenson 91

Amina Muse 35

Amy Tong-Yang Lee 24

Andrea Ortega 131

Angelica Pinto 13

Angel Morocho 139

Aniece Renard 135

Anonymous 14, 22, 23, 27, 33, 36, 46, 68, 95, 111, 128

Anthony Red Horse 136

Araceli Morales 35

Araceli Raya Hernandez 71

Asha Mohamed Yahya 45

Aura Olivares 63

Ayan D. 67

Ayub Mohamed 30

Aziza Ahmed 71

B

Bahja Mohamud 118

Barbara Beystrom 92

Ber Di 39

Bet Si Paw 113

Bianca Young 14

Blanca Mayorga 49

Bontu Ali 113

Brandon Kertscher 21

Brenda Romero 69

C

Cadna A 57

Caralys Santiago 36

Carmen Roa Mairena 72

Chaitanya Gundu 112

Christelle Baissat 112

Christian Porter 106

Christopher Drift 65

Clare Sierra 103

Colette Tinkpon 24

Cory Zerna 127

Cristiane Reis 20

Cristina Morozumi 22

D

Daisuke Ishizuka 42

Danielle Miller 82

Da Ra Paw 47

Darrell Ravitz 63

Devenoris McCraney 11

Devin Vu 105

Diep Ha 32

E

Edgar De Alba 19

Edwin Desintonio 94

Eh Moo Wah 56

Eh Ray 50

Eh Say Wah 115

Ekaterina Pershina 57

Elena Cheredova 136

Elizabeth Estrada 89

Elmi Bare 118

Elsa Amara 116

Elsa Olivera 34

Emily Richardson 93

Esmeralda Garcia 56

Ester Aye 94

Evan Mahmoud 26

Eya Aziadouvo 140

F

Fadumo Abdi 77

Fadumo Abdullahi 69

Fahima Yasin 35

Faiso Jama 117

Farhiyo Shirelle 16

Fartun Ismail 142

Fartun Mohamed 76

Fartun Omar 92

Fathi Ibrahim 72

Fatouma Abdi 64

Fatoumata Diakite 114

Fatuma Adan 37

Faytu Gemeda 87

Fetiya Ebro 83

Feyisa Bati 66

Filsan Ismail 26

Fosiya Shireh 15

G

Gabriela Celleri 58

Gabriela Lara Tello 26

Gana Ibrihim 44

Gano Hussein 37

Gize Lekulu 15

Gladys Del Valle Brink 109

Gutema Aliko 70

H

Habsa Ali 78

Hae Moo 38

Hae Thoo 35

Hali Abdi 33

Halima Adem 69

Halima Dualeh 68

Halimo Abdalle 18

Hameed Jaralla 92

Hana Borena 119

Hanad Mohamed 71

Hana Mohamed 140

Hanna Volkava 130

Hawi Jarso 108

Hayaat Mohamed Sheik Ali 11

Heather Riley 68

Hodan Farah 25

Holali Amekoudji 96

H. Pierrette Santanna 25

I

Ibtihaj Alzubaidi 43

Ifrah Aadan 63

Ifrah Warsame 117

Ignacio Sandoval 90

Ikram Yusuf 37

J

James Lee 135

Jartu Kennedy 129

Jay Li 140

Jessica Streich 79

Jialing Lin 23

Joeun Lee 117

Johanna Chavez Mendoza 34

John Higgens 100

Jolene (Jialing) Liu 50

Judy Kim 90

K

Kah Heh 129

Ka Ler 24

Kamonphat (Mai) Kerbel 133

Kannika Nelson 55

Kao Kalia Yang 7

Karen Ann Loe 97

Kariana Reyes 116

Karla Luna 36

Karl Hendrickson 101

Katherine Kasl 74

Kawsar Muse 73

Kemeriya Jara 115

Khadra Abdi 78

Kifah Mohamed 117

Kimberly Lesetmoe 79

Kyaw Win Nai 52

L

LarMay Paw 130

Laurent Guehi 18

Lemma Tufa 31

Leonard Miles 127

Leyla Iman 129

Lidia Lopez 43

Linda Chacon 48

Lorena Cruz Jiménez 122

Luciana Cardoso 47

Ludmila Leriche Leonne 22

Luisana Mendez 126

Luliya Lavriv 117

Lum Naw Chyau Hpa 110

Lyman Lowry 135

M

Manoj Yadav 118

Mariama Ann 136

Marilyn Gjerde 90

Marion Angelica 89

Marithza Rivera 56

Mark Wright 95

Marsi Pivaral 49

Martrell Jackson 73

Maryam Jamac 22

Matthew Miller 83

Maung Na 59

Maya Garcia Fisher 86, 138

Mekdes Trite 17

Meseret Fana 13

Michael Warren 11

Michelle Georgette Zabalou 33

Miriam Agustin 20

Miriam Flores Gonzalez 51

Miriam Omana Contreras 109

Miriam Sauz 22

Mohamed Duale 46

Mone't Spaulding 60

Monica Espinoza 97

Moraima del Carmen Castro 115

Moua Xiong 142

Mozhgan Pazoaki 39

Mu Aye 12

Mumina Kochi 111

Munira Rashid 109

Muse Dini 67

My Van Hua 132

N

Nalini Elumalai 74

Nasro Sheikh Abdullahi 45

Nataliya Krupatkykh 133

Naw Paw Htee Lah 93

Nga Nguyen 141

Nga Tran 51

Niky Noenurai 46

Ntxhi Vang 54

Nysomakorn South 53

P

Pah Day 52

Paola Vargas 132

Pat Strandness 88

Paw Ta Yaung 116

Paxoua Yang 17

Pi La Mu 59

Ping Mechter 48

Plae Meh 15

Q

Qin Sun 75

Quinn Robinson 75

R

Raghad Shareef Dhahad 64

Rahma Ahmed 98

Ramey Olson 76

Rashmi Jha 119

Rehima Keti 84

Rochelle Anderson 141

Roda Guled 78

Roman Tesema 113

Rongyun Ruan 111

Rosario Cortes 66

Rukiya Omar 73

Ruth Zhanay 88

S

Sadiyo Hassan 65

Safia Ahmed 21

Safiya Mahamed 77

Sagal Ibrahim 123

Sahmad Nakumbe 69

Sahra Ahmed 142

Sahra Wali 39

Sai Duong 12

Samar Mohamed 13

Sana Bangoura 53

Sandra Estrada 12

Sarah A 18

Sara Jama 31

Saw Bo 47

Seangchan "Sunshine" Gudim 58

Sedjiro Dossa Goubiyi 74

Sergio Chilel 134

Shada Adam 27

Shagitu Rafera 53

Shamso Omar 70

Sha Ruan 16

Shaymaa Jakjook 68

Shelly Bresnahan 75

Simon Ortega 66

Snow Yang 51

Soklim Tou 110

Sonita Soy Djoa 38

Steve Geheren 91

Sue Jansen 62

Suleka Ahmed 132

Sumeya Mohamed 118

Suphattra (Neng) McLeod 67

Svetlana Kartak 128

T

Tanya Trombley 12

Tatiana Ushakova 54

Teidy Ochoa 58

Tha Blay Eh 11

ThanThan Bo 88

Thany Kuong 39

Tianna Saltzman 134

Tigist Gebremariam 13

TJ Larson 44

Tomasa Romero 19

Tou Bee Xiong 104

Tresor Kempouk Hermen 17

Tri Duc Tran 133

Tufah Muhumed 127

U

Uel Olivier 76

V

Verónica Celleri 50

Veronica De Alva 10

Vicente Vital Cortez 33

Vicki Vialle Larson 96

Victor Manuel Ramos Chacon 59

Vimlesh (Vimmi) Sharma 46

W

Wei Liao 60

X

Xochitl Itzel Deniz Myrillo 123

Y

Yadira Salvador 25

Yan Bartel 120

Yasmin Ali 19

Yaxeng Vue 114

Yenework Woldeyohannes 109

Z

Zaynab Al Wahah 32

Zeinabou Maiga 131

Zeynab Mohamed 64

Zhanna Kim 34

Zong Xiong 57

Journeys Curriculum Unit

Overview

Literacy Minnesota is pleased to offer this curriculum unit to accompany *Journeys*. It is written for an audience of High Intermediate to Advanced ESL learners (CASAS scores 211-235). The learning objectives below are aligned with the College and Career Readiness Standards (CCRS) and the Transitions Integration Framework (TIF). For more information about the CCRS and the TIF, visit atlasabe.org.

In response to COVID-19, we have also suggested activity modifications for the virtual classroom. These modifications are labeled with the tag VIRTUAL CLASS IDEA and were designed to eliminate the need for printing and advance distribution of materials. These ideas rely primarily on the features available on the Zoom platform.

Objectives

After the unit, learners will be able to:

1. Discuss the concept of "storytelling" and its varied roles across cultures.

2. Read and navigate a table of contents, activating prior knowledge, making predictions about content and locating key information in a text. **(CCRS RI.2.5) (TIF LS 1a, 1b)**

3. Identify and analyze examples of literary genres in *Journeys*. Identify the main purpose of a text, including what the author wants to answer, explain or describe. **(CCRS R1.2.6) (TIF CT 1b)**

4. Read *Journeys* texts aloud with fluency, focusing on appropriate speed, accuracy and expression after successive readings. **(CCRS RF.4)**

5. Compare and contrast *Journeys* texts of the same genre using graphic organizers. **(CCRS RI.3.9) (TIF CT 1c)**

6. Use a personal response journal to synthesize and reflect on *Journeys* texts. **(TIF CT 1c)**

7. Write a *Journeys*-style narrative text, using a prewriting/rough draft/final draft process. **(CCRS W.2.3, W.3.4, W.3.5)**

Structure

This unit consists of eight cumulative lesson plans, including ready-to-use activities. Each lesson is designed to be approximately 1 to 1.5 hours long. Teachers are welcome to adapt the lessons to accommodate their unique classroom settings. Since class levels and sizes vary, a range of times is suggested for each activity.

Lesson Contents

Lesson 1: Storytelling

Lesson 2: Navigating a Table of Contents

Lesson 3: Literary Genres in *Journeys*

Lesson 4: Reading with Fluency

Lesson 5: Compare and Contrast Texts

Lesson 6: Culminating Activity: Prewriting

Lesson 7: Culminating Activity: Rough Draft

Lesson 8: Culminating Activity: Final Draft

Tech Tip

To copy handouts from the *Journeys* print edition onto 8 ½ x 11 sheets, use an enlargement ratio of 121%.

Lesson 1: Storytelling

Objective:

Discuss the concept of "storytelling" and its varied roles across cultures.

Materials + Prep:

1. *Journeys*: teacher's copy or class set; 2. Reference copy of the unit's learning objectives (see previous page); 3. Copy and cut Storytelling Mingle Cards (see next page) so each learner gets one card. Note: there are only four questions total, so learners will have duplicate questions.

VIRTUAL CLASS PREP: 1. *Journeys*: teacher's copy; 2. Storytelling Mingle Cards for reference; 3. PDF copy of a *Journeys* text.

Lesson Plan:

1. Introduce the Unit (10-20 min)

- Show and introduce *Journeys* as a book of stories written by Adult Basic Education (ABE) learners across Minnesota. It is published annually; this year nearly 300 learners' stories and poems are in the book.

- Explain that the class will be using *Journeys* to work on some reading/literacy learning objectives. Talk through the objectives in detail if appropriate.

- Explain that as a final project, learners will write their own *Journeys*-style texts; ask them to keep in mind what story of their own they would like to tell.

2. "Storytelling" Warm-up (15-20 min)

- Remind learners that *Journeys* is a book of stories, as well as some poetry. Write the word "storytelling" on the board and define/discuss. **VIRTUAL CLASS IDEA:** Use Zoom's Whiteboard or Google Slides.

- Lead a Think-Pair-Share activity with the prompt: "What do you think of when you hear the word 'storytelling'?" **VIRTUAL CLASS IDEA:** Use Zoom's Breakout Rooms to pair up learners. Then, type the prompt in the Chat.

3. "Storytelling" Mingle Activity (30-40 min)

- Introduce the four questions about storytelling—see the cards on next page.

- Lead the mingle activity: each learner gets one card. They mingle around the room, asking peers the question on their card and answering questions from peers. **VIRTUAL CLASS IDEA:** Use Zoom's Breakout Rooms to place your class into 4 (or fewer) breakout rooms. Before breaking out, assign each group one mingle question and designate a facilitator/reporter for each group. Note these assignments on Zoom's Whiteboard. Then, capture your Zoom screen to save these assignments. Once broken out, share the screen shot in the Chat. (Alternatively, type the assignments in the Chat, without sharing the screen shot.)

- To follow up, facilitate a conversation to discuss and summarize learners' answers to the questions.

4. Free Silent Reading (with any remaining time)

With any remaining time, invite learners to browse *Journeys* and get to know the book. If you only have a teacher's copy, make copies of a variety of pages of the book.

VIRTUAL CLASS IDEA: Choose a story to read aloud to the class.

Storytelling Mingle Cards

Who is the best storyteller you know? Why?	Who is the best storyteller you know? Why?
Is storytelling important in your family? In your culture? Why or why not?	Is storytelling important in your family? In your culture? Why or why not?
In your culture, are stories told mostly by speaking, writing, or both? What is an example?	In your culture, are stories told mostly by speaking, writing, or both? What is an example?
What are some reasons to tell stories?	What are some reasons to tell stories?

Lesson 2: Navigating a Table of Contents

Objective:
Read and navigate a table of contents, activating prior knowledge, making predictions about content and locating key information in a text. **(CCRS RI.2.5) (TIF LS 1a, 1b)**

Materials + Prep:
1. *Journeys*: teacher's copy or class set; 2. Make copies of the Table of Contents page; 3. Make copies of the Table of Contents Quiz (in-person class version).
VIRTUAL CLASS PREP: 1. *Journeys*: teacher's copy; 2. PDF of the Table of Contents; 3. PDF of the Table of Contents Quiz (virtual class version).

Lesson Plan:
1. Key Vocabulary Word: *Anthology* (10-20 min)
   - Show and re-introduce *Journeys* as a book of stories written by MN ABE learners; remind the class that at the end of the unit they will be writing their own stories.
   - Introduce and define the vocabulary word *anthology* as "a book or other collection with writings by many authors." Post the word on your word wall, board, Zoom Whiteboard or Google Slides.
   - Elicit the contexts in which learners may have heard/used this word. As a class, generate a sentence with the word.

2. Table of Contents/Prior Knowledge and Predictions: Activity 1 (15-25 min)
   - Give handouts of the Table of Contents page, and project using a document camera (or, in a virtual class, screen share.) Orient learners to the organization of the Table of Contents for this anthology.
   - Model reading the Table of Contents with a partner, making predictions about what types of stories will appear in each section. Model some creative predictions using this sentence frame:
       "I notice a section called _____. I think there will be stories about _____ in this section."
   - Ask learners to do this read and predict activity with a partner. **VIRTUAL CLASS IDEA:** Use Zoom's Breakout Rooms to pair up learners. Then, type the names of 1-2 Table of Contents sections in the Chat. Next, type the sentence frame in the Chat. Ask pairs to use the sentence frame to make predictions about the sections you shared.
   - Give learners the Table of Contents Quiz (next page). Ask learners to use the Table of Contents to find the answers. **VIRTUAL CLASS IDEA:** Do this activity as a large group. Screen share the quiz, then use Zoom's Annotate to fill in the answers as you discuss them. Ask learners to chat their answers or "raise their hand" in Zoom.

3. Table of Contents/Prior Knowledge and Predictions: Activity 2 (10-15 min)
   - Model reading the Table of Contents individually, marking the sections you're interested in with a * and the sections you're wondering/confused about with a ?
   - Ask learners to read and mark their own Table of Contents page. **VIRTUAL CLASS IDEA:** screen share the Table of Contents page. Instead of using a handout, ask learners to make notes in their notebook on the topic above.
   - Assess interest in each section by asking them to "vote with their feet": read the name of each section, and ask learners to respond by standing up to indicate high interest, a "so-so" gesture for medium interest and sitting down for low interest. **VIRTUAL CLASS IDEA:** use Zoom's Nonverbal Feedback feature to assess interest.

4. Free Silent Reading (with any remaining time). See Lesson 1 for notes. Remind learners to pay attention to which stories resonate with them, and what stories of their own they might want to write about. **VIRTUAL CLASS IDEA:** choose a story to read aloud to or with the class.

Journeys Anthology
Table of Contents Quiz (modified worksheet for virtual class)

Table of Contents

Foreword by Kao Kalia Yang 7

For My Loved Ones, Near or Far 9

Arrivals and Departures: Journeys to the U.S. 29

Pieces of the Past 41

We Persevere: Overcoming Challenges 61

Social and Racial Justice 81

Teaching and Learning in the Pandemic 85

Sketches and Snapshots 99

Exploring Culture and History 107

Fiction and Folktales 121

Wishes and Wonderings 125

Letters about Literature 137

Index 145

1. What page does the "Fiction and Folktales" section begin on? _____

2. What page does the "Pieces of the Past" section begin on? _____

3. What is the name of the section that begins on page 9?

_____

4. What is the name of the section that begins on page 107?

_____

5. How many pages is the "Wishes and Wonderings" section? _____

6. How many pages is the "Letters about Literature" section? _____

7. What section do you think will have stories about experiencing life in a new place? What words in the section title make you think this?

Journeys Anthology
Table of Contents Quiz (traditional worksheet for in-person class)

1. What page does the "Fiction and Folktales" section begin on? _____

2. What page does the "Pieces of the Past" section begin on? _____

3. What is the name of the section that begins on page 9?

_____

4. What is the name of the section that begins on page 107?

_____

5. How many pages is the "Wishes and Wonderings" section? _____

6. How many pages is the "Letters about Literature" section? _____

7. What section do you think will have stories about experiencing life in a new place? What words in the section title make you think this?

_____

_____

_____

Lesson 3: Literary Genres in *Journeys*

Objectives:

Identify and analyze examples of literary genres in *Journeys*. Identify the main purpose of a text, including what the author wants to answer, explain or describe. **(CCRS RI.2.6) (TIF CT 1b)**

Use a personal response journal to synthesize and reflect on the *Journeys* texts. **(TIF CT 1c)**

Materials + Prep:

1. *Journeys*: teacher's copy or class set; 2. Make copies and cut Genres Matching Cards, one set per pair (next page); 3. Make copies of *Journeys* texts: choose one text per genre; 4. Make copies of *Journeys*: Which Genre? handout (next pages).

VIRTUAL CLASS PREP: 1. *Journeys*: teacher's copy; 2. PDF of the Genres Matching Activity (virtual class version); 3. PDF of three *Journeys* texts of different genres;

Lesson Plan:

1. Key Vocabulary Word: Genre (10-20 min)

- Review the vocabulary word *anthology* from the previous lesson.

- Introduce the vocabulary word *genre* as "a type of writing with similar form, style or topic." Post the word on your word wall, board, Zoom whiteboard or Google Slides.

- Elicit the contexts in which learners may have heard/used this word. As a class, generate a sentence with the word.

2. *Journeys* Genres: Activity 1 (10-20 min)

- Explain that you'll be studying five different literary genres that appear in *Journeys*: Autobiography, Narrative Essay, Descriptive Essay, Verse and Folktale.

- Lead the genres matching activity: each pair gets a set of cards (5 vocab words, 5 definitions); they match each genre with the correct definition. **VIRTUAL CLASS IDEA:** Screen share the matching activity worksheet. As a class, read through each definition and use Zoom's Annotate to match each one to the correct vocabulary word at the top. Write in the correct vocabulary word next to each definition. Give learners time to copy the definitions into their notebooks.

- Follow up by checking comprehension of the genre definitions. Add the words to your word wall, board, Zoom whiteboard or Google Slides.

3. *Journeys* Genres: Activity 2 (30-45 min)

- Select a short text from *Journeys*. Read the text as a class. Ask learners: "What was the author's purpose for writing this text?" Decide together which genre this text belongs to and why.

- Select three or more texts of different genres from *Journeys*. Give learners copies of the "*Journeys*: Which Genre?" handout. Ask learners to work in pairs, reading the texts and completing the genres analysis. **VIRTUAL CLASS IDEA:** Select two or more texts of different genres. Use the Chat to pose the two key questions for analysis: "What genre is this text? Why?" Then, screen share the first story. Read the story as a class and discuss the key questions. Repeat with as many stories as is appropriate.

- In the "my notes" section of the worksheet (or in their notebooks), suggest that learners note any ideas for their own texts, and remind them that the class will be writing their own *Journeys*-style narrative texts soon. Follow-up by checking comprehension in the large group.

Genres Matching Activity (modified activity for virtual class)

Genres:

autobiography   narrative essay   verse

   descriptive essay   folktale

_____

Definitions:

1. A text that describes a person, object, event or place with many details, so the reader feels like they are there or makes a strong connection.

2. A fictional story where magical characters learn a lesson, often passed down by storytelling traditions.

3. A text about the author's own life or history.

4. A poem (may or may not rhyme)

5. A text about one event or experience that was important in the author's life, usually sharing a lesson learned.

Genres Matching Cards (traditional activity for in-person class)

Cut out the individual cards to prepare for a matching activity.

Genres	Definitions
autobiography	A text about the author's own life or history.
narrative essay	A text about one event or experience that was important in the author's life, usually sharing a lesson learned.
descriptive essay	A text that describes a person, object, event or place with many details, so the reader feels like they are there or makes a strong connection.
verse	A poem (may or may not rhyme)
folktale	A fictional story where magical characters learn a lesson, often passed down by storytelling traditions.

Journeys: Which Genre?

Text Title	What genre is this text? Why?	My notes

Lesson 4: Reading with Fluency

Objectives:

Read *Journeys* texts aloud with fluency, focusing on appropriate speed, accuracy and expression after successive readings. **(CCRS RF.4)**

Use a personal response journal to synthesize and reflect on *Journeys* texts. **(TIF CT 1c)**

Materials + Prep:

1. *Journeys*: teacher's copy or class set; 2. Make copies of two *Journeys* texts for fluency practice; 3. Make copies of the *Journeys* Personal Response Journal handout for each learner (next page).

VIRTUAL CLASS PREP: 1. *Journeys*: teacher's copy; 2. PDF of two *Journeys* texts for fluency practice; 3. PDF of Personal Response Journal handout.

Lesson Plan:

1. Key Vocabulary Review (10-20 min):

- Return to the key vocabulary words from Lessons 2-3. Use a vocabulary review activity to reinforce new vocabulary acquisition.

2. Reading Fluency Activity 1 (20-25 min)

- Choose a *Journeys* text that fits most learners' fluency level.

- Explain the purpose of fluency practice: today we'll read a text multiple times to practice reading accurately (with few mistakes), at a good speed (not too fast, not too slow) and with good expression (including pausing in the right places). This will help us become better readers and be more comfortable reading aloud.

- Model reading the text aloud to the class. Ask them to follow along, paying attention to your speed and where you stop to pause. After you read, answer questions learners have about the text.

- Lead a choral reading of the same text. Debrief to ask if they noticed the pauses and expression.

- Read aloud in pairs: one learner reads the text aloud; the other listens. Then they switch roles. **VIRTUAL CLASS IDEA:** Use Zoom's Chat to send a document with the text. Then, use Zoom's Breakout Rooms to break learners into smaller groups. Before breaking out, ask for 1-2 volunteers in each group to read the story aloud. (Allow extra time and model how to navigate from the breakout room to the chat and how to open the document.) Once in small groups, allow time for the volunteers to read aloud to the group.

3. Reading Fluency Activity 2 (20-25 min)

- Choose a new *Journeys* text that fits most learners' fluency level.

- Share (or screen share) the text with the class. Model a think-aloud, scanning the text for punctuation and the phrasing/expression conventions for each: commas, periods, question marks, etc.

- Read the text aloud to the class, with everyone tracking the text signals. After you read, answer questions learners have about the text. Next, lead a choral reading of the same text.

- Repeat the pair reading (or virtual class modification) from Activity 1.

- Ask if anyone would like to read the text aloud to the class.

4. Personal Response Journal (with any remaining time). Give each learner a Personal Response Journal handout. Explain/model the activity and ask them to write a response. **VIRTUAL CLASS IDEA:** Screen share the handout. Ask learners to write their response in their notebooks.

Journeys: Personal Response Journal

Instructions:

1. **Choose** a reading from today that interested you the most.

2. **Choose one** of the Response Questions to the right.

3. **Think** about the question, then **write** a few sentences in response.

Response Questions:

1. What connections did you make with this text? They could be from your experiences, others' experiences, or other texts.

2. What do you wonder after reading this text? Why?

3. What are some other titles for this text? Which one do you like best? Why?

4. What sentence(s) are the most important in this text? Why?

Name:_____   Date: _____

Text title: _____

Response to Question Number _____:

_____

_____

_____

_____

_____

_____

_____

Lesson 5: Compare/Contrast Two *Journeys* Texts

Objectives:

Compare and contrast two *Journeys* texts of the same genre using graphic organizers. **(CCRS RI.3.9) (TIF CT 1c)**

Use a personal response journal to synthesize and reflect on the *Journeys* texts. **(TIF CT 1c)**

Materials + Prep:

1. *Journeys*: teacher's copy or class set; 2. Make copies of two *Journeys* texts, making sure they're of the <u>same genre</u>; 3. Create a handout with comprehension questions about the two texts and make copies; 4. Make copies of the Venn Diagram handout (next page); 5. Make copies of the *Journeys:* Personal Response Journal handout (previous page) for each learner.

VIRTUAL CLASS PREP: 1. *Journeys*: teacher's copy; 2-5. PDF versions of materials 2-5 listed above.

Lesson Plan:

1. Read and Summarize the Texts (30-45 min)

- Introduce the two texts, explaining that they are of the same genre.

- Ask the class to read both texts. After reading, they answer the prepared comprehension questions. **VIRTUAL CLASS IDEA**: Choose two texts that are short enough to read them both as a large group.

- Review answers to the prepared comprehension questions as a class. Ask learners to point out where they found answers to each question in the text(s).

- Make a T-chart on the board with the names of the two texts at the top. Ask learners to scan the texts individually, noting a few key ideas in each text. **VIRTUAL CLASS IDEA:** Use <u>Zoom's Whiteboard</u> to make a T-chart. Then, use Zoom's Chat feature to <u>send a document</u> with the texts, so learners can refer to the texts during the large group discussion. Alternatively, use Zoom's <u>Simultaneous Sharing</u>: If you have a volunteer, class assistant or advanced learner: ask that person to pull up the text and share their screen, so the class can see the text and the T-chart at the same time.

- As a large group, discuss the ideas they noted. Through discussion, arrive at a consensus about the two or three most important ideas in each story. Note these in the T-chart.

2. Compare and Contrast the Texts (30-45 min)

- Ask for an example of one thing that's similar about the texts and one thing that's different.

- Next, model how to fill out the Venn Diagram with one thing that's similar and one thing from each text that's unique/different.

- After you model, ask learners to pair up and work together to fill out the Venn Diagram. **VIRTUAL CLASS IDEA**: Use <u>Zoom's Annotate</u> to fill out the Venn Diagram as a large group.

- Follow-up with a large group discussion, eliciting learners' responses to the activity.

3. Personal Response Journal (with any remaining time). Give each learner a Personal Response Journal handout. Explain/model the activity and ask them to write a response. **VIRTUAL CLASS IDEA:** <u>Screen share</u> the handout. Ask learners to write their response in their notebooks.

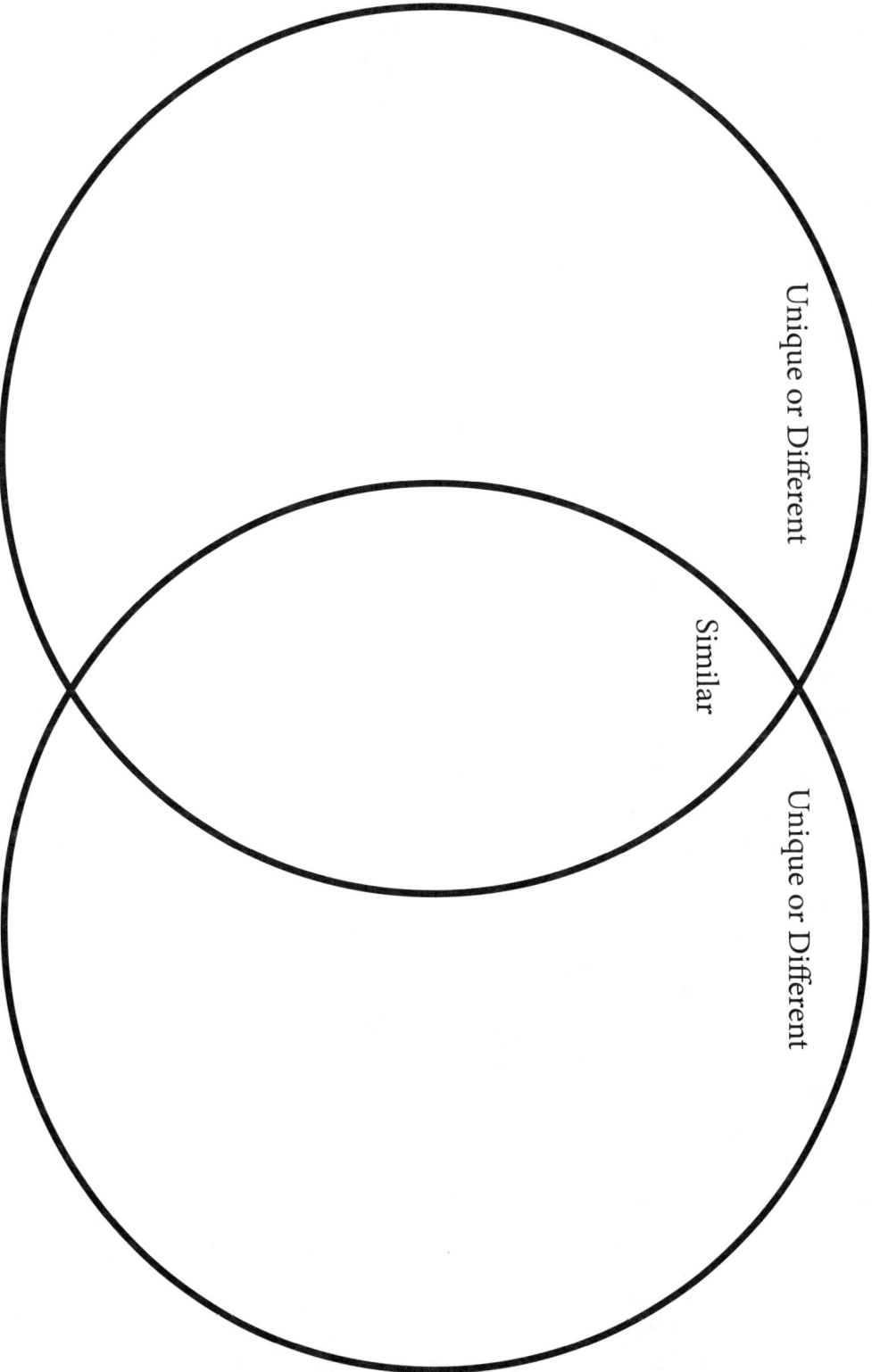

Compare and Contrast Journeys Texts

Text 1: _____

Text 2: _____

Unique or Different

Similar

Unique or Different

Lesson 6: Culminating Activity, Prewriting

Objective:

Write a *Journeys*-style text, using a prewriting/rough draft/final draft process. **(CCRS W.2.3, W.3.4, W.3.5)**

Materials + Prep:

1. *Journeys*: teacher's copy or class set; 2. Make copies of two examples of *Journeys* narrative texts; 3. Make copies of the Prewriting Narrative Essay Graphic Organizer (next page).
VIRTUAL CLASS PREP: 1. *Journeys*: teacher's copy; 2. PDF of two *Journeys* narrative texts; 3. PDF of the Prewriting Narrative Essay Graphic Organizer.

Lesson Plan:

1. Identify Descriptive Details in Narrative Essays (20-30 min)

- Introduce the two texts, explaining that they are of the same genre. Review the definition of a narrative essay from previous lesson.

- Write this question on the board or virtual whiteboard: What words does the author use to describe?

- Read each text aloud. Ask learners to think about the question as they listen and answer the key question with a partner after you read aloud. **VIRTUAL CLASS IDEA**: Skip the partner discussion and talk as a large group.

- After learners have answered the question, elicit examples from the class. Write descriptive details on the board, Zoom whiteboard or Google Slides. Ask learners to add to the list with their own ideas.

2. Identify Signal Words in Narrative Essays (20-30 min)

- Now, write this question on the board, Zoom whiteboard or Google Slides: What words does the author use to tell the order things happen in?

- Ask learners to read both texts again on their own. Ask learners to think about the question as they read and answer the question with a partner after they read. **VIRTUAL CLASS IDEA:** Skip the partner discussion and talk as a large group. OR, if level-appropriate: share a document containing the texts through Chat, so learners can refer to the texts during their discussion. Then, type the discussion prompt in the Chat. Next, use Zoom's Breakout Rooms to break learners into smaller groups and ask them to discuss the prompt.

- After learners have read and answered the question, elicit examples from learners. Write signal words on the board, Zoom whiteboard or Google Slides. Ask learners to add to the list with their own ideas.

3. Pre-Writing Activity (20-30 min)

- Introduce the Prewriting Graphic Organizer to the class.

- Model completing the graphic organizer by filling it out together, using one of the sample texts you read. Be sure to include descriptive details and signal words.

- After you model, invite the learners to think of their own story and complete the Prewriting Graphic Organizer on their own. Ask them to share their completed graphic organizer with a partner. **VIRTUAL CLASS IDEA:** Instead of using the handout, ask learners to note their prewriting ideas in their notebooks.

Prewriting Narrative Essay Graphic Organizer

What is the story about?

Who is in the story?

What **descriptive details** help to tell the story?

What happened **first**?
One day,
In (year),
To begin with,

What happened **next**?
Next,
After awhile,
Later,

What happened **last**?
Finally,
At last,
In the end,

What did you learn?
I learned that...

Lesson 7: Culminating Activity, Rough Draft

Objective:
Write a *Journeys*-style text, using a prewriting/rough draft/final draft process. **(CCRS W.2.3, W.3.4, W.3.5)**

Materials + Prep:
1. Prewriting Graphic Organizer, completed as a sample from previous lesson; 2. Optional: Make copies of the Narrative Essay Paragraph Frame (next page).
VIRTUAL CLASS PREP: PDFs of the two items listed above.

Lesson Plan:

1. Prewriting Review (10-15 min)

   • Ask learners to locate their Prewriting Graphic Organizers (or notes in their notebook) from the previous lesson. Give them a few minutes to review their work, then a few minutes to share their ideas with a partner. **VIRTUAL CLASS IDEA:** Use Zoom's Breakout Rooms to pair learners up.

2. Rough Draft (30-45 min)

   • Share the sample Prewriting Graphic Organizer from the previous class. Model transferring the story details into paragraph form using signal words and descriptive details. Optional: use the Narrative Essay Paragraph Frame to model.

   • Save this model rough draft for the next lesson.

   • Ask learners to transfer their prewriting ideas into paragraph form. Optional: share the Narrative Essay Paragraph Frame handout to support learners.

   • Reiterate that at this stage, they don't need to worry about spelling/mechanics. Encourage them to focus on the text's organization and development.

   • Give the class enough time to write a rough draft of their stories.

   • **VIRTUAL CLASS IDEA:** After learners have written their rough drafts, invite them to type and share their rough drafts with you through email, a Google Doc, a Google Form or another sharing method.

3. Reading the Rough Draft (with any remaining time):

   • If there's time, ask learners to read their rough drafts aloud to a partner and make any changes they need to. Reading aloud can help to identify sentences they may want to change.

Narrative Essay Paragraph Frame

This story is about _____

_____.

What
happened
first?

_____ , _____

_____.

What
happened
next?

_____ , _____

_____.

What
happened
last?

_____ , _____

_____.

What
did you
learn?

_____

_____.

Lesson 8: Culminating Activity, Final Draft

Objective:

Write a *Journeys*-style text, using a prewriting/rough draft/final draft process. **(CCRS W.2.3, W.3.4, W.3.5)**

Materials + Prep:

1. Make copies of the Editing Checklist (next page). 2. Sample rough draft, from previous lesson.
VIRTUAL CLASS PREP: 1. PDF of the Editing Checklist; 2. PDF or other shareable version of the sample rough draft, from previous lesson.

Lesson Plan:

1. Rough Draft Review (10-15 min)

- Ask learners to locate their rough draft from the previous lesson. Give them enough time to re-read their text.

2. Introducing the Editing Checklist (15-20 min)

- Introduce the Editing Checklist, project using a document camera, and model how to review/ edit the sample rough draft which you modeled in the previous lesson, checking for the items on the checklist. **VIRTUAL CLASS IDEA:** Instead of screen sharing the Editing Checklist, screen share the sample rough draft from the previous lesson. Then, one at a time, type each editing question (e.g., "Does each sentence have a punctuation mark at the end?") in the Chat. Model how to review/edit the sample rough draft as described above.

- Share with learners that they will use the Editing Checklist twice. First, they will review their writing on their own. Next, they will have a partner review their writing (or, in a virtual setting, they will review their writing as a group).

3. Review and Editing the Rough Draft (20-30 min)

- Ask learners to use the Editing Checklist to review/edit their own rough draft, putting a check in the first column for items that are completed. **VIRTUAL CLASS IDEA:** Ask learners to refer to the editing questions already posted in the Chat (from previous activity) and use them to edit their rough drafts. OR, share a document with the Editing Checklist through the Chat, so learners can refer to it while editing their rough drafts.

- Next, ask learners to work in pairs to review each other's writing using the Editing Checklist. Give them enough time to review/edit the texts. **VIRTUAL CLASS IDEA:** If rough drafts are typed in a Word Doc or Google Doc, ask a learner to share their screen and ask the class to help edit the story using the checklist. Repeat with as many learners as is appropriate.

- Give learners a "brain break" after editing.

4. Final Draft (20-25 min)

- Introduce the final draft process to the class and ask them to write/type a final copy of their text, incorporating the edits identified.

5. Share with Class (with any remaining time)

- Invite learners to share their texts aloud with the class.

Editing Checklist

1) Read your rough draft aloud, checking for the items below.
2) Have a partner read your rough draft, checking for the items below.

		My Edit	My Partner's Edit
Punctuation	Does each sentence have a punctuation mark at the end? . ! ?		
Capital Letters	Does each sentence begin with a capital letter?		
	Do all proper nouns begin with a capital letter? For example, names and place names.		
Grammar	Is each sentence a complete idea?		
	Can you break up any long sentences into shorter ones?		
	Is there agreement between subjects and verbs? For example, *she has* (not *she have*).		
Spelling	Did you circle words that are spelled wrong or words you are not sure about?		

Notes

Notes

Journeys 2021 Editorial Team

Allison Bares

COPYEDITOR

Allison is a senior at the University of St. Thomas, studying English with Creative Writing and Classical Languages. She has a newfound love of dramatic literature, so she is trying to read and see as many plays as she can, though musical theater will always have a special place in her heart. In addition to working on *Journeys*, she is part of a research team that is partnering with a local theater company to address grief in the Twin Cities. She is hoping this research and her work with *Journeys* will prepare her for a career in publishing or theater. In her free time, Allison likes ballroom dancing, baking, and sewing. It is her dream to one day own a fruitful lemon tree.

Maya Garcia Fisher

COPYEDITOR

Maya is a poet, writer, and researcher currently based in Minneapolis, Minnesota. She received a dual Bachelor of Arts in English and Puerto Rican and Latino Studies from Brooklyn College in Brooklyn, New York where she lived for four years. Her previous research has focused on exploring Latinx narratives in literature and she is an alum of VONA (Voices of Our Nations Arts) and The Watering Hole poetry workshops. Maya is currently working on an Advanced Certificate in Labor Studies from the Graduate Center of New York.

Journeys 2021 Editorial Team

Anna Pasno

COPYEDITOR

Anna is a senior at the University of St. Thomas majoring in English: Creative Writing and minoring in the Renaissance Program (a specialized business program for those pursuing a BA) and Justice and Peace Studies. She hopes to be continuously involved in nonprofits and work in publishing to amplify underrepresented voices; her own writing has been published in *The Summit Avenue Review*, as well as Flexible Press' *22 Under 22* anthology. Anna also loves to cook, spoil friends with leftovers, read, sing, and paint.

Emmalee Rabe

COPYEDITOR

Emmalee is a senior at the University of Northwestern—St. Paul, majoring in English with a Professional Writing concentration. When she is not copyediting for *Journeys*, she is working as an English tutor and executive editor on campus. Her own writing has been published in literary journals *Inkstone* and *Sonder Midwest,* as well as papers *Hometown Focus* and *The Examiner.* In her free time, she listens to too many true crime podcasts and carries on her late grandfather's love of poetry. She hopes to one day adopt a small army of rescue animals and perfect the art of baking bread.

Acknowledgements

Literacy Minnesota extends our heartfelt thanks to our 2021 *Journeys* copyeditors Allison Bares, Maya Garcia Fisher, Anna Pasno and Emmalee Rabe, who have donated their time and talent to the planning, design, editing and production of this book. Special thanks also to staff Debbie Cushman, Kasey Payette, Ellie Purdy and Kelly Rynda for helping make *Journeys* a success.

We are grateful for a partnership with the Friends of the Saint Paul Public Library and their generous support of the Letters about Literature chapter. Letters about Literature is a statewide writing contest for Minnesota students from elementary school through adult education. The program invites students to read a piece of literature of their choice, reflect on it, and write a personal letter to the author explaining how the piece changed their views of the world and/or themselves. Special thanks to Alayne Hopkins.

Finally, we are deeply grateful to donors Mimi and Todd Burke, who give in memory of Todd's late mother through the Burke Family Fund of the Minnesota Community Foundation. Their generous support helped make *Journeys* possible this year.

About Literacy Minnesota

The mission of Literacy Minnesota is to share the power of learning through education, community building and advocacy. We believe literacy has the power to advance equity and justice, and we envision a world where life-changing learning is within everyone's reach.

Contact Us

literacymn.org
651-645-2277
700 Raymond Avenue, Suite 180
Saint Paul, Minnesota 55114

Literacy
Minnesota